Edition of One

The Autobiography of Eugene B. Power
Founder of University Microfilms

UNIVERSITY MICROFILMS INTERNATIONAL

Produced and distributed by
University Microfilms Inc.
Ann Arbor, Michigan 48106

Library of Congress Cataloging in Publication Data

Power, Eugene B., 1905–
    Edition of one : the autobiography of Eugene B. Power /
(Eugene B. Power) with Robert Anderson.
        p.   cm.
    ISBN 0-8357-0898-5 (alk. paper) . — ISBN 0-8357-0899-3 (pbk. : alk.
paper)
    1. Power, Eugene B., 1905–   . 2. University Microfilms International—
History. 3. Publishers and publishing—United States—Biography. 4. Scholarly
publishing—United States—History—20th century. 5. Micropublishing—
United States—History—20th century. I. Anderson, Robert, 1930–1990.
II. Title.
Z473.P588   1990
070.5 ' 092—dc20
[B]
                                                                    90-10808
                                                                    CIP

British Library CIP data is available.

The paper used in this publication meets the minimum requirements of
American National Standard for Information Sciences—Permanence of Paper
for Printed Library Materials, ANSI Z39.48-1984. ∞ ™

For Sadye, Phil, and Nathan

Author's Note

It would be impossible to acknowledge everyone who has contributed in some way to this book. However, I would be remiss if I did not single out a few whose contributions were vital to it. My wife, Sadye, was closely involved, as she has been through the years in virtually every aspect of my life. I could not have completed the project without the invaluable perspective of Margaret O. Massialas, who has worked with me for twenty-three years. And the help of Mark Osborne, our office secretary, is greatly appreciated. I also extend special thanks to the various people who contributed their own recollections and observations.

I think it is fitting that this autobiography is published by the "Editions-of-One" process, an idea for which was my major contribution to the field of academic publishing. I selected the typeface, 13-point Times Roman, which is larger than that of most books, not because it would make the book thicker or give the impression of weightiness to my words, but because it is easier for me and my contemporaries to read.

An unexpected tragedy was the sudden death of Robert C. Anderson, who assisted me in the preparation of this book, one week after this manuscript was completed. He was a remarkable person, with varied talents. I will be eternally grateful that he had the opportunity to finish the work which we had started. He is sorely missed.

Introduction

by Robert Anderson

Eugene B. Power's autobiography provides a model for any entrepreneur who wants to succeed in business while enjoying life to the hilt and gaining the respect and admiration of his peers.

It was the uniqueness of his entrepreneurial career that first appealed to me when Mr. Power asked me to help him organize the voluminous records he'd kept over a span of nearly seventy years, combine them with his reminiscences in interviews, and assist him in setting them down in readable prose. As the former editor of *Success* Magazine and co-author of *Grinding It Out: The Making of McDonald's* with Ray Kroc and *Pizza Tiger* with Tom Monaghan, I had had considerable close contact with entrepreneurs in fast-food franchising and other conventional businesses. I was intrigued by Mr. Power's outstanding success in the "soft" field of academic publishing via microfilm. How, I wondered, had he managed to build University Microfilms after he founded it in June 1938 with an unproven new service, selling to a market so narrow and difficult to reach as universities and libraries? The first five years is a critical period for any startup company, and University Microfilms

I

labored under the additional handicap of unfortunate timing: its formative years straddled the end of the Great
Depression and the beginning of World War II.

The answer to my question came during our very first
day of work on this book. I stood in awe of Mr. Power,
because he had been a Regent of the University of Michigan
when I was a student there. But when I addressed him as
"Mr. Power" in our first meeting, he glanced at me from
under forbidding, frosty brows, and snapped, "Gene." Our
interview continued on a first-name basis until noon, when
he announced, "Come on, we're going to play water polo!"
I did join the game on another occasion, but on that first day
I chose to watch the play from the sidelines. I was glad I did,
because I saw Gene at age eighty-three, his hair snow white
and his body afflicted by Parkinson's disease, attack burly
football types a third his age and wrestle them strenuously
under water. I saw him use cunning for what he lacked in
speed to score five goals, more than any other individual
player. Obviously, I realized, such fierce energy and fear-
lessness must have been major factors in the successful
launching of his company.

After the game, the conversation at a ritual lunch with the
other water-polo players provided another insight. Several
of the players are academics, and Gene related to them as
easily as he did to other businessmen. He talked their
language. This point was reinforced many times during the
next year in various meetings we had with his wide range of
associates, representing both town and gown.

When we started work on the book, Gene had in mind a
brief history of his family, along with an account of the

II

INTRODUCTION

development of "Editions of One," his landmark contribution to the field of academic publishing. However, friends who read a draft persuaded him to expand it to cover the full sweep of his unique life. There was certainly plenty of material to draw upon for such an expanded work. Gene has been a dedicated if somewhat sporadic diarist for many years. Some of his daily records were jotted in longhand, but most were tape recorded, literally thousands of hours of tapes, which were transcribed and printed — as Editions of One, of course — and bound between black-paper covers into volume after volume of eight-and-a-half by eleven-inch books. In addition, there were two volumes of earlier autobiographical writings Gene had dictated, plus about twenty hours of an oral history done by Enid Galler, which Gene mentions in the last chapter of this book. Consequently, while the ordering of the material herein is mostly mine, the voice and the thoughts are pure Eugene B. Power.

In asking him to expand the book, Gene's friends urged him to give not only his reflections on business but to tell the wonderful love story he and his wife, Sadye, have lived for more than sixty years and to share his insights on philanthropy. The latter became a second career for him after his retirement from University Microfilms, Inc. (UMI). Incidentally, he doesn't like to use the word *philanthropy*, preferring to refer to his good works simply as *helping others.*

These three themes — business, Sadye, and helping others — are dominant in Gene Power's life. They are rarely isolated, however, but emerge as part of the texture of the events he recounts. The same is true of the lessons to be found in Gene's experience. He does not presume to provide how-to-do-it lists or the kinds of self-help formulas to be found in books or tapes that promise to help you learn to swim with sharks without being eaten alive or how to come out holding the trump card in any deal. Experience is still the best teacher, and Gene's long experience offers a wealth of instruction. For example:

While Gene Power is an urbane executive and his writing style has an academic dignity, he is also a master salesman. He follows all the conventional rules of good salesmanship. However, his approach is so original that he seems to reinvent those principles. For instance, one of the rules beginning salesmen hear repeatedly is *stay close to your customer*. Gene's customers were the heads of major libraries. As he shows without embellishing the fact, he stayed close to them by developing an entire reinforcing network of friendship, mutual assistance, and information sharing among them. His approach worked because he was sincere about wanting to help them (another basic sales principle). In fact, the network became as useful and important to his customers as it was to his business.

It is characteristic of Gene Power that he also demonstrates exceptions to some of the most sacred of business maxims, in particular the one that declares *the customer is always right*. Gene believed his customers were dead wrong in their resistance to his idea for putting their periodical collections on microfilm. His assertion that they should regularly discard periodicals they had already paid for and repurchase those same issues as microfilm seemed to them preposterous. He tackled the objections by applying two other sales fundamentals: *factual analysis* and *persistence*.

INTRODUCTION

He formulated his analysis of the facts into thorough cost comparisons and persuasive projections of how his idea would provide future savings for libraries. These arguments swayed his customers. His persistence changed their minds. Happily, the benefits he promised in long-term savings of both storage space and money have been realized. What's more, microfilm backfiles of periodicals have become a common library research tool that might not exist if Gene had been a less courageous innovator or a less persistent salesman.

Moving from the business theme of this autobiography to Sadye requires no shift of gears, for her influence is evident in every aspect of her husband's life. Some who know both of them well say that without her, Gene Power would never have developed his good taste and social graces. A few would maintain that without her, he would have been far less successful in business. Such assertions are, of course, empty speculation, like imagining what FDR would have been like without Eleanor, JFK without Jackie, or LBJ without Lady Bird. Not only empty but insensitive, for the magic in the relationship between Gene and Sadye lies in the fact that their characters and personalities complement each other to a remarkable degree. For example, Sadye is timid, having been overprotected by her parents; Gene is fearless, his rugged independence having been honed on the grindstone of his father's intransigence. In joint undertakings, such as supporting theatrical groups or Planned Parenthood, they combined these opposite traits to great effect. Another synergistic combination of opposite characteristics is in their leadership styles. Sadye is low-key, influencing others through subtle encouragement; Gene is forceful and demanding. She gentles his approach, says one close associate, so that instead of being like a bull in a china shop, he is more like a guided missile.

Their mutually fulfilling relationship should be especially interesting to entrepreneurs who, like Gene Power, are intuitive thinkers. Quite often such people find that their spontaneous flow of ideas puts them at odds with their more logical mates.

"Gene's thinking is saltatory, that is, it goes in jumps," says his son, Philip. "Sadye's, on the other hand, is strictly linear and logical. Gene's instinct was always to test his leaps of imagination against the logic of Sadye's thought."

Inevitably, this fire-and-ice difference in modes of thinking led to misunderstandings that could have shattered their marriage. The fact that both are such strong individuals would seem to have made a split even more likely. But the love Gene and Sadye share, and the trust implicit in that love, allowed them to endure their doubts and fears and resolve their differences.

The point needs no further elaboration. There is a wealth of instructive detail in the story of the fascinating life that unfolds on the following pages. But it would be unseemly to dwell too much on the book's practical aspects, because there is much in this autobiography for the reader who is interested only in the entertaining human dynamics and historical interplay of the story itself.

Contents

Contents

Edition of One

Chapter One

Quest

During my lifetime, Americans have altered their environment in many ways. I was born in Traverse City, Michigan on June 4, 1905, and things that in those days were deemed impossible have become commonplace. Now, in the declining years of the century, we take for granted electronic machines which, at the touch of a button, can perform the work of hundreds of people; we are no longer amazed at the phenomenon of sound and pictures transmitted across vast distances to be viewed in nearly every home in the nation; we have become blasé about air transport that allows us to cross the continent in less than half a day. Yet if a dinner guest in my parents' home had predicted that this newborn son of theirs would one day live in a world of computers, television, and commercial air travel (not to mention such things as nuclear power or satellites or space shuttles), his ideas probably would have been dismissed as idle conjecture.

In contrast, a dinner guest at my home in Ann Arbor today would be hard put to imagine an advance in future technology so exotic as to be considered impossible. William Van Dusen Wishard, a special assistant to the U.S. Secretary of Commerce, stated recently that, "Ninety percent of all scientific knowledge that exists has been acquired in the

1

past thirty-five years."[1] Our culture has passed from the industrial age into the information age, and the transition has wrought a fundamental change in our attitude toward progress. We now believe that literally anything is possible.

But while information has become an *open sesame* for business and industry—as well as for literature, science, the arts, and education—the very rate at which it proliferates erects barriers to those who seek to use it. Every day sees fresh accumulations of new information released by legions of publishing houses, print media, research organizations, and educational institutions across the land. Over time, this steady flow grows into veritable mountains of paper. Much of it, for the purposes of the researcher, is evanescent, being in the form of newspapers and periodicals or typescripts and computer printouts, all of which deteriorate relatively rapidly and are cumbersome to store and handle. (It must be noted that the paper used in modern books also deteriorates rapidly; instead of lasting for centuries, these volumes decay within fifty to one hundred years.) The glut of new materials also competes with scholarly works and historic books and documents for space in the various library collections, making the problems of storage and access increasingly difficult.

My life's work has been in preserving the ideas contained in this ever-growing mass of material and making them available, at a reasonable cost, in a form that is permanent, manageable, and accessible. This was the mission, the *raison d'être,* of University Microfilms, the company I

---

[1] "Challenges for the Twenty-First Century" by William Van Dusen Wishard in *The Futurist,* September-October 1987, p. 60.

2

founded in 1938 and built over the next three decades into an operation that by 1989 had sales of well over $80 million.

In the pages that follow I will detail the influences that helped shape my life. I will attempt to show the sources that gave rise to my most creative idea: a method of using microfilm as a publishing medium. This concept was the foundation of my enterprise. It allowed me to reverse the economic pattern of traditional publishing, and though it was hailed as "the first completely new technique to be introduced to the field of publishing since Gutenberg," [2] its real significance, as I saw it, was that it allowed me to provide scholars with information they needed at a price they could afford.

While describing the people and events that have influenced me, I will try to trace my intellectual development. I want to show how my particular concern for preserving man's heritage in the form of books, coupled with an abiding entrepreneurial spirit, resulted not only in the unique firm I founded but in the urge to help my fellow man that has given me a very satisfying second career. The things I have accomplished since my retirement have been equally as interesting and rewarding as anything I did in business.

The gratification of my second career is intensified by the fact that it comes after having been "turned out to pasture" by mandatory retirement, a shortsighted policy that was in vogue in American corporations during the 1960s and early

---

[2] *Information Media & Technology* The Journal of Cimte—the National Centre for Information and Media Technology (UK)—Volume 21 Number 6, November 1988. Editorial.

1970s. That was not the only policy I disagreed with. My entrepreneurial approach to management often clashed with the highly structured world of Xerox. But I will tell that story in some detail later. For the moment, here is a brief summary of what happened:

After nearly twenty-five years of success in building University Microfilms, I decided to merge my little company with Xerox Corporation. There were several reasons for this. I did not think it wise to continue carrying all my eggs in that one basket. Had anything happened to me, my wife, Sadye, would not have been able to handle the business. Our son Philip had no interest in running UMI; he was more interested in carving his own niche in the business world as a newspaper publisher. I considered the alternatives of taking the company public or merging with one of my direct competitors. But in the end, the Xerox merger seemed best. It was a sound move, by and large. It greatly enhanced my personal financial position, since I acquired quite a lot of Xerox stock, which went up sharply soon after the merger. It also gave me influence, in the form of a seat on the board of directors of Xerox. There was a benefit, too, in gaining some freedom from the burden of managing day-to-day operations. I could spend more time pursuing my interest in creative developments for the company. However, when my sixty-fifth birthday rolled around, I *had* to retire. Never mind that I was in good health, full of energy, enthusiastic, and, I think, very effective as an executive and producer of new business. Fortunately, in recent years, the deplorable practice of mandatory retirement has been going out of favor in corporate America.

At this writing, I am eighty-four years old. I think this is an ideal age to be setting down one's thoughts and observations on life, for as Lacey Baldwin Smith wrote in his biography of Henry VIII: "If the conclusions of geriatrics are correct, it is during the final stages of life that man casts off a portion of the protective shield hammered out during childhood and adolescence and reveals the raw personality beneath."[3] I believe I am past the point where writing a book would be mere self-indulgence, an exercise in ego gratification. Therefore, I can concentrate on ways in which the events of my life might be enlightening to others. After all, one of the principal things that distinguishes human beings from the other animals is our ability to pass on to subsequent generations the knowledge we gain from experience.

Being old doesn't mean one is wise, of course, or that one's experiences will be instructive for those who come after. But I do think I've learned some things that are worth passing on from my career in business—both as an entrepreneur and a corporate executive—as well as from the various other parts I've played during my turn on the world's stage, including those of public servant, patron of the arts, fundraiser, and champion of scholarship.

The University of Michigan opened its School of Business Administration in 1924, and I was a member of the sixth class to receive the MBA degree from it. My entry into the world of commerce came at an inauspicious time—the

---

[3] *Henry VIII: The Mask of Royalty* by Lacey Baldwin Smith, Houghton Mifflin Company, Sentry Edition ISBN: 0-395-13694-6, Copyright © 1971 by Lacey Baldwin Smith, pp. 11-12.

spring of 1930—just eight months after the great stock-market crash of October 1929. Yet I had high hopes. I was buoyed by my year-old marriage to Sadye Harwick, who was then and is to this day my personal polestar.

Sadye and I had agreed that we would stay in Ann Arbor after my graduation, even though I had a job waiting for me with the Celotex Company in Chicago if I wanted it. We believed that Ann Arbor offered decent housing and all the cultural amenities, including free concerts and lectures and exhibitions, that people in the big city had to work and struggle to get. Sadye had a master's degree in psychology, and she was working at the University of Michigan's Student Health Service, where she established the Mental Hygiene Clinic. For my part, I believed I could earn a living anywhere, so I marched forth in search of gainful employment in Ann Arbor.

My first job was one I had no business accepting. It was a high-risk venture, because the company, Windsor Tractor Equipment, was small and had been in operation only a short time. It probably was undercapitalized, too, since it was backed by only three local investors. On top of all that, the firm had a very narrow market niche, having been formed to develop and distribute a particular kind of truck trailer hitch invented by Jim Windsor. I think the people at the business school were disappointed that I didn't get a position with Eastman Kodak or one of the other large firms that had been recruiting on campus. Nonetheless, I became bookkeeper and office manager for Windsor at a salary of $150 a month. Sadye was making about $220, so we were able to get by quite nicely. I don't think I was a very good

6

QUEST

employee for Windsor, because I didn't contribute much to the company, but the situation lasted only about five months. Sales of trailer hitches were few and far between. By October it became obvious to me that the company was going to go under. The time I'd spent with Windsor wasn't a complete waste, though, because I made several good contacts there, including Roscoe Bonisteel, one of the investors, who later became my attorney.

In retrospect it seems that the decisions I was making at that time, based mostly on intuition, were unaccountably the right ones. In choosing to stay in Ann Arbor, for example, Sadye and I were identifying with University of Michigan people with a kind of certitude that, if we remained in their milieu, we would somehow grow and find fulfillment. This certainly was not the result of any logical thinking I'd learned in business school. Nor, as I've indicated, was taking the job at Windsor Tractor Equipment a smart move. Yet if I hadn't marked time in the office at Windsor for those five or six months, I probably would not have been hired by Edwards Brothers, the publishing company where my idea for microfilm publishing was formed and from which I launched my own business. Other places might have served as well, I suppose, but Edwards Brothers provided a set of circumstances that probably was unique. Certainly Bill Edwards, the owner, provided me with challenges and opportunities I would have found difficult to duplicate anywhere else.

My interview at Edwards Brothers came about completely by chance. I happened to meet Paul Brumfield, a casual acquaintance, on the steps of the Ann Arbor post

7

office. We stopped to chat for a moment and I asked him how things were going. "Terrible," he said, explaining that he'd just been fired by Edwards Brothers. I commiserated with him, of course, but as we parted, I was thinking that since they'd fired him, they probably needed somebody. So I went over to their office and talked to the manager, an Englishman named Harold Scarth, who was Bill Edwards's brother-in-law. I think my description of a mail-order honey business my brother and I had started made a favorable impression on Scarth, because the next day he called me up and told me to report for work on November 1.

I had no idea what I was supposed to be doing at Edwards Brothers and no one seemed able to tell me. Scarth spoke vaguely about sales, but he gave me no specific duties or responsibilities. Consequently, I floundered around and asked a lot of questions. In those days the firm's principal business was in printing limited-edition university textbooks. These were usually draft manuscripts by professors who wanted to test them on students. The professors would make successive revisions based on experience in the classroom. In due course, they would be satisfied that the text was in final form, at which point they would submit it to a regular textbook publisher. Edwards Brothers had started off as a mimeographing house, but by the time I joined them, they had acquired Rotaprint offset presses from Germany. The offset method[4] is now widely used, but at that time it

[4] Offset, also known as photolithography or photo-offset, involves making a photographic negative of copy to be printed: in the case of Edwards Brothers' work, a page of typescript. The negative is etched onto a thin, sensitized zinc or aluminum plate, which is then placed on a cylinder of the press. Ink is picked up from rollers by the etched portion of the plate and is transferred to another cylinder covered with rubber called the blanket. This image is picked up by the impression cylinder, which transfers it to paper traveling around it.

was new to Ann Arbor. The Rotaprint presses printed on a continuous roll of paper called a web, eleven inches wide, and cut it into pages every 8-1/2 inches. This was perfect for the short runs the company's customers required, and the quality was equal to that of other forms of printing.

Another job the company had acquired was for printing the automobile-license lists for the Secretary of State of Michigan. The contract called for a specific quantity of these lists to be supplied to other agencies, and we had the right to sell additional copies to anyone else who wanted to buy them. They sold for about $300 a set and were updated at regular intervals during the year.

Shortly after Christmas, Scarth told me that Bill Edwards wanted me to go out and sell the auto-license lists. I had to sell a minimum of two thousand dollars' worth in the next month, he said, if I wanted to keep my job.

This was the kind of direction I'd been looking for, and I wasted no time getting on the road. I drove across the state, calling on garages and any other agencies I thought might have use for the lists. After ten days, I returned to the office with four thousand dollars' worth of orders.

Not long after that, I came up with what proved to be a major improvement in the company's method of operation. We had been photographing manuscripts that were type-written on 8-1/2-by-11-inch paper, single spaced, with one-inch margins all around. This resulted in books that were virtually impossible to read, which was to my mind an intolerable state of affairs. When I was working in Chicago for Celotex, I learned a formula which stated that a line of type would not be easily readable if it exceeded 30 times the point size [5] of the type. The average line in our books was nearly 60 times the point size of our elite type. My suggestion to Bill Edwards was that we type our copy on larger sheets, in two columns, using pica type instead of elite. These oversize pages would be reduced in making the negative, so we would wind up with printed pages on which there were two columns of 9-point type, each about 3-3/8 inches wide. This greatly increased readability. The eye could follow the shorter line of letters much more easily, and the letters themselves were sharper due to the reduction, which eliminated small imperfections. Moreover, the method reduced the overall number of pages required and, therefore, the cost of any job. The market accepted this change with enthusiasm.

Bill Edwards was impressed by my performance, so he assigned me the task of calling on members of the university faculty to solicit manuscripts for printing. This worked out well. Sadye's contacts on campus opened doors for me. Most of our friends were connected with the university, so I understood the academic attitude toward publication, which was quite different than the commercial approach. I was comfortable in talking to professors at Michigan and the other universities I called on about their teaching needs. Bill, on the other hand, was ill at ease in the academic environment. He envied my rapport with scholars, but he

---

[5] Point size refers to the height of a letter according to a system of measure invented by French printer Francois Amrose Didot (1730-1804) and now used almost universally. A point is equal to 0.013835 inch (about 1/72 inch), and there are 12 points to the pica. Elite type is 10 point, or two points smaller than pica type. The body type of this book, for example, is 13 point.

was secretly relieved, I think, to have me take over that part
of the business.

One day Bill came in and asked me if I knew anyone who
could keep books. Alice Plough, who had sat next to me in
business school, immediately came to mind. She had
majored in accounting and was currently without a job.
Alice was hired, and it soon became apparent that she was
exactly right for the job. She and I worked well together.
Bill was mercurial, both in temperament and in his involvement with the business. He'd come in and stir things up and
then go away and leave us to our own devices for weeks on
end. After about a year, he reorganized the staff. He
dismissed Harold Scarth, assigning accounting and finance
to Alice. He gave responsibility for production to Bert
Cushing, and sales and marketing to me. Then Bill went
away again, which was just fine with us. We were a great
team, and we got the place humming. Business increased by
20 percent that year.

One of the places on campus that I called on from time to
time was The Clements Library, a collection of early
Americana that had been the personal library of former
regent William L. Clements. He donated it to the university
and provided a certain endowment for acquisitions. Randolph Adams was the director, and I have him to thank for
teaching me about the value of old books and giving me an
appreciation for typography, printing, and binding. We
would spend hours talking about books he had acquired.
His enthusiasm for them, both as cultural artifacts and as
historical records, was contagious. I must say that Randolph was one of the most intelligent and imaginative

11

people I've known. He was also arrogant and impatient with people who didn't share his love of history. Yet he had a great capacity to inspire others.

At that time Clements was acquiring only books published prior to 1800, which made it, by nature, rather exclusive. This exclusivity was projected into the very atmosphere of the library by Randolph's assistant librarian, Edith Steer. She was a formidable person, about six feet tall. She also was a woman of the type who is never wrong. About anything. If Miss Steer rendered an opinion on something, that was it. You could depend on it. One day she was giving a visiting professor a tour of the library, and after being thoroughly intimidated by her and anxious to curry favor, he observed that the students must make a lot of use of the library.

She said, "Oh, no, the students don't use this library."

"I suppose the graduate students do quite a lot of work over here?"

"No," she assured him, "the graduate students don't use this library."

"I suppose the faculty members use it?"

"No, the faculty members don't use it."

"Well, then, who does use the library?"

"Mr. Adams," she replied loftily, "and Mr. Clements."

R andolph Adams was extremely interested in new ideas. One day I was explaining our process of photographing pages in order to make offset plates, and I said to Randolph, "We could make facsimiles of these books you have here, for example, in limited editions. They would look exactly like the originals." He was immediately intrigued, suggesting that perhaps we should produce a facsimile of Hariot's *Virginia,* [6] an eyewitness account of life in the Roanoke Colony, the first settlement in what is now the United States, during 1586 and 1587. There are only seven known copies.

I became excited about this, too. We decided we could produce an attractive facsimile of Hariot which we could sell to pay the cost of printing plus a profit. Randolph brought the original to our office, where it was photographed. After much experimentation, we produced the facsimile in an edition of 300 copies, bound in parchment by R. R. Donnelly in Chicago. The books were very attractive and got some favorable reviews, which pleased us. But I really had no idea of how to market them, and only managed to sell about a hundred copies.

Though it wasn't financially profitable, the Hariot experience solidified my interest in early books and typography, and it paved the way to another, much more rewarding, undertaking.

I kept a copy of the Hariot facsimile in my briefcase during my wanderings around campuses, and one day I showed it to Professor Charles Fries of the University of Michigan English Department. He was in charge of work on the *Early Modern English Dictionary* being compiled at the university, and he discerned in the facsimile process I was describing a method that might be a great aid in that effort.

[6] The full title of this volume by Thomas Hariot is: *A Briefe and True Report of the Newfoundland of Virginia.*

His staff was faced with the task of copying entries from early books by hand, an approach that was both time-consuming and open to all sorts of transcription errors. The only other possibility was to cut up these rare old books, as Sir William Cragie, a former editor at Oxford, had done in order to mark the examples of usage and file them for compilation into manuscript form. Professor Fries's idea was to photograph a carefully selected list of books from the Pollard & Redgrave *Short Title Catalogue of Books Printed in England, Scotland, & Ireland from 1475 to 1640* (STC) and produce one hundred copies of each page, printed on one side of the sheet. A lexicographer would take a stack of copies of a given page of a particular title and underline the first word of interest in the first sentence. Parentheses would be placed around that portion of the text which illustrated the underlined word's usage, then the whole sheet would be filed under that particular word, and so on, through every word of interest on a page. (See Appendix A.) There were about 150 books Professor Fries was interested in at the time, and most of them were in the British Museum in London. Some were in the libraries at Oxford and Cambridge.

I set up a conference with Professor Fries for Bill Edwards and me, which resulted in the decision that I would go to England and attempt to obtain permission to photograph the books and arrange for the work to be done. That trip, in the summer of 1931, with Sadye and my brother Frank, was memorable for many reasons, which I will detail later. Suffice it to say here that being introduced to early printed books, particularly those listed in the STC, has had a

14

lifelong effect on me.

The trip was a success insofar as getting the titles Professor Fries wanted photographed, but a side expedition to Germany in hopes of purchasing some plates for our Rotaprint presses was a failure. The Germans had imposed tight controls on these materials. After we got back home, I learned a good lesson from the photographer I had hired to make the negatives of the STC books. He decided to charge more than we'd originally agreed upon, and my hands were tied. I vowed never again to enter an agreement in which I was totally dependent on a single source unless I had complete control. Failing that, I would always arrange an alternative supplier or have a fallback plan.

In any event, the negatives began to arrive from England just as Edwards Brothers was entering its slow season of the year, fall and early winter, so they were a godsend even at the higher prices. They allowed us to keep our presses rolling and our crews employed and, of course, my status in the company was thereby improved.

One of my jobs during the increasingly frequent absences of Bill Edwards was handling the company's correspondence, and one day the mail brought an inquiry from Professor Robert Binkley, who taught history at Western Reserve University in Cleveland, Ohio. It concerned a short manuscript titled "Methods for Reproducing Research Material," which he had written in 1931 as chairman of the Joint Committee on Materials for Research of the Social Science Research Council and the American Council of Learned Societies. I responded to Binkley's questions, and he brought the manuscript for the second edition to us to have it printed.

I found Professor Binkley to be a fascinating and stimulating individual, and we were soon on a first-name basis. Bob's chief interest was in creating a systematic chart of the various methods of print reproduction available so scholars could determine whether hectograph, mimeograph, offset, or letterpress would be best suited to their specific purpose. I helped him write the section on offset, which he strongly favored for small editions with typewritten composition.

Bob had surrounded himself with a small group of individuals who were interested in this subject of methods of reproducing research materials. One of them was John Marshall, who later became an assistant to David Stevens in the Humanities Section of the Rockefeller Foundation and who was at that time secretary of the Medieval Academy of the American Council of Learned Societies. Binkley and Marshall organized a meeting in Cambridge, Massachusetts in late 1931 to discuss methods of production and distribution of scholarly information.

That meeting had great significance for me, because it was there that the concept of somehow being able to produce copies of academic material in small quantities or one at a time, on demand, first formulated itself in my mind. This concept was to become my personal holy grail, which I would pursue all the rest of my publishing career.

At that time, my concept seemed as remote as the moon. All known methods of reproducing information involved an edition process, which is to say that most of the expense or work of a given printing was incurred "up front," before the first copy could be made, for such things as typing or setting type, proofing, makeready, and printing. This had long been accepted as a necessary condition in publishing. There was no economical method of producing a single copy. With offset printing, for example, even on the extremely narrow webs and tiny plates we were using at Edwards Brothers, the absolute minimum edition we could produce at practical cost was one hundred. That, I might add, was only true for certain types of books. For most projects, the minimum would more likely be two hundred copies or more.

Impossible or not, my vision would not be dismissed. It kept creeping back into my mind in the months and years that followed the Cambridge meeting to tantalize me with how wonderful it would be for scholarly publishing if some process could be developed that would make possible the production of a single, readable book at a low unit cost.

Why?

Well, simply because scholars were being deprived of certain information that might be immensely valuable. Many scholarly manuscripts were considered unpublishable because demand for them was small and unit cost was, therefore, prohibitive. Shorter manuscripts could be published in journals, but long monographs often were not. The knowledge they might contain was hidden away from human use. There was a certain irony in the situation, because it was the very possessors of knowledge who were stifled by the limitations of our vaunted technology. Men and women whose ideas might enlighten others or aid in eradicating disease or ease the pangs of hunger were cut off from communicating these ideas.

My quest was encouraged by another of my contacts on

the Michigan campus, the university's librarian, William Warner Bishop. An impressive-looking, white-goateed scholar, he was widely respected in his profession, and I was in awe of him. When I told Bishop I was going to England on the project for Professor Fries, he gave me some letters of introduction that proved very helpful. He was extremely interested in the project, because some years earlier he and a Yale librarian named Andrew Keogh had gotten together with the librarian of the New York Public Library to attempt to arrange for a photostatic copy of every STC book to be made and deposited in the United States. American libraries had been late in starting their collections of these titles, and although certain collections were sizable, such as those at the New York Public Library, the Huntington Library in California, the Folger Library in Washington and, to a lesser degree, the libraries at Yale and Harvard, the American holdings were far from complete. Bishop had a broad perspective on the role of libraries as national resources, and he provided me with much scholarly guidance and advice. Unfortunately, he did not live to see my idea developed successfully.

All the while we were working on the dictionary project for Professor Fries, the economic Depression was deepening. It put a damper on things, including facsimile editions of three STC books I had printed with negatives left over after the dictionary requirements had been met. I designed the typography for the titles and someone on the dictionary staff wrote a brief introduction. The books turned out to be very attractive little volumes, but we couldn't get our investment out of them even though only three hundred were printed; to do so required that we sell all three hundred, and people were much more interested in putting food on the table than in purchasing facsimiles of rare books, however fine they might be.

That experience served to intensify my interest in finding a way to produce editions of a single copy. But I could not give it a great deal of attention at this point. I had some much more serious ramifications of the Depression to deal with if Edwards Brothers was to continue expanding.

Chapter Two

Discovery

Ann Arbor did not suffer as much from the Depression of the '30s as did many other communities across the country. The University of Michigan helped provide the area with stability in employment. But no one could avoid being affected by the problems banks were having in the wake of the 1932 Presidential election. Franklin D. Roosevelt had won; however, he would not take office until March 4, 1933,[1] and people were losing confidence in banks during Herbert Hoover's final lame-duck months as President. Several local banks scattered around the Midwest had declared holidays, closing their doors temporarily to ease the pressure of withdrawals by their depositors. On February 4, 1933, the governor of Louisiana proclaimed a weekend bank holiday for the city of New Orleans. Troubled banks had little hope of help from the Federal Reserve System, because it was strained by the need to put more and more currency in circulation at a time when its stock of gold was dwindling due to domestic hoarding and heavy demand

---

[1] The Twentieth Amendment to the U.S. Constitution, which provides that the terms of the President and Vice-President shall end at noon on the twentieth day of January (rather than in March), had been passed and ratified by the states, but was not declared in effect until February 6, 1933.

21

from foreign banks.[2]

On February 14, 1933, Michigan's Governor William Alfred Comstock announced the first statewide bank holiday. All banks were closed, all accounts frozen, for eight days. I thought this action was likely to spread to other states. If it did, our business would be paralyzed. We would not be able to cash bank checks received from our creditors and, therefore, we would be unable to pay suppliers or meet our payroll. I shared my concern with Alice Plough, telling her I thought we'd better try and get in our accounts receivable. Alice agreed, and that evening after work, she and I telephoned everyone outside the state of Michigan who owed us one hundred dollars or more and asked them to pay us, if possible, by postal money order. We explained our apprehension, telling them that if we could get the money immediately, it would help us and probably would help them as well. In fact, that's exactly what transpired. A few days later, the Michigan bank holiday had precipitated what came to be known as "the national banking crisis of 1933"[3] and banks across the country were closed. But we had cash coming in daily in the form of postal money orders—in all, we received just over $50,000 worth of them. This cash allowed us to continue meeting payrolls and paying our suppliers. We even made some loans to other businesses in Ann Arbor.

I'm afraid I displayed my immaturity and false pride by

[2] *Since 1900* Oscar T. Barck, Jr. and Nelson M. Blake, The Macmillan Company, pp. 486-487.

[3] *Encyclopedia Britannica*, 1973, Vol. 15, p. 371.

not telling Bill Edwards what I had done. I feigned ignorance when he said, "Isn't it great that all these people are sending in postal money orders?" He learned the facts later, when customers wrote to say how pleased they were that Edwards Brothers had made the request, because they got that money out before their bank was closed or went under. Some said they had lost everything else.

Among the many problems the banking industry had at that time was verification of checks drawn by depositors. After a statement was prepared for an account, the bank made a list of the checks pertaining to it, but it sent the canceled checks back to the customer along with a copy of his statement. A few unscrupulous customers would come in and contest a charge on the statement, claiming they never wrote such a check. The banks had no way of disproving the claims. George L. McCarthy, vice president of the Empire Trust Company of New York City, was an amateur photographer, and since about 1923, when he was a bank clerk, he had been tinkering with photographic devices designed to make such fraud difficult.[4] His work was backed by the Eastman Kodak Company, and in 1928 he finally came up with a "flow" camera that would photograph checks rapidly on 16mm film. The term *flow* derived from the fact that the material being photographed was fed into the device in a steady, uninterrupted stream and photographed while moving. "Photographing the documents

---

[4] *The Kodak Magazine* January 1929, Vol. IX, No. 8.

automatically was one thing," stated a report from Kodak.[5] "But to view these images in readable size for reference purposes required a special reader. This was designed as a companion unit to the photographing machine. . . . The first reader, designed to rest on top of a desk or office table, projected the images onto a horizontal white surface. . . . The rolls of film [were] moved quickly by means of a hand crank." The camera and reader, which were rented to banks as a unit, would give the institutions a permanent record of canceled checks and end any question about charges to an account. In March of 1928, Kodak formed a subsidiary, the Recordak Corporation, with McCarthy as president, to promote microfilming in banks and businesses.

My friend Bob Binkley had seen McCarthy's flow camera. Bob kept abreast of all the new developments in the field of print and photographic reproduction. For example, he was keenly interested in a method of research note taking, which was just on the horizon, involving the use of a Leica camera to copy books and manuscripts. Scholars working in foreign libraries needed such a technique. Bob invited me to join him in his experiments with the Leica on my frequent trips to visit him in Cleveland. After exposing the film,[6] we would take it into his darkroom and develop

---

[5] *The History and Progress of Modern Microfilming,* an undated historical memorandum prepared by Recordak Corporation; reference courtesy of the Eastman Kodak Company Archives.

[6] The film used was orthochromatic black-and-white, which had a fairly high resolution. At that time, a negative could resolve (make visible) 50 to 100 lines per mm, the quality being controlled by the lens.

it. If we got a recognizable image, we rejoiced.

Bob had decided that McCarthy's flow camera would be useful for the assignment he had of copying records from the files of the Agricultural Adjustment Administration in Washington. These records consisted of a large number of unbound 8-1/2-by-11-inch mimeographed pages, the useful life of which was extremely limited because the paper tended to tear easily and the print faded quickly. Bob's assistant, Ted Schellenberg, did the copying work. Ted and I were good friends, too. He was to come to Ann Arbor on September 19, 1934 to discuss the new edition of Bob's book, *Methods for Reproducing Research Materials,* which Edwards Brothers was preparing to print, and Ted was eager to show me the results of his efforts with McCarthy's camera on 16 mm film. I'll never forget that night.

I had picked Ted up at the train station that rainy Wednesday afternoon and driven him to my office at Edwards Brothers. We went through the page layout and my proposed changes for the Binkley book; then I took Ted to the Michigan Union, where I had arranged for him to stay. Since the weather was so nasty, we decided to have dinner there in the Union and then go to Ted's room to see his flow-camera samples.

At dinner, Ted told me about an interesting new camera designed by R. H. Draeger for copying books. It seemed that Draeger, a captain in the Navy, had been assigned to China and wanted to take a lot of books with him—more than he could afford to buy. So he designed a camera mounted on a mast over a flatbed, on which an opened book could be pressed flat beneath a glass cover. Lights on both sides of the holder illuminated the pages without creating shadows. The camera held 100 feet of roll film that was advanced electrically after each exposure. Presumably, Captain Draeger had gone off to China with a hundred books captured in miniature on his rolls of 35mm negative film, which he could enlarge and print on paper in his spare time. His book-copying camera had been moved from the Department of the Navy and placed in the Department of Agriculture Library, where it was being used by Biblio-Film Service, a subsidiary of Science Service, a business established by Watson Davis, who had obtained permission from the Department of Agriculture to photograph journal articles and extracts from its library's books and periodicals. Davis filled requests for copies by sending the negative film to his customers.

I was excited by Ted's description of the way Watson Davis was using the Draeger camera. I wasn't sure what made it so appealing, but I felt there was something tremendously important about it.

After dinner Ted set up his projector to show me the sample rolls of film he had made with the McCarthy flow camera. As he loaded the negative film into the projector, I experienced a strange, almost giddy feeling of anticipation. I could not explain it. Then, when Ted flashed the image of a page of mimeographed manuscript onto the screen, the idea I had sensed lurking just beneath the surface of my consciousness emerged. It was as if a great light had gone on in my mind; for here, before my eyes, was the long-sought answer to the problem of how to produce a single copy of any printed document "on demand."

DISCOVERY

The idea came to me full-blown: *If the film in Ted's projector were a positive instead of a negative, it would be projected onto the screen black-on-white, reading exactly like the page of a book. I could photograph a page and print a positive-film copy for the customer, keeping the negative in my file to be duplicated over and over again in filling future requests. There would be no need, as there was in traditional publishing, to maintain a warehouse inventory of finished copies or to rephotograph the original material. Each copy made would be to fill a specific order. I could keep a vault full of negatives; therefore, no title need ever go out of print.*

"That's it!" I shouted.

Ted Schellenberg was baffled. He had expected a polite word of approval of his work, but here I was practically bouncing off the ceiling with enthusiasm. I began an excited explanation, and Ted got caught up in the spirit of it. We talked about it until almost two o'clock in the morning. Then I went home and woke Sadye up to tell her about my great discovery.

I knew my concept was solid. All that remained was to work out the details.

As a matter of fact, in the months and years that followed, the "details" would prove to be significant challenges. An entire system of making microfilm positives had to be devised, and I would have to publicize the process and solicit orders for it, not to mention such tasks as setting up a means of producing the positives and packing and shipping them. I envisioned customers "reading" the positive film by use of a projector like the Recordak machine Ted

27

showed me. In practice, this machine would not prove to be entirely satisfactory. It was cumbersome and relatively expensive. It did not provide the adequate substitute for the printed page that my idea would require.

However, on that night of discovery, no foreseeable obstacle could overshadow the shining pinnacle of my idea. The concept of "publication or production on demand" glowed for me like a snowcapped peak in the moonlight. I knew it would work, and I knew its publishing advantages would far outweigh any time and money it would take to develop it.

A few days later, I made a trip to Washington, D.C. to examine the Draeger camera. I spent nearly two days looking it over and discussing it with Watson Davis and a Department of Agriculture employee named Vernon Tate. The construction of the camera was straightforward enough, and I felt I could build something like it without much difficulty. I liked Vernon Tate; we shared many of the same interests, and he knew a lot about copying library materials on 35mm film with a Leica camera. He had employed this method in Mexico while studying for his doctorate at the University of California. I invited him to dinner that evening, and we began what would prove to be a long and close friendship.

When I returned to Ann Arbor, I was bubbling with enthusiasm for building a Draeger-style camera and using it to do the microphotography or microfilming for a test of my idea of publication on demand. It seemed to me that photographing STC books would be an ideal trial, since the collection was extensive, some 26,000 titles, and demand for them would be certain; American libraries, having been established relatively recently, were generally lacking in STC titles. I talked the idea over with Randolph Adams and William Warner Bishop, both of whom were encouraging. Then I proposed to Bill Edwards that we get into this new field of microfilming. I told him I was certain that it had great possibilities. Bill was lukewarm about it, but he did hear me out and finally told me to go ahead and see what I could do.

With the aid of a machine shop in Ann Arbor, we converted parts of two movie and still cameras into what was the second microfilm book-camera in existence. Its film advance was set to move the film ahead three-quarters of an inch each time the shutter was tripped. This movement was half a standard Leica frame (a full frame being 1-by-1-1/2 inches) of the double-perforated film. When the camera was completed and working smoothly, I told Bill I was ready to take it to England, install it in the British Museum, and begin having the STC books photographed. My plan was that when the negatives began coming back to Ann Arbor, I would set up a subscription service in which Edwards Brothers would provide libraries with 100,000 pages of STC titles annually on positive film for $500, or one-half cent a page. I felt this would be profitable. Bill remained skeptical about the viability of the venture, however, and so did Alice Plough.

In August 1935, with the camera secured in a big packing case, Sadye and my mother and I sailed for England from Quebec on the S.S. *Rotterdam*. I had written in advance to

29

Arundel Esdaille, the secretary of the British Museum, about the plan. He was most cordial when I called on him, and gave me permission to place the camera in the museum's photographic studio. He also arranged to have STC books sent there to be photographed from the Bodleian Library at Oxford and the University Library at Cambridge. The arrangement worked very well, although there were the usual hitches and minor problems to be ironed out. (One was that the photographer whom I had engaged to operate the camera wanted to increase his charges after I returned to Ann Arbor. This had been anticipated as a possibility, so Esdaille agreed to have one of the museum staff operate the camera for a fixed charge per exposure, and this was done.) I announced the new service—the first use of microfilm as a publishing medium—at the Spring 1936 meeting of the American Library Association (ALA) in Chapel Hill, North Carolina.

I had my regular job to perform at Edwards Brothers, of course, so I could not devote as much attention to the microfilm business as I would have liked. Nor could I seem to get a supplier to provide positive microfilm of the quality I desired. Finally, I asked Bill Edwards if he would approve of my making the positives myself, in my spare time. I would charge Edwards Brothers the going rate of six cents a foot. He agreed. I had only a general idea about darkroom techniques, so I sought expert advice from people like Bob Gach, who ran a photo shop in the Nickel's Arcade near the U of M campus. Bob was very helpful. I also obtained Eastman Kodak's *Motion Picture Laboratory Practice,* which I read three times before I really began to understand the darkroom process. A young man named Jan Vanden-brock, an instrument maker for the university's psychology department, was helpful in making some of the equipment I needed. The only space I could afford to rent was two small rooms on Maynard Street, in the rear of Ray Dolph's Funeral Parlor. I converted one of these rooms into a

darkroom; the other was used as a workroom. I hired a young man who had some darkroom experience to help me. We had a small printer, which we had to turn by hand at a uniform rate, to make the contact prints on 35mm positive film. This film was wound into a Stine-man spiral reel in 200-foot lengths and placed in the developing tank, then fixed, washed, and dried

This 1936 photo shows me after a full night's work in my funeral-parlor lab.

on a large drum-style rack. Some nights we would finish a thousand feet of film. We cut the film into 100-foot rolls, each containing approximately 3,000 book pages, and placed them in labeled boxes for shipment. As I look back on those methods now, they seem crude, but they did produce readable positives. Also, in retrospect, I can see that those nights of feverish work amid the caskets and embalming odors of Dolph's Funeral Parlor were the real beginning of University Microfilms.

By the fall of 1936, six libraries had subscribed to our service of supplying STC books as microfilm. Filling these orders required diligent effort in the darkroom every night of the week. I worked from 7:30 P.M. until midnight, back there among the corpses. But I didn't mind. I was enjoying every minute of the process of making "publication on demand" a reality.

My cause was advanced unexpectedly by Argus, Inc., an Ann Arbor camera maker, when it came out with the first practical, inexpensive microfilm reader. I learned about it from an Argus representative named Benjamin Gilbert, who called on me one day and showed me a demonstration model. The reader sold for $75, and it was to play a significant role in making microfilm a practical means of disseminating information. Gilbert was a likable chap. His wife was an interesting person—she was a granddaughter of John D. Rockefeller who, in accordance with a stipulation of the old man's will that all his heirs must support themselves for a period of time, had worked as a nurse. Sadye and I saw quite a lot of the Gilberts during the year they lived in Ann Arbor. Ben and I discussed the notion of tie-in sales, in which I could earn a commission for offering the Argus reading machine in conjunction with our microfilm sales, but I never seriously considered it. I wanted to sell our film service exclusively and be free to recommend whatever equipment seemed best. Looking back now, I can see that my approach was a good one. Tie-in sales might have led me astray and prevented me from concentrating on the microfilm business.

While all these interesting developments were taking

place at work, Sadye and I had news of a major change in our life at home. She had come to the conclusion that the fact that we had not had a child in our seven years of marriage was due to the stress of her work in the Mental Hygiene Clinic of the University Student Health Service. So in 1937 she gave up the job she loved so much and, sure enough, she became pregnant. We were delighted.

At that time, I was regularly attending ALA meetings, at which there was always considerable interest in microfilm. Vernon Tate attended these sessions, too. He had been appointed head of the microfilm laboratories at the National Archives, where he was already using microfilm negatives as a method of preserving certain holdings, so he was extremely knowledgeable. After the regular ALA sessions, Vernon and I and a few others would get together for discussions about microfilm that sometimes continued late into the night. In one of these informal meetings, someone suggested that we needed a journal dedicated to microfilm. Charles Rush, associate librarian at Yale, said he would talk to David Stevens of the Rockefeller Foundation about obtaining a small grant to get it started. He was successful, and Vernon Tate was appointed editor of the publication, *The Journal of Documentary Reproduction,* which Edwards Brothers printed (see Appendix A), beginning in 1938.

My work life was becoming increasingly complicated. For a little over a year I had been, in effect, handling two jobs: directing the sales efforts for Edwards Brothers—both the regular printing and the microfilm service—during the day and working in my funeral-parlor darkroom at night.

There was a conflict between traditional printing and microfilm that was becoming increasingly apparent. It was not a matter of interest or energy—I had plenty of both. It was a more fundamental difference in approach. Traditional publishing is geared to producing large quantities of a single title. Microfilm publishing, on the other hand, produces single copies of a large number of titles. For Bill Edwards, this translated to a conflict in sales point of view. I now think Bill was justified in the approach he took, but at the time I thought he was being stubborn and short-sighted. I think he considered my manner arrogant, and perhaps it was; I certainly did not have a high regard for his business judgment. My longtime friend Neil Staebler also knew Bill Edwards very well, and in order to be fair to Bill, I asked Neil to dictate his recollection of the situation for this book. He said:

> Yes, Bill Edwards was a good friend of mine. He tended to be rather rigid in his thinking, and Gene Power's prolific ideas were upsetting to him. All Bill wanted was to concentrate on doing a good job of printing. He went along with the microfilm thing for a time, but finally he told me that he gave Gene an ultimatum: "Either you throw that Goddam thing out, or you take it with you and leave!"

I chose to leave. Bill didn't want any payment for the equipment, which included the microfilm copy camera that was in the British Museum. I had a $1,500 bonus due me for work I had done during the previous year, and that seemed to me sufficient to develop my business, since I already had a start with the STC book orders. Perhaps I should have been apprehensive about giving up my secure position at

Edwards Brothers, but I wasn't. On the contrary, the feeling of being on my own was exhilarating! I located a small building at 313 North First Street in Ann Arbor, which had been a contractor's office and garage, and there I rented two of the three offices for, as I recall, fifty dollars a month. I shared a secretary with Connie Wageman, an advertising-space salesman for *American Builder* magazine, to whom I rented the other office, and University Microfilms was in business.

It never occurred to me that I might fail. I left Edwards Brothers on June 1, 1938. Two days later, our son, Philip, was born.

Chapter Three

Heritage

H aving a son is, paradoxically, one of man's most ata-
vistic yet grandest experiences. From fulfilling the
urge to procreate and ordain the future comes his most
poetic sense of human love and belonging in the ranks of
time. I felt this deeply when Phil was born, because I came
from stock that was proud of its sturdy heritage.

My ancestors were from England. The earliest I have
been able to trace was Nicholas Power I, whose son,
Nicholas II, came to the New World before 1670 and settled
in Rhode Island. Nicholas II was one of a group that was
killed in King Philip's War (1675-76) between the colonists
and the Indians. An estimated six hundred settlers lost their
lives in that war. Nicholas Power III had two sons, both of
whom lived in Providence, Rhode Island, and fought in the
Revolutionary War. The first son was killed in battle. The
second son, John II, had a son named Arthur, who in 1822
or 1823 was reported in Farmington, New York, and came
to Michigan via the Erie Canal and a boat trip across Lake
Erie to Detroit. In 1824, Arthur took the plank road north-
west from Detroit into the forest and blazed a trail to what
is now Farmington. He settled there because there was a
stream suitable for powering a grist mill, and he home-
steaded about 150 or 200 acres of rolling, fertile land.

Arthur Power was a Quaker and in 1826 he established the

first Quaker meeting in the state of Michigan. In clearing his land for farming, he burned the logs because there was such an abundance of wood. While engaged in this work he was visited by representatives of the University of Michigan, which had just been established in 1817. They were seeking a section of land in the center of that county to purchase for the university, as decreed in one of the first acts of the territorial government (Michigan did not become a state until 1835). Each county was to make available to the university, at its choosing, a section of land to be used to support the fledgling institution. In this case the parcel they decided upon was almost in the center of Arthur Power's homestead. The university wrote to him offering to buy his land for $1.25 an acre. He did not answer the letter. Then they offered $1.50. He did not answer that letter either. Finally he sold to them at $2 an acre. (This was a good price for such land in those days. H. Wirt Newkirk, a probate judge in Washtenaw County, observed in 1924 that the Ann Arbor property on which the University of Michigan's main campus was built had been purchased in 1825 for $3.75 an acre). The university later sold Arthur Power's land at a profit and the proceeds were used to build the first building of the University of Michigan in Detroit.

Arthur was an influential man in his community. Arthur's son Nathan Power was even more influential—a very solid citizen. He kept a diary that covered about thirty years. Each entry was about three lines long, usually about daily events, the weather, and general observations on farming. But there was an occasional memorable entry such as the description of some travelers who came through on the boat from Buffalo, "bringing with them the cholera." They stopped at Nathan's home, and the next entry, on what he described as "the saddest day of my life," Nathan wrote: "8th mo. 20th, 1832: Selinda Pain, my first wife, died of the Asiatic cholera, being 32 years old. She died at 7 A.M. My only daughter Phoebe Minerva 5 years old died the same day at 11 A.M. They were buried in our ground the same day at 6 o'clock. The first grave opened in our cemetery." There followed quite a long period in which he made no entries. Nathan's diary is in the possession of Bob Power, who is from

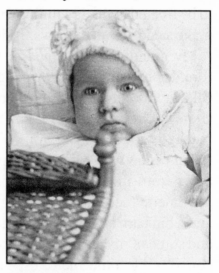

My first portrait, at age three months.

another branch of the family, and both Nathan and Arthur are recorded in the Farmington, Michigan Historical Museum. Nathan sired several children, among them my great-grandfather, Gideon Power.

I don't know exactly where my grandfather, Eugene Power, was born, but he was a farmer who apparently also had considerable organizational and management skills. At any rate, he was selected to manage a farm corporation that a group wanted to establish in Cuba for the purpose of raising cattle and harvesting valuable tropical timber. The capitalists who hired him had not done an adequate job of research prior to embarking on the project, however, and

39

when my grandfather reached the island with the first boatload of cattle, he discovered that the water was too alkaline for the animals. The timbering venture also failed because the tropical hardwoods they sought were too dense to be floated to the sawmill. Worse yet, the water would not make steam to run the saws: it simply foamed in the boilers.

My grandfather returned to Michigan and got a job as foreman of a large farm owned by the Antrim Ironworks in Elk Rapids, a few miles north of Traverse City on the east shore of Grand Traverse Bay. It was a large farm and when management of Antrim Ironworks decided to close it down (I don't know why) Grandfather purchased about one hundred acres from them. He lived there with my grandmother, Antoinette (nee Cloyse), tilling the land. He built a house and a big barn and had a lot of livestock. It was a fine farm, and some of my earliest memories are of that place. I spent considerable time there, especially during the summers. One of my recollections is of my father talking my grandfather into planting a cherry orchard. I was only four or five years old at that time, so it would have been about 1909. I remember my father standing behind a transit as a man placed stakes where trees were to go; he sighted down the rows of stakes, signaling for adjustments, to be sure the rows would be perfectly straight and the trees properly spaced. That was the beginning of the cherry industry up there in northern Michigan.

Grandmother Power was a strong person; she was taller than my grandfather and robust, but she also was extremely intelligent and had a wonderfully happy disposition. I can remember standing at her knee beside her kitchen table as she washed dishes and chatted away to me about one thing and another; for example, she'd look out the window and say, "There's old Joe Smith coming up the road and he's got a new bay horse." She had a lovely voice and she often sang as she worked, songs like "On the Banks of the Wabash" and " 'Way Down upon the Swanee River." Grandmother also loved to talk with her neighbors on the party line—the telephone was a great socializing factor on the farm, for it allowed everyone to participate in everyone else's business. The phones were the old magneto crank type, of course, and I recall that my grandparents had to remember to pull a switch at night or whenever there was a thunderstorm. There were no lightning arresters, and if you failed to pull the switch, lightning could flash into the house through the phone. I remember it doing so once, a sizzling flash that darted from the phone to a stovepipe on the opposite side of the room.

Another thing I remember about Grandmother Power was going with her to the lye box, which she kept out in the backyard. This was a box with a spigot in its bottom and she kept it full of wood ashes. Every so often she would go out and pour a pail of water into the box. The water would seep through the ashes to leach out lye, which she combined with fat saved from butchering pigs, to make soft soap. Nothing went to waste on the farm. Grandmother would test the strength of the lye water obtained from the ashes by putting an egg into it: if the egg floated, it was good; if the egg sank, this meant that the ashes were worn out and had to be replaced. The lye soap was used for washing clothes and dishes; it was too soft to form a cake and too strong to use

41

on one's skin. But I did get a bath in Grandmother's dishpan once a week when I was little.

The farm was pretty much self-sufficient in those days. My grandfather would go to town, once a week, two miles by horse and wagon, to peddle eggs and the butter my grandmother had made to the townspeople in Elk Rapids. I loved to go with him on those trips. Neither of my grandparents had much formal education, but Grandmother had an appreciation of the value of learning and my father told me that she was the one who insisted that he get a college education. Grandfather thought my father, whose name was Glenn Warren, should settle on a farm. But Grandmother said, "No, that boy is bright and we aren't going to do that. He's going to college."

My father went to Valparaiso University in Valparaiso, Indiana for a couple of years; I don't know what kind of degree he got, but I know he studied engineering. When he returned to Elk Rapids, he took a job as a teacher. It was a custom in those days for the bigger farm boys to gang up on male teachers and toss them out the window. My father was broad-shouldered, as I am, and very strong, and when one of these older boys began to act up, Father marched up to him, grabbed him by the back of the collar, held him out straight with his feet off the ground, and dropped him. The boy never gave him any trouble after that.

A short time later, Father moved to Traverse City and became an insurance agent for Fidelity Mutual Life Insurance Company of Philadelphia. He traveled around the northern part of the state by train and horse-and-buggy, and he must have been a pretty good salesman, because he was able to save money and establish himself in the community. He met my mother in about 1903.

Mother was born in Ypsilanti, where her father, Frank H. Barnum, operated a jewelry store. In the early 1890s, he moved his family to Traverse City and opened a jewelry store, Barnum and Earl, in partnership with a cousin of his named Frank Earl. Grandfather and Grandmother Barnum, whose name was Florence, had three daughters: Edna, Annette, and Blanche. Edna married Dr. Percy Lawton, a general practitioner; Annette married my father; and Blanche married John Coolidge, an Episcopal minister. Edna and Dr. Lawton always lived near us and she and my mother were very close all their lives. I mention this because I think that the warmth and cohesiveness of our family had a great influence on me and the manner in which I cultivated friendships throughout my career.

My maternal grandparents had a cottage on what we called Carp Lake, now called Lake Leelanau, and they went out there often in their Franklin automobile. Grandmother Barnum was a very positive woman, small and alert; she had a quick mind and a very sharp tongue, which she didn't hesitate to use when the occasion required. I remember one day when I was about eight years old, my father was driving the Franklin out to the cottage, with my mother and me and Grandmother Barnum as passengers. We got about halfway there and the driveshaft broke or came loose. They finally got it fixed, but the car wouldn't start. My grandmother said to my father, "Glenn, you aren't doing something, I'm sure."

"What do you mean?" he asked.

"Well, I saw a man kick the tire of his car the other day and

43

it ran."

"Don't be foolish," he said. "The tires have nothing to do with the engine."

"All right, then, I will do it," she declared. She walked over and kicked one of the tires. "Now try it," she said. And the damned thing started.

I was three years old when my brother Frank was born on September 12, 1907. I stayed at Aunt Edna's house that night. Next morning I was taken home to see him, and my mother asked me if I didn't think he was very nice and just what I wanted. My only comment was, "I wish he were gum."

Three years is a large difference in age when you are a child, so Frank and I weren't particularly close until his last year in college, when he lived with Sadye and me and we were the best of friends. I don't recall much about Frank as a youngster, except for dramatic things like the time he almost drowned at the cottage on Carp Lake. I was swimming nearby and saw him go under, and I thought, "Well, he is learning to dive." My father had been working on the launch motor, which happened to stop just then, and he heard Frank gurgle. Next thing I knew, Father jumped into the water and pulled Frank out. He was OK, but it was a frightening incident.

Grandfather Barnum made his own fishing rods during slow periods in his jewelry shop, and he took me fishing with him. He and my grandmother liked to row out onto the lake and still-fish for bass, which were plentiful. That was great fun, but I learned to like stream fishing for trout much better. My first experience at this came when I was in the third grade. About two blocks from my home was a small stream we called Asylum Creek because it ran through the grounds of the State Mental Hospital. The stream was only three or four feet wide but it provided a home for numerous speckled trout. One day I noticed a man drop his line through a storm drain in a bridge that crossed Asylum Creek. He waited a moment, then pulled out a trout. After he left, I dropped my line down the drain, and to my surprise, I caught one, too. I kept at it and caught several more of what I called "sewer trout." Because of the grating over the storm drain, I thought the fish came out of a sewer, but in reality they came from the stream under the bridge. I spent a lot of time on that stream and learned all the spots where trout liked to hide under the overhanging banks. By the time I was ten, I had worked out a method of impaling a single worm, hooking it just once, which left it free to slither naturally along the stream bottom. This was deadly. I could follow after other fishermen, fishing the very water they had just covered, and hook more trout than they had. I think I knew the location of virtually every fish in that stream; at any rate, if my mother had unexpected guests for dinner, she'd just call me and off I would go on my bicycle and return in short order with three or four more fish.

My father was a dedicated fly fisherman, and on May 1, 1914, he went off with some friends for the opening of trout season. I asked to go along, to no avail. However, I did not pout. I would go fishing anyhow, up at Asylum Creek. I was back before noon. Father returned late that evening empty-handed, and later that week the local paper ran a little feature story describing how Mr. Glenn Power had been upstaged by his young son, Eugene. Mr. Power had journeyed far to a river famous for its fishing. He was equipped with waders and hundreds of dollars' worth of fancy gear, but caught nothing. Meanwhile, little Eugene had walked barefoot to a local creek with a willow pole and line (which was not quite true) and caught five!

I was not introduced to the mysteries of fly fishing until I was thirteen. Had my mother been the one to take me hunting and fishing, I'm sure I would have learned earlier, for she was a more relaxed kind of parent. She also was more intuitive and quicker to reach a decision. My father tended to be disciplined and deliberative. I guess in this respect their marriage was a demonstration of the principle that opposites attract. The difference in their temperament could be quite evident, for example, when they played bridge. Father would drive Mother crazy with his mulling over a decision on what to bid. Her style of play was rapid-fire. It seems to me that one of the more important elements of success in life is a careful selection of one's parents. I don't mean to sound immodest in asserting that I chose mine well. I took my physique from my father who, as I have said, was strong and broad-shouldered. I suppose I also inherited his cautious approach to matters of finance. He was careful in his investments and he believed in saving, as I do. However, he was an authoritarian, which sometimes was hard for me to cope with. I took my mental capacities from my mother. Like her, I think intuitively. When I deal with a problem, I usually see the solution whole, without an intervening process of logical deduction—for example, the way my idea for microfilm publishing came to me that night with Ted Schellenberg. (If I seem to digress here from the subject of my introduction to fly fishing, please excuse me. Fly fishing is a sport full of lessons in living and tends to make its devotees philosophical and patient.)

To go on with my story. . . . On Decoration Day, May 30, the year I was thirteen, my father took me along on his annual fishing trip to Stone's Pond on the Cedar River near Alpena. We got up at four A.M. to be picked up by the other men in the party and drove to a place near Rapid City, where we had breakfast. Since I had no waders, my father had arranged for Mrs. Stone to take me out on the pond in her boat. It was interesting to see the schools of trout moving ahead of us, and I caught a few of them. But my real thrill came in the late afternoon when we went to a place called the Boat Houses on the lower Rapid River and my father let me use one of his spare fly rods. I waded into the river in my tennis shoes; the water that gripped my hips and legs was so ice cold it took my breath away. But I soon forgot the discomfort as I flailed away with the delicate rod and began getting the fly to fall somewhat gracefully at a respectable distance. Casting a fly requires a good sense of timing, and I seemed to have a natural bent for it. I soon had a series of strikes. Then I landed a fish, and *I* was the one hooked.

Throughout my high-school years I haunted the rivers in the Traverse City area—the Platte, the Rapid, the Boardman, and numerous lesser streams—learning the ways of trout and of the insects they fed upon, which I strove to imitate. I learned to tie flies from Ralph Hastings, my father's partner in his fire-insurance agency, and from Don Martinez, a Chicagoan, who was the best fly fisherman I have ever known. Don later moved to West Yellowstone, Montana, and I used to buy flies from him from time to time. The tragedy in Don's life, apart from being married to a woman who detested fishing, was alcohol.

Fishing teaches patience and perseverance, but the attentive fisherman learns more about himself than about his quarry, and so it was with me.

My most memorable fishing experience, strangely enough, was not on a trout stream but on the calm waters of Spider Lake, about fifteen miles southeast of Traverse City. I went there first with Ralph Hastings and his wife and their children, Bob and Elizabeth. There were no buildings at all on the lake, which was in the midst of cut-over pinelands, and local lore had it that its waters were barren. We disproved that the very first night by catching three or four large bass. Spider Lake got its name from its extremely irregular shoreline, which was a tangle of old roots and stumps and downed logs that made excellent cover for bass. I know of few greater pleasures in fishing than cruising silently along such a shore in a canoe and casting a surface plug into the holes. The bass would explode from the water like depth charges and grab our lures. The five of us camped there for ten wonderful days.

The following two summers, Bob and I camped by ourselves on an island in the middle of the lake. Bob was two years older than I, but we got along like Tom Sawyer and Huck Finn. Accompanied by Bob's cocker spaniel, we swam and fished and told lies. We each had a .22 rifle, and I regret to say that we reduced the turtle population considerably, thinking it great fun to pick them off as they sat sunning on logs. Had we realized how helpful turtles are in keeping a lake clean, we never would have shot them. We were blissful in our ignorance, I guess, and I would not change anything else about my memories of that lake. My favorite time was the wonderful evenings after the sun went down, when a family of loons would form a shadowy convoy under the rising moon and their odd, forlorn call would hang eerily in the peaceful, pine-scented air.

My brother was not a fisherman. In fact, he thought he was some sort of jinx or, as he put it, a hoodoo, and that whenever he went with me, the fishing was always poor. He loved winter sports, though, especially skiing. Our equipment was primitive by today's standards: heavy flat skis with no bindings, just a simple leather strap over the toe of one's boot. Our technique was commensurately Neanderthal: we stood at the top of a hill and went straight down. It was exciting to be going fast down a big hill and see a bit of brush or limbs jutting out of the snow ahead of you, for there was no turning—one just became a human snowball.

I became a competitive swimmer as a young boy. This happened because my parents belonged to the We-Que-Tong Club, which had a swimming beach on Grand Traverse West Bay. The club had a party every Saturday night during the summer, and part of the entertainment was a swimming race for the youngsters. One of my friends, Walt Thompson, always came in first and I invariably took second. Second prize was $1.50, which I used to buy fishing flies. I loved to swim and became good at it after I had some instruction at the University of Michigan ... but I'm getting ahead of my story.

There was one other aspect of my boyhood that was to become a lifelong characteristic, and that was my love of dogs. An English setter we called Joe was my constant companion. I even took him fishing with me sometimes. Joe lived a dog's life. For example, one time I took an especially long ride on my bicycle with faithful Joe trotting behind all the way. When we got back home I discovered that he had worn through the pads of his feet and they were bloody. I was remorseful, of course.

A boy could lead a dog's life sometimes, too, as I learned one day when Joe and I were crossing the alley, following my mother to my Aunt Edna's house. A strange cat had been hanging around the area, and when my mother spotted it in the alley, she impetuously said, "Sic 'im, Joe!" Joe did not require further urging. He and the cat went 'round and 'round. The animal altercation inflamed human emotions because, it turned out, the cat belonged to our neighbor. The offended cat owner apparently had not seen my mother on the scene, just Joe and me. She complained to my father, and I got my backside paddled before my mother could intercede and explain that it had been her fault.

Old Joe and I shared a lot of adventures. He was an affectionate dog, and I was heartbroken for a long time after he died. I was a senior in high school when Joe was hit by a car out at the farm and left in a ditch. We brought him to town and tried to nurse him, but it was no use. I realized then what a dog can mean to a person.

I suffered a series of mishaps in my high-school years that I think affected my performance as a student and, to some extent, my personality. First, in jumping from the second floor of the We-Que-Tong Club to the sand below, I caught my heel and fell onto the boardwalk. That put me in bed for ten days with internal injuries. Then, the next year, Frank stabbed me in the elbow with a fork during horseplay at the dinner table and I contracted blood poisoning, which was serious business in those days before penicillin.

Then, in the winter of my junior year, I developed encephalitis or "sleeping sickness." The physicians did not know how to diagnose or treat it, although Dr. Fleming Carrow, who had been chairman of the Eye, Ear, Nose, and Throat Department at the University of Michigan Hospital and once was chief medical officer for the Chinese Army, knew that since I had double vision there was some sort of brain infection. I did not regain normal vision for eight or ten weeks. I missed the entire last semester of school.

My parents thought I needed building up after that, so they sent me to Citizens Military Training Camp, which was run by the United States Army at Camp Custer, near Battle Creek. It was a miserable experience. Instead of being built up, I lost 15 pounds. The food was awful, the weather was unbearably hot, and my experience in riding horses—I selected the cavalry even though I'd never been on a horse before—was inglorious. I did learn something about military drill, however, and I enjoyed shooting on the rifle range.

Toward the end of that summer I spent ten days at a YMCA camp on Torch Lake, Camp Hayawenta. There I met Neil Staebler. I'll let him tell about one experience:

> Gene Power and I were assigned to the same tent. We became unhappy with the dictates of our tent counselor, a much older

51

boy, so we got together and decided to throw him in the lake. It took two of us to do it, and it was our first joint effort.

I felt peculiar and out of place, when school resumed for my senior year; I think it was a consequence of the encephalitis. My classmates seemed to avoid me. I think they felt I was acting strange as well. Up to that point, I had been rather popular; in fact, I was president of my junior class. Now even my relationship with my closest friends— Walt Thompson, Chuck Varney, and Albin Johnson—was strained, although we saw a lot of each other and spent considerable time driving around in Chuck's father's Nash automobile. Prior to my senior year, I had been a reasonably good student. But that year I had less than a *C* average and it was impossible for me to concentrate for any length of time. Unfortunately, we were never taught good study habits. I don't believe I really knew how to study. So what I learned was largely through osmosis. I wish it had been otherwise.

The summer of '23, after my graduation from high school, I got a job as a chemist for the local cherry cannery and cider mill run by the Morgan family. It was interesting work that utilized the chemistry I had learned in school. Each day, I tested the cider and vinegar for acid content and I estimated the fermentation rate. I also tested the effectiveness of the pectin which the plant produced from apples, to be sold commercially.

I took time that summer to visit the University of Michigan, staying with my cousin, Lathem Lawton, who was attending summer school there. I had taken the college-preparatory course in high school: Latin and French (I saw no purpose in studying French, and consequently did not do well in it), chemistry and physics. The man who taught the latter courses was creative and inspiring. (We had a science club and we performed all sorts of interesting experiments. Those of us who went on to college took chemistry and physics, thinking it would be a continuation of our interesting work in high school. We were disillusioned. The college courses were dry and dull. I often thought that the professors in beginning physics at the university probably discourage more potential physicists than any other influence.) But I digress. My point is that I always assumed I would go to college. When I graduated from high school, it seemed natural that I should apply to the University of Michigan. I did, and was accepted; admissions standards were not as high then as they are now. Of our gang of four—Thompson, Varney, Johnson, and me—I was the only one who went to college, which was unfortunate, because the others all had ability.

My summer visit to Ann Arbor did nothing to change my impression that college was mostly fun and games. I really did not understand the importance of academics. So it was a very naive young man who bade farewell to his parents in Traverse City that fall and headed south to begin life as a freshman at the University of Michigan.

Chapter Four

Passages

During my first few weeks on campus as a freshman in the fall of 1923, I was like a kid in a candy store. Enchanted by the lists of extracurricular activities, I signed up for one after another. I was not concerned about studies, because I had never really learned to study in high school. I thought it was just a process of reading over the text once and going to class. The process of digging into an assignment and really thinking about it eluded me entirely.

I enjoyed my extracurricular activities and learned something from each, but there were some bitter lessons among them. One of the latter was the swim team, which I approached with great confidence based on my experience in races at the We-Que-Tong Club in Traverse City and at summer camp.

The U of M swim team worked out off campus in a small pool in the old Ann Arbor YMCA building. I went up to the coach, a Mr. Barnes, and told him I wanted to try out. He said, "OK, just dive in and swim a couple of lengths." I did so with gusto. I was thinking as I clambered out of the pool that I must have impressed the coach. So you can imagine my chagrin when he turned to one of the other boys and said, "Take him down to the shallow end and show him how to swim." It proved to be worth the humiliation, though, because I did learn to swim properly; in fact, I became an excellent swimmer.

My experience as a reporter for *The Michigan Daily* was less salutary. I joined an eager bunch of fledgling journalists in the organizational meetings and was full of enthusiasm as I went out on my first assignment. Then the editor held a staff meeting and used the article I had turned in as an example of "how not to write a story." That cured me of the itch to see my byline in the paper.

I lived in a rooming house run by Mrs. Elmer Beal. I had planned to share a room with Don Weaks, one of only four other boys from my high-school graduating class who went on to college. At the last minute, though, Don got a scholarship to Michigan State and went there instead. So I roomed by myself. I was rushed for several fraternities, but did not want to join them. I was never lonely, though: there were too many fascinating things going on. The Michigan Union had a dance every Friday night, and I usually went with a redheaded girl who was in my geology class, a subject I liked especially.

Freshman boys had to wear a pot (beanie) in those days, and of course there was a bit of hazing from upperclassmen. But that merely added zest to interclass contests, such as tug-of-war and climbing a greased flagpole. Home seemed far away, and indeed it was a nine-hour trip by train—too long for the short Thanksgiving Day holiday. I had Thanksgiving dinner in Ypsilanti at the home of friends of my mother's, two maiden ladies named Jessie and Florence Swain. But my parents came to visit me once during that first semester, and I went home at Christmastime. Toward the end of my freshman year I went on a date with Frances

Light, a very popular Alpha Chi Omega. She liked to dance, too, and we dated regularly. I enjoyed some of my classes very much, especially rhetoric, which taught me to read more widely and wisely.

During the summer of 1924 I had a series of jobs. The first was weighing cans of cherries as they came off a canning-plant conveyor belt. It was the most mindless and boring job I'd ever done. A switch to stacking boxes in the plant's warehouse wasn't much better. Then I worked as a cement-mixer's helper for a contractor. It was hard work, but I managed to find time on weekends to do quite a lot of trout fishing. Then I got an opportunity to take a much more interesting job—teaching canoeing and organizing tent trips at a girls' camp near Traverse City—and I jumped at it.

B ack on campus and in the same rooming house for my sophomore year, I pledged Theta Chi Fraternity in the middle of the first semester, because I liked the members, it had a good reputation, and its house was near the campus. I began taking my meals in the fraternity, but I didn't move in until the beginning of my junior year. Apart from that, there was little change in my interests until the beginning of the second semester, when I enrolled in a course in beginning psychology. On the first day, before the professor began his lecture, an attractive graduate assistant walked up and down the aisles taking attendance. In the weeks that followed I felt a growing desire to talk to her personally. This was not a romantic interest—after all, she was already working on her master's degree—I simply thought she was an interesting person I would enjoy knowing better. At midterm I was writing a paper on the human ear for the psychology class and, as a pretext for a personal chat, I thought up a good question to ask her. I went to her office, which had a card on the door attractively engraved with her name: *Sadye L. Harwick.* She was personable, helpful, and very easy to talk to, although she did not know much about the human ear. I began dropping into her office on a regular basis.

One spring day, Neil Staebler, my former Torch Lake tentmate who was now a U of M junior and a fraternity brother of mine, asked me if I had a girl I would like to take on a picnic with him and his girl friend, Mina Miller. I was not dating anyone in particular at the time, but it occurred to me to ask Sadye. Somewhat to my surprise, she accepted. Neil tells about it in the transcription of his tape-recorded recollections:

> Gene came up to me a few days after I'd asked him to come on a picnic and said, "Neil, I am going to bring a girl who is a grad student. She's a big brain, a Phi Beta Kappa, and it's going to take both of us to keep up the conversation. Will you help me out?" I said I would. When we met and drove out to some property my family owned on Dead Lake, near Whitmore Lake, just outside of Ann Arbor, it was clear that his girl was a brain and a beauty as well. I asked him later how he'd ever met a girl like that and he said, "I don't know; just lucky, I guess." I don't recall much about the picnic itself except that all the wood was soaking wet. It had rained a lot during the previous week and began to drizzle again as we prepared to cook our hot dogs. But Gene was a master fire builder. In no time at all he had a blaze going, and Sadye was impressed by that.

We had a good time at the picnic. We laughed and sang

"It isn't raining rain, you know, it's raining violets." I was glad the others were along. Neil and Mina and Sadye talked animatedly while I sat wondering what the devil they were talking about. They shared ideas on moods and feelings, what motivated people, and religion and politics. I was speechless. I knew nothing about such topics. My father did not believe in introspection. He thought it was bad for a person—I'm not sure why. Anyhow, their conversation was quite a revelation to me.

Sadye as a high-school girl.

One day toward the end of the semester, Sadye and I were in her office talking about the upcoming final exams in my psychology class, and she appeared baffled by some of my remarks. Finally she said, "You don't know a thing about this course, do you!"

I could only shrug and shake my head.

"Let us review it together then," she said.

We went to the University Arboretum, sat under a tree, and she began reviewing the text. Suddenly, it all came clear to me. I had been a middling student at best, but after Sadye's explanations I wrote a 94 final, one of the few *A* 's I got that year.

My visits to Sadye's office had grown more frequent. I held her in great respect and valued her judgment, and I was delighted with her indulgence. We frequently took long walks together and discussed without restraint a wide variety of aspects of life. Our relationship was purely platonic, intermingled perhaps with a bit of role-reversed Pygmalion.

Gradually, however, a subtle undercurrent of emotional tension, unbidden yet undeniable, began to develop between us. I suppose it was inevitable that, sooner or later, I would kiss her. It happened in her office on a May evening in 1925, and I remember the occasion as clearly as if it were three days ago instead of sixty-four years ago. Both of us were surprised by the intensity of our feelings. We locked her office door and went out for a walk, hand in hand, through the Arboretum, trying to sort out what had happened to us. I realized then that my affection for Sadye was much greater than any emotion I had ever known. That evening changed both our lives—and the change was much more profound than I realized at the time. All I knew was that Sadye was a wonderful girl and I wanted to be with her.

I told Sadye I had mixed feelings about the impending summer vacation. On one hand, I was looking forward to it, because Matt Mann, who had taken over as U of M's swim coach that year, had asked me to be a counselor at his boys' camp in Canada. I accepted enthusiastically. However, summer now meant being far from her, which was not a happy fact to contemplate. Sadye said she understood, and she proved it a few weeks later with a message that was delivered by Neil Staebler.

I had gone home to Traverse City for a few days prior to leaving for camp; it was a joyless situation with Sadye far away—she had returned to her home in Detroit about the time I left Ann Arbor. My loneliness was dispelled, however, when Neil telephoned and said Sadye had told him she would be visiting her uncle in Dundee, Michigan, down near the Ohio border, for a few days and wanted to know if I would like to stop and visit her on my way to camp. If so, he would drive me down from Ann Arbor. Naturally I said yes, I would like that very much. Sadye and I spent three magical days together. Her uncle and aunt were there, of course, but I can remember nothing at all about them. My mind was on nothing but Sadye. We took long walks down country roads and basked in the moonlight—it seemed as if a full moon shone each night I was there.

I reached Matt Mann's camp by train from Detroit. The rest of the summer, while not occupied with the energetic young boys at camp or practicing for canoe races, I thought about Sadye and exchanged letters with her. Our almost-daily correspondence brought us closer together both intellectually and emotionally. It made me realize that I was truly in love with her and that she was the one I wanted to marry. For whatever it's worth, Sadye was and is the only woman I ever felt that way about. She still has all our letters, neatly bundled, and she has said from time to time that she was going to burn them. I hope she will not. I'd like to put them in a historical collection and seal them for fifty years. The letters are of great personal value to us, and I think they preserve an impression of the manners and mores that young people observed in the mid-1920s, which one day might enlighten the work of some social scientist.

The canoe-race practice mentioned above was inspired by Dr. Frank Lanham, who was the camp physician for Matt

Mann. Dr. Lanham was about sixty-two years old then, sturdy and well built, and he was the best canoeist I have ever known. He used an extra-long paddle, about six-and-a-quarter feet from top to tip, and he stood half crouched in the canoe, just aft of the center. This posture allowed him to attain tremendous leverage with his stroke, which ended in a modified *J* in order to keep the craft on course. I learned Dr. Lanham's stand-up technique that summer, and I was never beaten in a canoe race thereafter.

When I went back to Ann Arbor to begin my junior year at the university, I was troubled by my lack of direction. How could I possibly get a job and support Sadye after I graduated if I didn't even know what field to enter? I took a few vocational tests, and the counselor said my scores indicated that I had ability in construction. Since I had not taken engineering courses, major construction work seemed out of the question. The counselor agreed, but he suggested there was a lot of opportunity in developing residential real estate. This appealed to me. At least it was something I could work toward. I could visualize myself building and selling houses. I discussed my aspirations with Dean John R. Effinger of the College of Literature, Science, and the Arts, and he allowed me to enroll in a series of courses I had selected in engineering, business, and the humanities. I felt this would give me the background I would need as a developer.

My mind was not on my studies, however, because Sadye had come back to town and was staying at the Kappa house while doing some research at the psychiatric hospital with Dr. J. Barrett. They were investigating hereditary transmission of schizophrenia.

Sadye and I spent nearly every evening together; it was a period of exploring each other's thoughts and ideas. She opened a whole new world of ideas for me; I had been primarily action-oriented and I found the world of ideas totally fascinating. This concentration on Sadye had an adverse effect on my grades. But Dean Effinger was tolerant and understanding. He allowed me to repeat the work in summer school, and I got better grades.

In the late spring of 1926, Sadye got a job at the Illinois State Mental Hygiene Clinic. She lived in the Women's City Club on the Near North Side of Chicago. While attending summer school, I got my first taste of selling—representing a Detroit real-estate firm, selling residential lots. I managed to sell one, for about a thousand dollars, and my 10 percent commission paid my way to Chicago to visit Sadye.

When Sadye took a job in Milwaukee with the County Mental Health Department that fall, I drove over there to see her three times. I bought a Model T Ford from my friend and classmate Bob Straub for thirty dollars, and a roommate of mine named Newt Detzer shared the upkeep and use of it with me. The car had no top, so driving to Milwaukee in midwinter was a frigid experience. I would bundle up like an Eskimo and make the drive, straight through, in about thirteen hours. Once on the trip back I ran low on money. I had just enough to buy a tankful of gas in South Bend. Whether I could make it all the way to Ann Arbor was questionable. It was late in the evening and there was almost no traffic. I got a quick picture of a headline in the *Ann Arbor News:* "UM Student Found Frozen in Car." But I decided

63

to push on. I turned the carburetor adjustment all the way down to conserve gas and drove eastward on the snow-covered road. Fortunately, I had a strong tail wind, and I think that's what got me to Ann Arbor at two o'clock the next morning with half a gallon of gas left in the tank and six cents left in my pocket.

Sadye had visited my home in Traverse City during the spring of my junior year, and she and my mother took to each other instantly. They became very close. But in order to describe their relationship, I must tell more about my mother and father.

Mother's sense of humor was always at the ready. For example, she once accompanied my father to his life-insurance company's annual convention in Philadelphia, and some of the Easterners thought it was fascinating that Mr. and Mrs. Power lived "on the frontier," which I suppose meant anywhere west of the Alleghenies. "Do you have any Indians up there in northern Michigan?" one asked. Mother, who had jet-black hair, brown eyes, and a deep suntan, said, "Oh yes. I'm half Indian myself." They believed her.

Although Mother was jesting about having Indian blood, she really had great compassion for Indians in our area, most of whom were poor. She adopted an Indian village, called Shobbytown, up near Northport, as her personal social project. She raised funds for them, took food to them, and drove them to town when they needed to get to a doctor. There were no welfare agencies helping the Indians in those days and no civil-rights movement. Mother simply saw a need and filled it, out of the goodness of her heart.

Mother was a civic booster, too. She taught me the value

64

of community spirit. She also taught me to appreciate the outdoors and share her pride in the wonderful, wild surroundings in northern Michigan. We treated the environment respectfully, and we made use of its abundance—wild berries, which Mother used to make jams and jellies, and morel mushrooms. Every spring we would go hunting for the flavorful morels that grew in abundance in the hardwood forest and these outings would often be family picnics, with Mother's sister Edna and her three children—Latham, Mary, and Betty—joining Mother, Frank, and me.

Sadye's rapport with my mother pleased me, of course. She also had a good relationship with my father.

For my part, I found it difficult to talk to Father, even though we loved each other and were companions on many fishing trips. It is difficult for me to describe this situation, although I am sure it's not uncommon in relationships in which a father and young son are both strong-willed. Father and I had difficulty understanding each other or being close until later, after my mother died.

Sadye's presence in our family home gave me a new perspective on the place and a new appreciation for the pleasant life we had there. It was a big frame house, painted yellow with white trim, built about 1900; as I look back, its design wasted a lot of space, but its large rooms and spacious hallways were wonderful for the games children play. We would sail paper airplanes from the stairway into the big main hall, where we always put the Christmas tree; Frank and I would go into the woods to chop our Christmas trees, and we chose taller ones each year.

My mother's elderly uncle, Delbert Chapman, lived with

us during the summers and spent his winters in California. He was a character, six feet tall, gaunt, and stern-looking; he fascinated me with stories of his adventures as a captain of cavalry in the Civil War. He had been with Sherman on the March through Georgia. About the turn of the century, Great-Uncle Del had opened a tannery to make lap robes of buffalo hides. He said he received a hundred carloads of hides a year for processing. Most people had a horse and cutter in those days, and a warm, windproof buffalo robe was virtually standard equipment in the winter.

Great-Uncle Del used to startle me with his cavalryman's gift for colorful curses. Let a cutworm take a single plant in the big backyard garden he used to tend for my mother, and Great-Uncle Del would unleash a hair-curling blast of invective. At one time he had owned Signal Hill in Los Angeles. Unfortunately, he sold it before oil was discovered there. He was well-off, though, and when he died in about 1914 he left all of us some money. Mother received about $80,000. He left Frank and me $2,000 each, which my parents invested for me, and it provided a good lesson in finance. My father would take us to the bank with him twice a year to cut the coupons on our bonds, and I was amazed to see how our money grew.

In my senior year back at the U of M, I took twenty-one hours, mostly to fill the time I had on my hands since Sadye was in Milwaukee. I worried about all the other fellows who wanted to date her. One of them was a chap named Frank Lee. Sadye was coming over for a football game on the ferry from Milwaukee, and I was to pick her up in Muskegon in my Model T. She said she had agreed to see Frank and I couldn't deny her that, of course. But I called Frank and informed him of what the time for his visit would be, keeping it short. He got the message.

I guess I was not the most popular fellow in our fraternity house either, as Neil Staebler notes in another incident from his taped recollections:

> Gene had a reputation in the fraternity for being a distinctive character. Since my family lived in Ann Arbor, I stayed at home instead of in the Theta Chi house, and I was able to observe what went on in the house with some detachment. The rest of the brothers referred to Gene as "Hunter, Trapper and Trader Power" because he kept a cache of candy bars for sale or trade and because he was from the "wilderness" of northern Michigan; he obviously took pride in being the rugged outdoor type. One day Gene felt they had carried this "Hunter, Trapper and Trader" business too far, and he decided to show them what it was like to have a real backwoodsman in their midst. He got up about six o'clock in the morning, put on a pair of showshoes he kept under his bed, and stomped around the third-floor dormitory of the house. The brothers awoke shivering with alarm; it sounded like a bull moose was on a rampage up there. Then BANG! Gene fired a WWI Mauser automatic pistol through an open window. He stomped across the room to another window and was about to fire again, but a visiting alumnus, who happened to be sleeping next to the window, bolted when he saw Gene standing over him holding a smoking pistol. BANG! Gene fired again. The visitor left that morning and was never heard from again. I don't recall ever hearing the phrase "Hunter, Trapper and Trader Power" around the fraternity house again either.

After my graduation from U of M in June 1927, I was not sure what to do. I felt aimless. I went back to Traverse City and did nothing for an entire month but prowl along streams fishing for trout. I guess I regarded this as one last fling of freedom before entering the world of work. It might have gone on longer, but my parents suggested that perhaps it was time I got a job. So off I went to Chicago, which I selected because I had a place to live there and because it was close to Milwaukee and Sadye. I moved into an apartment on Goethe Street on the Near North Side with my friend Bob Straub and two other U of M grads. Then I proceeded to enroll in a trade-school course in reading construction plans and blueprints. The school had a low level of instruction; I completed the eight-week course in three weeks and managed to get a refund on my fee by arguing that since the school's policy was to charge more if a student failed to finish the work in eight weeks, its charge must be based on class time, not course content.

My first job was with the Western Foundation Company, owned by a man named Oscar West, who was a friend of my Uncle John Coolidge. Mr. West had met my brother Frank on a canoe trip in Canada and liked him, so I guess he thought any brother of Frank's would make a good employee. I have to admit that he probably regretted the decision—at least *I* don't think I was a very good employee. I was supposed to be the timekeeper on jobs involving the driving of wooden piles and capping them with cement to form foundations. But I did not grasp the necessity for keeping accurate records of every phase of the work, so after a time I was relieved of the job.

I then went to work as an inspector of pilings for the Turner Construction Company. I did reasonably well at it, and the pay, about $35 a week, was not bad for someone of my experience. But an opportunity to expand my horizons in the field made me realize that I had no real future in major construction. The operator of the pile-driving subcontract whose work I inspected suggested that I bid on a small foundation job; he said he would lend me the necessary equipment and help me organize the work. I knew it would be over my head, so I declined. I also knew that my future was not in this kind of work and it was time for me to move on. My next employer was the Parker-Holliday Company, which created and sold motivational posters intended to improve the morale of factory workers. The promotional aspect of this work appealed to me, but I soon began seeing shortcomings in the product—it lacked substance—and I felt I could not sell something I considered inferior.

My difficulties in the job market were not unusual. Bob Straub was going from one company to another, too, mostly in proofreading jobs. Our roommates, Stanley Armstrong and Tom Furlong, were both working as reporters for the *Chicago Tribune,* but even though they had jobs in the field they wanted to pursue (both eventually became top editorial executives with the paper), they shared the same sense of struggling to get established that Bob and I felt. We lived in one large room and slept dormitory-style on a screened porch that was open to the weather year 'round.

I was fortunate in having Sadye nearby. She was my polestar: no matter how lost I felt, her presence sustained my hope for the future. We saw each other as often as possible and got together with friends like Fred and Vera Wolff, who lived in the same building as Vera's father, Frederick Stock, the famous conductor of the Chicago

Symphony. Vera had been Sadye's roommate when they were undergraduates at the U of M, and I enjoyed being with her and Fred because I had developed a keen interest in classical music and the arts, thanks in large measure to Sadye's influence. When I first went to the university, I had never heard a symphony, listened to an opera, or attended a play. In my first semester I bought tickets to a series of performances by the Detroit Symphony because someone told me I should, and I sat bored stiff and uncomprehending through the concerts, counting the lights on the chandeliers to pass the time. I took a course in music appreciation, but got little out of it. Later, Sadye and I took a similar course together at night with a different teacher and we learned how to listen.

My search for a job led me to the Celotex Company and here, at last, I landed a job I liked. It was in the advertising department, at $30 a week. I wanted to learn everything I could about the field, so I enrolled in night-school courses in advertising and marketing at Northwestern University's School of Business Administration. My job did not have much responsibility; it consisted principally of taking orders and supplying dealers with advertising materials. However, it taught me some basic things about type and type specification and how to dictate correspondence, all of which would prove useful to me later. At the same time, my courses at Northwestern were giving me an insight into the value of possessing an MBA degree. MBA's were starting at $5,000 to $6,000 a year, which seemed to me a tremendous income—enough, certainly, to allow me to marry Sadye, which was my chief concern. In those days a man would not think about marriage until he had a steady job with income sufficient to support a wife.

My father had told me he would underwrite the cost of any additional training I needed, so after considerable discussion with Sadye, I decided to return to Ann Arbor in February 1929 and enter the newly established U of M School of Business Administration. I felt that, with the credits I'd earned at Northwestern, I could complete the two years of work in one and one-half by carrying nineteen hours each semester. When I interviewed with Dean Clare Griffin for admission, he looked over the admittedly weak transcript of my undergraduate grades and said, "Well, you can take the additional hours, but I will tell you now that by the end of the semester you will be out." I accepted the challenge and, for the first time in my scholastic career, threw myself wholeheartedly into my studies. I hired an underclassman, a boy named Maxwell Katzen, to type my dictated expansion of the detailed notes I took in class. I found this allowed me to absorb and retain the ideas. To Dean Griffin's amazement and delight, I proved him wrong by finishing near the top of my class.

I lived that semester in a house owned by a Professor Florer, who had been hounded out of the university during World War I by some faculty members who accused him of being pro-German because he taught the German language. I was not particularly interested in politics then, but I was opposed to such bias, and I had no compunction at all about being associated with Professor Florer. I took my meals at my fraternity house and being an "older man," a graduate student, I was assigned to the head of a table. Each noon, I would choose some topic of current events for discussion, and the freshmen and sophomores at my table would chew it over thoroughly. Those luncheon discussions were recalled fondly in the fraternity house for years afterward.

I never proposed to Sadye. We both came to take it for granted that we would be married as soon as we could. Her parents were rather surprised at this because they had not taken me seriously. Sadye had some boyfriends who were substantial citizens, and her mother, as I recall, thought I was just a passing interest, a kind of will-o'-the-wisp. Both her mother and father came from farm families in southeastern Michigan. Her father had taught school in various towns around the state, and when I met Sadye he was assistant principal and head of the commercial department at Southwestern High School in Detroit. The Harwicks were strict Methodists; life was serious business for them, although her father had a good sense of humor. Sadye had had a sister, Ida, who was unusually bright and talented, but she had come down with typhoid fever at age fourteen and died when her nurse mistakenly gave her carbolic acid instead of castor oil. I think Sadye always felt she had to extend herself and accomplish enough to compensate for the loss of her sister. Her mother reacted to the daughter's death by becoming overprotective—she would not let Sadye take part in athletics or anything that could possibly involve any danger.

I don't remember much about the night I told Sadye's father that I wanted to marry her, except that he had a habit of twisting one foot and sliding it back and forth when he was concerned, and that foot was going like a power hacksaw. I don't think the Harwicks were overjoyed about the match, but they resigned themselves to it. In April of 1929, in the hope that somehow we would be able to get married that summer instead of waiting until I got my MBA, Sadye resigned her post in Milwaukee and moved back to her parents' home in Detroit. It was fortuitous, because one day when she was visiting me in Ann Arbor, she happened to meet an old friend of hers, Dr. Margaret Bell, who was in charge of women's medicine for the Student Health Service and also was Director of Physical Education for Women.

Sadye positively glowed with excitement as she told me about the meeting: "Margaret said, 'You are just the person I am looking for, Sadye. We want to start a Mental Hygiene Clinic in the Student Health Service, and we need you to head it up.' Isn't that grand?"

It certainly was. The job would give her an income, and that—in addition to the $120 a month I was getting from my father, and my inheritance from Great-Uncle Del, which had now grown to $4,000—would allow us to get married right away.

The date we chose was June 17, 1929. Sadye wanted our wedding to be small and private, so she selected a place to which only the most dedicated family members and friends would trouble to journey—a cottage on the shore of Lake Michigan near the little town of Ootsburg, Wisconsin, about thirty miles north of Milwaukee. There, in a natural bower of cedars facing the lake, we were wed by my Uncle John Coolidge, who had a flair for drama and tied the mat-

On our wedding day, I stood proudly at Sadye's side, with her bridesmaid, Joyce Yost, next to her with Frank, who was my best man, on the right.

Our guests lined up in front of the cottage before going to dinner.

rimonial knot with rhetorical flourishes that left us feeling bound for life. My brother Frank was best man (a post that meant he had to prepare a place for us in our natural altar by pulling up a patch of poison ivy with his bare hands; the guests had to stand in the stuff, though) and Joyce Yost was Sadye's maid of honor. There was a small reception with chicken salad and angel-food cake. We then went to Milwaukee for a wedding dinner with both our families and some of the guests like Neil Staebler, who had driven over from Ann Arbor. Then everyone departed and Sadye and I returned to the cottage. With the dawn, we went for a cold swim in Lake Michigan, then opened the icebox to get breakfast and found nothing in it but chicken salad and angel-food cake. So we ate that. We did the same for lunch, and again at dinner. Breakfast the next day also consisted of chicken salad and angel-food cake. Ditto for lunch. That night I suggested that we go out for dinner even though I had only fifteen dollars in cash, which shows how naive I was about practical matters. We suspected our families had conspired to leave us on a diet of chicken salad and angel-food cake, but we were never sure. One thing was certain, though: it was a long time before either of us could confront chicken salad again.

Our honeymoon lasted the whole summer. I had arranged with Ken Marantette, a fraternity brother of mine, for Sadye and me to be counselors at his oddly named Touring Boys Camp on Jackson Lake in Jackson Hole, Wyoming. (The appelation *Touring* referred to the fact that the boys went west by train, and while there would take several excursions in a camp bus, with a truckload of camping gear following behind.) We had a wonderful time: we lived in an umbrella tent and Sadye, bless her heart, endured the hardships—

awakening to cold that froze the water in our canteens, and incursions by unbelievable swarms of mosquitoes and other biting insects—as if she had been roughing it all her life. We started out our days with an icy dip in the lake; then we'd saddle our horses for rides into the backcountry, whose wild beauty was a perfect complement to our soaring emotions. Occasionally I went fishing for cutthroat trout, and we "toured" to rodeos and took hikes on the high alpine meadows with our boys. Working with them was not at all demanding since there were only ten of them. The summer passed all too quickly.

But once we got on the train for the two-day trip back to Ann Arbor, we could hardly wait to begin settling into married life in the house we had arranged to rent from Everett Brown, a professor of political science, and his wife May, who was an abstract artist. The house was on Day Street; it had a room and bath downstairs, which we decided to rent out, as well as an extra bedroom upstairs, which we told my brother he could rent and live with us. This proved to be a very satisfactory arrangement.

Frank and I had grown much closer since the fall of my senior year in college, when we went into the honey business together. This came about because, like other owners of cherry orchards in the Traverse City area, our father kept bees to pollinate his trees. The chief byproduct of the insects' work, of course, was honey. They produced quantities of the stuff—so much that the price was very low in the area. You could buy honey for ten cents a pound. Frank and I saw this as an opportunity. We would take the honey from Father's twenty-five hives, pack it in attractive containers, and market it as *Pooh-Bear Honey.* Sadye loved the idea, and she accompanied us on a trip to a ceramics factory in Urbana, Illinois, where we arranged to buy a quantity of jars that would hold a pound of honey and looked like the kind of container an imaginary bear might store his honey in. We had some problems figuring out the best way to seal the jars, but beeswax proved to be the answer. We sold our product to specialty stores, who retailed it for a dollar and a half a jar, and we cleared about $900 the first year. Then the holder of the copyright on *Winnie the Pooh* threatened to take us to court if we didn't stop using the name Pooh-Bear. We bought different jars, shaped like beehives, and continued under the name *Cherry Blossom Honey.* But it lacked the market-

My father, Glenn Power, in 1929.

ing magic of our original idea; sales fell off, though we continued the business for two more years.

Our household on Day Street was a lively place—too lively sometimes to suit the cook/housekeeper we had hired in order to let Sadye keep her job at the Student Health Service. She was a black woman named Mrs. Laura Jackson, and we were fond of her, especially since we had tried three other cooks in succession who had not worked out. Mrs. Jackson was a great cook—almost as good as my mother—and she had a wonderful laugh. But at times she must have thought we were a trio of lunatics. For example, Sadye was determined to be a dutiful wife and build up her husband's constitution by giving him cod-liver oil. I hated the stuff. She insisted, I resisted, and she and Frank persisted. He was a member of the university's wrestling team, so after a good deal of threshing about he was usually able to pin me. Then Sadye would pour that horrible gunk down my throat.

Sadye did not like to disappoint Mrs. Jackson, which she felt she might do if she did not fulfill her role as mistress of the house by giving directions. So she bought a book of hints on housekeeping. Whenever Mrs. Jackson would ask a question on how something was to be done, Sadye would say, "Excuse me for a moment. I have to go upstairs. I'll tell you when I come back down." Then she would go to our bedroom and consult the book before returning to give her instructions. Mrs. Jackson probably knew what Sadye was doing, but she never let on.

One day Mrs. Jackson approached Sadye and said she was very sorry but she was going to have to leave us: "I have had a call from the White House."

"Oh, really? That's wonderful!" Sadye said. "You're moving to Washington then?"

"No, I mean the White House on South University Street," Mrs. Jackson said. She meant the home of the president of the university.

As I mentioned earlier, Sadye and I decided to remain in Ann Arbor after I received my MBA in 1930. I went to work for the Windsor Tractor Equipment Company and then, on the first day of November that year, I joined Edwards Brothers. Incidentally, I think one of the things that got me the job was that Harold Scarth was impressed by my story of our Pooh-Bear Honey enterprise. Frank, meanwhile, had begun his senior year at the U of M. He did well after he cleared up a foreign-language requirement that had given him a great deal of difficulty. He simply could not learn French. The following spring, when Bill Edwards agreed that I should go to England to arrange for the photographing of STC books for Professor Fries's dictionary project, Sadye and I hoped Frank would be able to accompany us. But he couldn't afford it. My parents had come down for Frank's graduation, and when he drove away with them to return to Traverse City, Sadye and I felt sad.

Later that evening, Frank telephoned and said his acceptance into Northwestern University's Medical School had been at home awaiting his return. "This day has been too much!" he exclaimed. "I graduated from college, I've been admitted to medical school, and . . . " with a gleeful laugh, "my parents have given me a great graduation gift: they told me I can go to Europe with you two!"

We sailed from New York on the S.S. *Pennland,* a one-class boat, in July 1931. Sadye was the experienced traveler among us—she had visited Europe three years earlier. Frank and I were absolute greenhorns, although we did our best to conceal the fact under our dashing knickers with socks that matched our colorful sweaters. Frank had come down from Traverse City with enough gear to outfit a touring company of actors. Sadye took charge of our packing and promptly cut Frank's luggage down to manageable size. This was accomplished with good-natured banter that set the tone for the entire trip. The spirit of our journey was exactly like the youthful foolishness described by Cornelia Otis Skinner and Emily Kimbrough in their book *Our Hearts Were Young and Gay*. Of course, I had to tend to business at the British Museum and the libraries in Oxford and Cambridge, but we still had plenty of time and opportunity for adventure.

Frank and I bought raincoats in London, which was swathed in fog and drizzle, and with Sadye between us we cut Sherlock Holmesian figures through the city's streets. A mysterious young man attached himself to us the first night, introducing himself as Arthur. He spent two evenings showing us the sights. On the third evening, he handed me his card, which said: *Arthur Cain, Special Branch, Scotland Yard.* "What the devil?" I muttered to Frank. " 'Special branch' means he's a detective." Later, we speculated excitedly

Arthur Cain of Scotland Yard.

about why Scotland Yard would be interested in us: *They had mistaken us for a trio of American anarchists . . . the suitcase full of photographic chemicals I had brought with me was believed to contain materials for making bombs* . . . and so forth. In the end, Arthur Cain proved to be simply a nice young man who wanted to be friendly to three young Americans.

One of the places Arthur took us was the Caledonian Market. A large number of silver items was displayed there, flea-market style, and Sadye and I bought a Sheffield tea set for about seventy dollars. We considered this outlay long and hard, visiting the dealer several times, and even going to his home before making up our minds. But we were happy with our purchase; it was a real bargain, and we continued to deal with that merchant by mail, buying many silver items from him through the years. I also bought some interesting early books in the Caledonian Market.

Moving on to The Hague, we had some difficulty getting a good rental car, but after considerable haggling we wound up with a fairly new Essex that served us well. Sadye and I had learned that Frank would become cranky if he didn't get his meals on schedule. We had been given a whole stalk of green bananas when we sailed from New York, and we still had plenty left, so whenever Frank started to get testy as we drove along, one of us would grab a banana and feed it to him. He would respond with contented ape sounds, which never failed to make us laugh ourselves silly. Frank didn't much care for Continental cooking; he suffered from diarrhea, which we called "traveler's complaint." But I learned something that has always stood me in good stead: most digestive problems will disappear if you drink the local wine.

We drove to Kiel, Germany, where I tried unsuccessfully to buy some Rotaprint plates for Edwards Brothers. There was a little restaurant in Kiel that served a crab soup Frank liked very much. For three straight days he dined on crab soup; it kept him from being crabby. Driving down the coast to Lubeck, we saw some German Frauleins swimming in the Baltic so merrily that we were eager to try it, too. We changed, plunged in—and popped right out again. How were we to know those women had ice water in their veins? We agreed that they must be Valkyries—the sea was too cold for warm-blooded humans.

In Berlin, Sadye wanted to go to Haus Vaterland, run by a wine merchant named Kempinski. It was an eight-story building with two restaurants on every floor, each representing a different country. Frank did not feel like going; he preferred to stay in the pension where we had checked in. But Sadye and I were determined to have a grand time, and we dressed to kill—she in a long evening gown, I in a tuxedo—and off we went to the eighth floor of the Haus Vaterland, which was a nightclub. We dined and ordered champagne, which I had never drunk before. We danced and drank some champagne, then danced and drank some more. Poor Frank. He was awakened at three o'clock in the morning by his companions, who laughed giddily and tried to explain why they had walked back to the pension in the rain. We thought our ruined formal wear was tremendously funny, and we tried to imitate one fat German couple's dancing for Frank's benefit. But he failed to see the humor in it.

Since there were no Rotaprint plates to be had, we decided to see as much of Europe as possible. We made our way down to Leipzig, then drove south to the marvelous medieval walled city of Rothenburg. We were spellbound by the atmosphere in Rothenburg, whose foundations were laid by Romans in 900 A.D. Then we pushed on to Munich and ended up in Vienna.

Our drive back to Paris by way of Switzerland was a series of delightful interludes. We stopped frequently to savor the sights and try whatever Gasthaus or restaurant struck our fancy. We saw the museums and famous churches, of course, and went to concerts and operas. Frank had a terrible time at operas. He fell asleep during *Carmen* in Paris. When he woke up during the second act, he nudged me, whispering, "Which one's Carmen?" In Paris we also visited a dressmaker Sadye had been referred to. She made three dresses for Sadye, one of them from some voile material embroidered with rosebuds that we had bought in Switzerland. I was not allowed to see Sadye in this dress until she wore it on her birthday, September 17, while we were steaming homeward aboard the S.S. *Westernland,* a sister ship to the *Pennland.* It was a stunning dress, and Sadye was beautiful in it, but unfortunately neither Frank nor I could stay awake during dinner. Sadye went off in a huff and never wore the dress again.

Sadye's irritation soon dissipated, and we found ourselves looking back on our European experience somewhat pensively. It was as if we had passed through an invisible doorway in our lives. Ahead of us was a parting of the ways: Frank was going on to medical school; Sadye and I were looking forward to new professional challenges. It was unlikely that we would ever recapture the excitement and spontaneous laughter of that first trip abroad. On the other hand, our memories of it would always be with us.

The next time Sadye and I went to Europe was our 1935 trip with my mother, when I was setting up the project of microfilming[1] STC books. Along with my copy camera in the hold of the S.S. *Rotterdam* was a new Ford V8 coupe my father had loaned us for the trip.

I called on Arundel Esdaille at the British Museum and again he was very cooperative. I used a small wall projector to show him samples of the type of copies we would be making from the STC books, and he helped me get our camera set up in the museum's studio. I visited the Bodleian Library at Oxford and the University Library at Cambridge and arranged to have them send books to the British Museum in London to be photographed until such time as I could have a camera placed in each of those institutions. While I was thus occupied, Sadye showed my mother around London during the day. At night, Arthur Cain, the Scotland Yard man we'd met in 1931, escorted us around the city he knew so well from his days as a patrolman. After I was satisfied that the microfilming would run smoothly, we shipped the car, and ourselves, across the channel to Holland.

It was a bit crowded with three of us in the Ford's single seat, but we had a delightful time. Mother had never been abroad before; in fact, she had been outside the State of Michigan only rarely. So she was agog as we drove through

---

[1] The work I did in 1931 for Professor Fries's Early Modern English Dictionary project was full-size photography rather than microfilm and, incidentally, it used paper negatives as a means of reducing cost.

Rotterdam, The Hague, and on to Berlin. I called on libraries in these cities and the others we drove to: Munich; St. Gall, Switzerland; and, after touring the French Riviera, Madrid, and then Paris. Without exception, the librarians I spoke to were interested in the possibilities of our microfilm service. By the time we arrived in Paris, my mother had a cold and said she felt bad. Sadye and I were concerned because Mother had insisted on drinking the local water everywhere. We put her in the American Hospital at

I paused during our 1935 visit to Paris to peruse the offerings of a Left Bank print dealer. Below is our trusty Ford coupe on a busy avenue in Nuremberg.

Neuilly, where the doctor said there was nothing wrong with her beyond complete exhaustion. After she got some rest and recovered her energy, we returned home on the S.S. *Normandy.* It was a rather uncomfortable trip. It was the ship's first year of operation, and the owners were anxious to set speed records—never mind that vibration caused by the madly turning screws seemed to be shaking the vessel apart. One day the vibration caused the door on my mother's cabin to jam. She got locked in and, being claustrophobic, became panicky. I finally managed to free the lock with my jackknife.

When we arrived back in Ann Arbor after the long drive from New York, my father was there waiting for us, much to Mother's delight. We regaled him with stories of our adventures abroad.

Those two trips to Europe established some important patterns for Sadye and me. In the first place, we always included Frank in our travels whenever we could. If Frank could not come, we usually included someone else on our trips. Another pattern we established was that of melding business and pleasure on our excursions. Pure vacation trips were rare for us—I always felt that I could make any trip pay for itself. This was especially true after I left the employ of Edwards Brothers and became an entrepreneur.

Going into business for yourself after you have been an employee for someone else brings about an immediate change in attitude. When everything depends upon you, all aspects of the business command your attention. I shoveled snow from walks, I carried in the freight, I swept the floors, I operated the cameras, and I established the processes and sold them. I loved every bit of it!

Even with a new baby, Sadye and I didn't need much money to live on — five dollars would buy a lot of groceries in those days. I paid myself $350 a month—$4,200 a year— which was well above the average income,[2] so money was not a major concern. However, having three people to provide for gave me a new sense of responsibility; I knew that our carefree, footloose days were over, and I would have to make a go of this new business I had started.

With that motivation, I was fairly bursting with energy and ideas to push University Microfilms ahead.

[2] Pretax income of families and unattached individuals (in current dollars) fell from an average of $2,335 in 1929 to $1,631 in 1935 and 1936. *Historical Statistics of the United States*, Part I, U. S. Department of Commerce, Bureau of Census.

Chapter Five

Beginnings

O ne of the first things I did after getting my company's doors open for business was to write a pamphlet outlining my idea for publishing doctoral dissertations via microfilm. I'm not sure where I got this idea, although its genesis probably was in conversations with Randolph Adams and William Warner Bishop. I thought it was a breakthrough idea, because the existing system of publishing dissertations was wasteful of resources, costly to the scholar, and completely ineffectual as a means of preserving and providing access to important scholarship. Policy varied from one university to the next but, generally speaking, the scholar was required to pay a fee to cover publishing of the dissertation. In some instances the fee was "in lieu of publication," as was the case with the University of Michigan, which charged $75. In other cases, actual publication with typesetting and case binding was required, which could make the fee as much as $300. The published theses were then distributed to university libraries; the problem was that since there was no index or other guide to what they contained, they simply gathered dust.

I titled my pamphlet *A Plan for Publication of Scholarly Material by Microfilm* and opened it with a thumbnail sketch of the economics of traditional publishing, pointing out that:

> Our printing facilities today are all geared to the production of a large number of copies on an extremely economical basis. However, they are not able to produce a small number of copies economically, and with the [relatively small] size of the market [for dissertations], scholarly publishing becomes an increasingly difficult problem unless accompanied by subsidy.
>
> What scholarly publishing needs is a method of distribution that gives sufficient and adequate publicity to a title or list of titles so that the information regarding what is offered is readily available to prospective users, combined with a means of production which can produce as demand materializes at an economical and uniform rate.

I then proceeded to describe why the "newly developed microfilm technology meets these needs in a singularly satisfactory manner" and outlined in twelve points how University Microfilms' program would operate (see Appendix B). One important point explained my idea for printing abstracts of the dissertations, which would be "distributed without charge to two hundred of the leading libraries in the United States and abroad." I made clear, too, that UMI would not be responsible in any way for the content or scholastic standard of the dissertation, and that the abstract would have to be approved by the candidate's committee before it was accepted. I also stressed that the only cost to scholarship for publishing a dissertation under my plan would be $15—"less than the cost of typing it."

Concluding my draft of the pamphlet with a sample abstract and a catalog card for a "typical dissertation," I had it professionally typed and printed as a 5-1/2-by-7-inch booklet by Edwards Brothers where, by the way, I was still on the board of directors. I was quite pleased with the finished product. It was simple and scholarly in presentation, yet it contained a sales message that I thought was persuasive. Whether, indeed, it was or not, I would soon find out, for I sent a copy to Clarence Yocum, dean of the graduate school at the University of Michigan. Dean Yocum was highly regarded as a scholar. He had the reputation of being very careful and deliberate, and of seldom saying things directly; his way was to state things obliquely. After a few days, I gave Dean Yocum a call. He said yes, he had read *A Plan for Publication of Scholarly Material by Microfilm.* Whereupon I took the bit in my teeth and asked him if he would be kind enough to visit my office. "I would like to give you a step-by-step demonstration of the process and show you a finished dissertation on one of our Argus reading machines," I said.

"Well, I don't know. I'll have to see about that," he replied.

He left me on tenterhooks for a few days, but finally he came over. I was nervous—I had not entertained such a distinguished visitor before. I gave him my presentation and when I finished, Dean Yocum amazed me by leaning back in his chair and asking straightforwardly: "Well, what can we do to put this across?"

He meant it, too. He championed my idea to the Association of Deans of Graduate Schools. This effort gave my proposal credibility.

Like any new concept, however, unforeseen problems arose in my procedures. I had the abstracts printed and sent them out to libraries according to plan, but the librarians

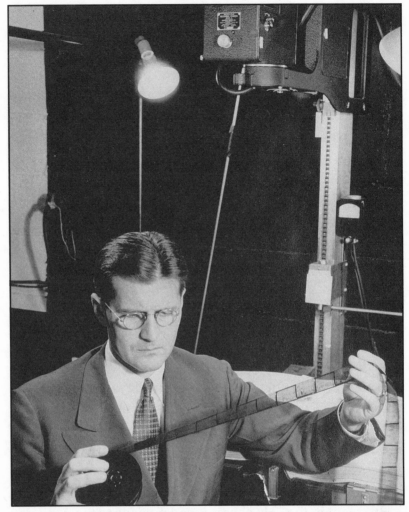

I am working here at a favorite task — inspecting my company's product.

often treated them as advertising—which, in a way they were—and threw them away. Later, these librarians would realize they had a need for the material referenced in the abstracts and would request a new copy. After the second year, we received so many of these requests that it became necessary to make them available only on a subscription basis. This made the point, and many libraries subscribed.

Finding a method of storing and preserving the negatives of all these documents was a major challenge. I experimented with various approaches. Originally I had a cabinet with numbered pegs inside and we would hang rolls of film on the pegs. This was dangerous, though, because the cabinet was of wood and if there were a fire, everything would go up in smoke. I had a vault built with fireproofing in the area in which the negatives were stored, and over the years we built better vaults. Nowadays, UMI's vault is in a separate, air-conditioned building. The original negatives, being extremely valuable, are used only to make duplicate negatives. This plan met the publication requirements for the doctorate degree at the various universities. In addition, for the first time, copies were available on demand for widespread use by a sizable number of researchers across the country. By 1989, UMI had well over 900,000 negatives of dissertations, touching all fields of knowledge. The volume of work is vastly greater now, of course. As I mentioned earlier, UMI now publishes 98 percent of all dissertations accepted each year by American institutions, as well as many Canadian and some foreign universities.

During the company's first six months of operation, while developing my idea for microfilming doctoral dissertations, I also was working with Vernon Tate on getting our brainchild, *The Journal of Documentary Reproduction* off the launching pad. The first issue came out— in about November, I believe—dated *Winter 1938,* and contained an article I wrote, "A Report of Progress on Filming English

Books before 1550."[1] In it I noted that it had been just about one year since we began distributing copies from the first negatives made in England. At that time, sixteen libraries[2] had subscribed to the service, receiving approximately 100,000 pages a year at an annual cost of $500, or half a cent per page. I also touched on some of the problems we had experienced, both in the making of the negatives in England and making positives. "A considerable amount of experimentation has been done [on the latter problem] with the result that we now feel we can produce a positive which is clear, sharp, and, for most purposes, a satisfactory substitute for the original book," I wrote. I then went into detail, describing how we had changed the original system of numbering the films as an aid to identifying and accessing the material contained in them. I noted, too, that a Graflex Photorecord camera then in the British Public Record Office would soon be available for "photographing books at the Bodleian Library and in the small outlying libraries of London and in other cities. A second Photorecord is located at the Vatican Library in Rome so that books and manuscripts may be secured from that library and the other principal libraries in Italy with whom arrangements have already been made. . . ." (The latter observation evidenced

---

[1] This date was later extended to 1640, to include the entire STC calalog.

[2] The sixteen libraries were: Yale University Library, Harvard College Library, University of Rochester Library, University of Michigan Library, Duke University Library, Library of Congress, New York Public Library, University of Virginia Library, University of Illinois Library, University of Chicago Library, Public Library of the City of Boston, University of Pennsylvania Library, Public Library of Toronto, University of California at Berkeley Library, University of Texas Library, and (jointly) Mount Holyoke, Smith, and Amherst College Libraries.

some of the fruits of my visits to various libraries during the 1935 trip I made to Europe with Sadye and my mother.) I concluded the article with the observation that I believed our problems were behind us and that the "coming year should go much smoother." Also that we would be filming "not only books printed in English but all books printed in England before 1550, irrespective of the language."

The article proved to be effective as an advertisement for our STC book-subscription service. We signed up six additional subscribers immediately after it came out. Such a result had been in the back of my mind when I wrote the piece, but I had no idea it would be so well received. Writing such articles became a regular practice for me thereafter. In addition to *The Journal of Documentary Reproduction,* these pieces appeared in such periodicals as *Library Journal, College Art Journal, FID Review, Michigan Alumnus Quarterly Review, The Journal of Higher Education,* and *College and Research Libraries Journal.* [3] Over the years, they proved to be my most effective means of advertising.

As an aside, in mentioning the articles I wrote over the years, I should add that Warner Rice, who was chairman of the U of M's English Department and later also the university librarian, helped me a great deal with them. Warner was my best critic, both of my humble literary efforts and of my ideas for new ventures in scholarly publishing at UMI. Warner is a skeptic by nature, and I found that if he could not see something wrong with an idea, it probably was a good one. Warner and I share a great interest in early printed

---

[3] *Miscellaneous Articles by Eugene Power,* UMI. Available on special order, microfilm or Editions of One.

books—his specialty is English literature of the Renaissance—and I sought his advice frequently. I owe him a great deal. He and I also played squash regularly. We had some rousing games.

The STC book-subscription service provided me with an established base from which to build my business. The $1,500 bonus I received from Edwards Brothers helped provide working capital. But I needed more equipment, so I went down to the local bank to arrange a loan. My father had been chairman of the board of one of the main banks in Traverse City, and he taught me to respect bankers. "Don't wait until you need a loan to call on them," he told me. "Cultivate their interest in you and your business even if you have no immediate need for money." I think this is good advice for any entrepreneur. Following it, I had introduced myself to my banker in Ann Arbor, Mr. Herman Gross. He was from the old school, in which you started as a runner and worked your way up to teller, vice president and, if you lived long enough, one day you got to be president. The president dealt with any loan requests personally. I dropped by and chatted with Mr. Gross, told him about my company, and said I would like to have a business loan. He said, "I see. Well, I'd like to have a look at your financial statement." I brought one in and he looked it over thoughtfully, then said, "Well, I guess we could loan you $250." What I needed was about ten times that amount, so Mr. Gross and I did not do any business at that time. I was disappointed, but I appreciated his approach. Although he was more conservative than I would have liked, he knew his individual depositors personally and he paid attention to them. This is a banking ethos that unfortunately has been largely lost in the process of mergers and computerization of the last decade. I borrowed the money I needed by using as collateral some insurance policies I had taken on my father's advice. Later on, I did get loans from Mr. Gross, and the day came that I had a line of credit at his bank for $250,000. If I needed money, I would simply write a note and send it to him.

In 1938 Sadye and I were living, as we had been since 1932, in one of the oldest houses in Ann Arbor. It was a one-story yellow-brick home, built in 1827, and was framed like a barn with 12-by-12 hand-hewn walnut beams—I used to say it was built like a fortress. The interior had more room than one would guess: it had three bedrooms, a kitchen, dining room, and sitting room with the best fireplace I ever saw. After we had lived there about two years, the owner agreed to build on a fourth bedroom off the kitchen for a young girl who was our live-in housekeeper. The house was situated on a knoll with a view out over the countryside, and this suited us very well. In the back were two large elm trees, between which we hung a hammock; there was also a barn where, for a time, we stabled Sadye's horse, Lady. Sadye loved to come home at the end of the day, throw the saddle on Lady, and ride off on the gravel roads in the area. Later on, we stabled Lady on a farm in the area, where Joe and Betty Hayden also kept their horses. Joe was chairman of the U of M Political Science Department. Ben Wheeler, a history professor, also had a horse, and the five of us would often ride on Sunday mornings. We had connecting fields of about six hundred acres of meadowlands to ride over, and it was great fun.

Sadye gave up riding the whole time she was pregnant with Phil. In fact, we didn't even drive much, and she was careful not to get tired or excited. When her time approached, her obstetrician, Dr. Norman Miller, said it was going to be a difficult breech delivery and recommended a Caesarian. I was present, and Sadye was given a local anesthetic, so she was conscious the whole time. It was a

Sadye with Lady in 1936.

tremendously exciting experience. Dr. Miller's decision proved very sound, because the baby had the umbilical cord wrapped twice around his neck and tied in a knot, so he probably would not have survived a breech delivery.

We had been married nine years when Phil came along, so he was an eagerly anticipated and much-loved baby. I considered his birth a wonderful gift for my thirty-third birthday, but becoming a father was a sobering experience for me. Realizing that I was now responsible for the welfare of three people made me redouble my efforts in establishing my new business. I often went back to the office at night and worked late. This effort paid off in sales, which for that short first year—June through December, 1938—were $30,000. I was pleased with that performance. We made a profit that year and every year thereafter.

Sadye and I lived modestly. I drove a secondhand Buick coupe, and our household furnishings were mostly things we had bought from the back porches of farmhouses. I refinished these pieces on weekends with satisfying results. Our greatest pleasure was in having friends for dinner or going on picnics. Most of our friends were university people, but there were others like Neil Staebler and his wife, Burnette. Sadye had introduced Neil to Burnette when she was alumni adviser to Kappa Kappa Gamma and Burnette was one of the girls in the sorority. When Neil was slow in following up and asking for dates, Sadye pushed me to badger him a bit, which I did. Neil came up to us at a party in 1985 and said he was grateful that we had been so insistent that he date Burnette—the occasion was their fiftieth wedding anniversary.

In the fall of 1938, at the urging of Robert Binkley, the American Philosophical Society and the American Council of Learned Societies held a joint meeting at the American Philosophical Society's headquarters in Philadelphia to discuss methods of publishing scholarly materials. I was invited and so were Vernon Tate and a number of other people I knew, such as Keyes Metcalf, of the New York Public Library, and Charlie Rush, associate librarian at Yale. Waldo Leland, secretary of the American Council of Learned Societies, chaired the meeting. I had a lot to say about the various production methods — what could be done with offset printing, what was possible with microfilm, and so on. At the end of the first session I was a little worried that I had seemed too brash or overeager in the company of these distinguished scholars.

During the second day of the meeting, a note was handed down to me and I fleetingly thought, "Uh-oh, I am going to be told to quiet down." But the note simply said, "Next time you are in New York, come and see me—Frederick Keppel."

I didn't know who Frederick Keppel was, so during the next break I asked Charlie Rush. He arched a brow at me and I handed him the note. "Well," he said, "if I got a note like this, I would be heading for New York City tomorrow. Frederick Keppel happens to be head of the Carnegie Corporation."

A few weeks later I was in New York and made an appointment to see Mr. Keppel. He asked me what I was doing, what I was interested in, and I told him. When I finished describing my company's work and my plans for it, he leaned back in his chair and asked, "What would you *like* to do if you could?"

"Well, sir, I would like to go to Europe and visit the principal libraries there and arrange to place a copy camera in each of them so I could form a network to obtain research materials. An American scholar would then be able to contact us and request documents from a foreign library and we could obtain them quickly and inexpensively for him via microfilm."

"How much would this cost?" he asked.

"About nine hundred dollars," I replied.

"When you get ready, let me know, and I will send you the money," he said. We shook hands and I floated out of his office.

Sadye and I immediately began making plans to go to Europe the following April. We knew we could stay in bed-and-breakfasts for a dollar a night, so we could stay for three months, and my mother would take care of Phil. I should point out here that Sadye's training in psychology was Freudian and she believed there was absolutely nothing wrong with parents leaving children in the care of others during the first two years. Dr. Ted Raphael, the eminent psychiatrist and Sadye's mentor, concurred with this approach. So Sadye always accompanied me on my travels. I did not observe any adverse effect on Phil from these separations. He was a bright, alert youngster, always smiling and gurgling. However, Sadye later concluded that she had been wrong in leaving Phil at that early stage of his life, and she has suffered great pangs of guilt and remorse over it.

It happened that Neil and Burnette Staebler also were planning to go to Europe, so we decided to travel together. Neil was an interesting person (his father was mayor of Ann Arbor from 1927 to 1931); he was a liberal Democrat and pretty feisty when we were undergraduates. He made a trip to the Soviet Union in 1926 with a group of students led by Sherwood Eddy, who was prominent in the YMCA. That made him an ardent supporter of our democratic system and started him on his career in politics. We knew that traveling with Neil and Burnette would never lack for excitement and stimulating conversation.

Neil Staebler

We arranged to travel on the freighter S.S. *Nordam,* which carried only sixty passengers, one class, and we were able to take my Buick coupe over and back for $100 extra. My habit, whenever I was at sea and the ship developed a roll of more than two degrees, was to immediately become seasick. The *Nordam* was fast, and as soon as we had cleared the harbor I found a place at the rail and stayed there. By the time we landed in Holland, I was feeling fine and called on two libraries in The Hague while Sadye and the Staeblers went sightseeing. I explained my request that they allow me to install a copy camera in their institutions and

102

gave them a presentation of how microfilming worked, complete with a projection of the finished product. They agreed, as did the librarians in Brussels, Paris, Zurich, and Berlin.

The assistant librarian at the Bibliothèque Nationale in Paris was Jean Le Roy, and he and I discovered that we would both be attending the meeting of the International Federation of Documentation in Bern, Switzerland later in the summer. We arranged that Sadye and I would meet him near Paris and he would follow us to the conference. He said he had never been beyond the borders of France before and he was concerned that he might not be able to get any edible food in Switzerland.

I found interest in microfilming in Switzerland, although none had yet been done in the country. A Dr. Sevensma, head of the League of Nations Library in Geneva, had purchased a microfilm reader before he retired, but it was sitting there unused. I had some potentially useful discussions with a Miss Bartlett in the League library about the possibility of microfilming the index to the International Peace Conference and certain out-of-print materials. Mr. J. W. Haden, librarian of the International Labor Office in Geneva, had received a Graflex Photorecord just two days before I called on him, but he did not know how to operate it. I helped him set it up and demonstrated how to use it and how to go about processing the film. As a result, I was able to arrange with Haden that he would send his camera anywhere in Switzerland where we might need work done, with University Microfilms paying expenses and cost of the operator. I also called on Dr. Joseph Möller, Abbott of the

Monastery of Saint Gall, about photographing its collection of manuscripts, which was said to be the best in Europe.

We then headed into Italy, where my plans were thwarted by the language barrier. I had been told when I called to make an appointment with the librarian of the Ambrosiana Library in Milan, that he was a highly educated man who spoke fifteen languages. Unfortunately, English was not among them, and he was incensed when he discovered that I spoke neither French nor Italian. The experience made me sincerely regret my cavalier attitude toward foreign languages when I was in school. Having struck out in Milan, we went to the Laurenciana Library in Florence, where, in addition to asking permission to set up a camera, I hoped to fill a request I had received from an American scholar to copy all the manuscripts of the Don Juan story. This time my trouble was less linguistic than emotional. Specifically, the librarian, a Dr. Teresa Lodi, was a dark and moody Italian woman who treated my requests as an imposition on her time. After a week of fruitless effort, I decided to give up. Walking toward the Laurenciana, however, I passed a flower stall and bought a bouquet of carnations.

"Dr. Lodi, I am sorry we were unable to reach an agreement," I told her. "I must leave now to visit the Vatican Library in Rome, where I have a camera in place. So, goodbye. But please accept these flowers as a token of my esteem."

"Just a moment," she said. "What was it you wanted?"

I patiently repeated my request and she agreed. As for the *Don Juan,* she said she had a local photographer who could make the negatives right away with his Leica and she would be glad to send them to us.

Moving on to Rome, I found that the principal work in microfilming was being done by the Vatican. The camera I had placed there on my previous trip was in daily use, and a complete photographic department had been developed around it and was operating very efficiently. The prefect of the library, Rev. A. M. Albareda, a Spaniard from Montserrat, was extremely helpful in establishing a system by which we could access Vatican materials on an ongoing basis. My interpreter was a Miss Adele Kibre, who was spending six months each year in Italy on a grant from the University of Chicago. She was a good photographer in her own field of paleography, using a Leica; moreover, as an accredited scholar, she knew how to dig up material and was familiar with most of the principal European libraries. I arranged with her to work for us on a regular freelance basis.

After Rome, we went to Naples, because Sadye had fond memories of Sorrento and wanted to stay at the same hotel she'd been in the last time she was there. Our stay was enlivened by a lot of hilarious word play occasioned by my birthday. I was thirty-four. We forged on to Venice, a first visit for all of us, and we steeped ourselves in its romantic decay like four characters out of a novel by Thomas Mann, who, incidentally, had been stripped of his German citizenship by Hitler just a year or two earlier.

Hitler's chauvinistic ranting and raving were worrisome to everyone, especially Neil, whose sensibilities were offended by Hitler's venomous anti-Semitism. But we drove into Germany nonetheless, taking the lovely way to Cortina d'Ampezzo in the Dolomites and through the Brenner Pass to Munich. I called on the Munich Library once again, and then we pushed on to Berlin, where the librarian at the famous Staatsbibliothek, Herr Dr. Kruse, was a model of kindness and cordiality. He showed me some of his treasures: two Gutenberg Bibles, a beautiful Aldine book printed in about 1490 on parchment, and other choice items. He also directed me to a Berlin firm operated by one Willi Kramer, who used 35mm film to make enlargements of documents for the German government and industry. I was awed by Kramer's equipment and the crispness and detail he was able to attain in reproductions. I felt I learned quite a lot from him.

While I was visiting the Staatsbibliothek and Kramer's shop, Neil was doing some investigative work of his own, as he explains in this excerpt from his taped recollections:

I went to the American Embassy in Berlin and told them I was a graduate student in economics and would like to see "how Germany is being run—in particular, how they set prices and allocate capital." They sent me to the minister of propaganda, where some appointments were scheduled for me. One of these was to the Office of Foreign Exchange. I started to excuse myself, indicating I felt it would be a waste of time, and the man I was talking to said, "Just a moment; please don't be in a hurry. I was a graduate student in the United States. I married an American girl, so I like to talk to Americans." I learned that he had studied at the University of Wisconsin and that Bill Haber, whom I knew quite well, had been best man at his wedding. Haber was by this time an administrator in Michigan's state government, in charge of social-welfare programs, and he was Jewish. This suddenly put the discussion between the German and me on a different footing. We knew something about each other—we were not crazy Aryans. So he asked me again, in a

106

conspiratorial tone, "What kind of appointments would you like to make?" I told him I wanted to know the real facts about Hitler's treatment of Jews and his political operations. He put me in touch with some members of the underground, a small faction of Junkers. I got an inside picture of what was taking place, and it was spine-chilling.

One general observation I have about that trip of ours with Gene and Sadye Power was that it made a Democrat out of Gene. We talked politics incessantly during it, and he came around to my point of view.

Sadye was eager to visit Dr. Hans Von Hatingberg, who had been her psychoanalyst in 1934 and '35 when he was visiting Ann Arbor and lecturing at the U of M. He had moved back to Berlin four years earlier. We arranged to have dinner with him and his wife in a private dining room of a restaurant, but it turned out to be a terrible mistake. Von Hatingberg had been a reasonable man when he lived in Ann Arbor, rather liberal as I recall. But after he returned to Germany, he read no foreign newspapers and listened to nothing on the radio but state broadcasts, and he had swallowed Hitler's propaganda hook, line, and sinker. Neil and I had watched the Nazi troops goose-stepping on parade that very afternoon, and his German underground contacts had told us that an invasion of Poland was scheduled for the twenty-eighth of August. They did not think this would mean war because, they said, "The British will not fight." Of course they had British Prime Minister Chamberlain's equivocal "peace with honor" in the Munich Agreement as an example of Britain's distaste for what Chamberlain called "a quarrel in a faraway country between people of whom we know nothing."

Dr. Von Hatingberg also was sure there would be no war. He and his wife thought Hitler was the best thing that had ever happened to Germany, and that rumors about persecution and internment camps were lies. They thought Hitler's annexation of Austria was proper and that the destruction of Czechoslovakia was merely to put Bohemia, Moravia, and Slovakia "under the protection of the Great German Reich." Von Hatingberg and Neil got into a very heated argument. Frau Von Hatingberg shushed her husband and we tried to shush Neil, but he would not desist; he kept at it like a puppy worrying a boot. Finally, we had to call the evening off.

Our drive from Berlin to Holland, where we took a ferry to London, was somber. We had seen firsthand how honest people could be deceived by an evil government if there was no free press. At times in later years I was annoyed by our press and was a target for abuse by some newspapers, but I never lost my respect and appreciation for our freedom of the press.

The view we got from the English of what would happen if Hitler invaded Poland was quite different from that of the Germans. It would mean war, they said, in no uncertain terms. They were far more disposed to identify with Winston Churchill's belligerent attitude than with Chamberlain's policy of appeasement. I remember writing in a letter home that I now felt war was inevitable. Neil and Burnette set off to bicycle around England and then return home. Sadye and I paid a visit to Arundel Esdaille at the British Museum and stopped in to check on affairs at the libraries in Oxford and Cambridge. Then we were off again to the continent, to pick up Jean Le Roy on the outskirts of

Paris. He cut a dashing figure in an aviator helmet, kid gloves, and pullover sweater—his togs for the sport of driving. His wife and small dog were along; they were to stop at the French border and await his return from Switzerland. Apparently he did not want his wife to be victimized by Swiss food. M. Le Roy had arranged for us to drive sixty miles out of our way to have a final lunch of edible food at a remote restaurant. The dog joined us and sat on a chair at our table, where his mistress occasionally handed him a bit of food. The poor beast had a terrible time eating because his teeth were all loose. I remarked that he would do well to gnaw on a few bones to strengthen them. Mme. Le Roy was horrified. "Oh, monsieur, *non!*" she exclaimed. "He has never eaten a bone!" I believed her. But I could think of no polite way to explain that canines, unlike French people, were not meant to eat cake.

The city of Bern welcomed our international conference with a series of official ceremonies full of European pomp and circumstance. I was distinctly in the minority there, not only as an American but as the lone voice speaking up about the importance of microfilm. The rest of the conferees seemed only vaguely familiar with the term and knew practically nothing about microfilm's potential for their work in documentation. M. Le Roy was excited, not by the meetings but by the fact that the Swiss actually knew how to cook and produced good wine as well. Herr Dr. Kruse, the charming gentleman from Berlin, made a speech prevailing on the conferees to designate his city as the site for the organization's meeting the next year. Someone asked, "What if there is a war?" "Impossible," he assured us.

"There will be no war." He was serious, and I am sure he would have been startled by the scene that greeted Sadye and me when we got back to Paris on August 24.

The entire city was electric with tension. Notices of army reserves called up were being posted daily. There were no porters in the railway stations, which were jammed with people trying to get out of the country. We drove to Le Havre on the twenty-fifth to board the *Neu Amsterdam* for New York. The tender headed out to the ship three times, only to be called back each time by taxicabs arriving from Paris. The cabs would come screeching to a stop on the dock, blowing their horns frantically as their passengers stood on the running boards and waved handkerchiefs to hail us.

Although the *Neu Amsterdam* was a large vessel, she was overflowing with passengers. People were sleeping on mattresses in the gymnasium. Sadye and I had a tourist cabin reserved well in advance, so we were comfortable, but the mood on board was very serious. The news from Germany was not good. Hitler had signed an agreement with Stalin which he felt assured that British intervention on behalf of Poland would not be possible. We were well out to sea when we learned that Hitler had ordered troops into Poland.

On September 3, as we reached mid-Atlantic, word came from the radio room that Britain had declared war on Germany and that a German submarine had sunk the passenger ship *Athenia* with a heavy loss of life. All my efforts of the last three months in Europe were for naught. There would be no easy exchange of scholarly knowledge now. Of course, those were small and selfish considerations, given

110

the monstrous reality of a world at war and the catastrophic consequences it could have.

Sadye and I held each other close and wondered aloud about the future and what kind of a world our small son would know as he grew up. We felt with certainty that it would be far different from the one we knew, especially in those lovely European countries we had just left behind.

B ack in Ann Arbor, there was a great deal of catching up to do after my three-month absence. Jan Vandenbrock, whom I had left in charge, had done a good job of filling orders, but the process of generating new business was lagging. I plunged in and soon had the place humming again.

The development of creative new applications for microfilm was more than an intellectual exercise for me now. It was vital to my nascent enterprise. Even though the hostilities between Britain, France, and Germany were bogged down in what journalists were deriding as the "Phony War," mail service from England had grown erratic, and if the conflict became a shooting war, my flow of negatives of STC books—80 percent of my business— would be cut off. I contacted American libraries that had STC holdings and arranged to do some alternative photographing with them so that, if the worst happened, we would still be able to continue our service, which now had sixteen subscribers.

One day an important new business opportunity walked into my office in the person of a Mr. Lee White, who represented the *Detroit News*. Mr. White asked if I knew about Eastman Kodak's arrangement with *The New York Times* to photograph that paper's back files. Of course I did. Kodak had come out with a new camera, the Microfile Camera, specifically designed for photographing full-size newspaper pages, and I had read about it with keen interest.

"Well, then," Mr. White said, "would you be able to take on the job of photographing the back files of the *News*?"

"I certainly would," I replied.

The instant Mr. White left my office, I got on the telephone to my friend Charlie Case, who was a vice president of the Eastman Kodak Company. Charlie and I got to know each other at the American Library Association conferences and, in addition to our mutual interest in the photography business, we enjoyed some knock-down, drag-out after-hours poker games. I used to kid him that his only job was to sit up there on the eighteenth floor of Kodak's headquarters in Rochester and stare out the window. This was true, to a point—the point being that he was paid to make his staring time produce a lot of ideas for the company. Charlie arranged for me to obtain one of Kodak's $1,800 Model C Microfile Cameras on loan, with an option to purchase it for one hundred dollars a month. This was a great boost for us. The Microfile Camera was a superior piece of equipment. It had a large bed with a glass platen which would press bound newspapers flat and hold them in place to be photographed. Its cradle would shift back and forth in order to get a complete page on each exposure.

Once the *Detroit News* back-file operation was in progress, I called on the *Detroit Free Press* and signed them up. Then I approached the area newspapers of the Booth chain, which included *The Ann Arbor News*. Our service was a real boon to these papers, because microfilm requires only a tiny fraction of the storage space required for the cumbersome old spindle hangers and bound volumes, and it is far more permanent. After about fifty years, newsprint begins to crumble to dust.

The new operations taxed our production facilities to the limit. We were still developing film by hand, using Stineman reels holding two hundred feet of film each and processing it as described earlier. On a good day, if we hit the ball hard, we could produce 3,000 feet of positive film. We worked a lot of nights and Saturdays, too.

E arly in the summer of 1940, Sadye and Phil and I were visiting my parents at their cottage on East Bay in Traverse City, and I mentioned to my father that Jan Vandenbrock had decided to build a small house for himself in Ann Arbor. I was pleased that Jan's work for my company had enabled him to do this.

"Well, I think that sometime you ought to build yourself," was Father's response, and it set me to thinking.

Not long after that, I discovered Barton Hills subdivision outside Ann Arbor through Willett and Vera Spooner, who were building a house there. The area was being developed by Detroit Edison, whose original plan had been to sell lots of 5 or 10 acres to automobile executives. For some reason that had not worked out and they were selling lots of 1-3/4 to 2-1/2 acres. Sadye and I toured the area and found a lot we liked for $2,500. We arranged to buy it with the savings I had from my inheritance from Great-Uncle Del. It was a

Sadye and Phil, age seven, with her parents, C. A. and Caroline Harwick.

secluded piece of property, nicely wooded, and ran from the brow of a hill down to the shore of Barton Pond. Now we had to figure out what sort of house we wanted to build.

Sadye had been going over to Kingswood School once a week to work as a counselor. Irene Murphy, whom she had known as a social worker, was doing some work at Kingswood, too, and Irene told Sadye about the house she was building. She had used a "wonderful free-spirited architect from Birmingham, Michigan named Wallace Frost." We drove over to see the place and liked it. We were told that Frost had inherited two or three fortunes and went through them all. He had lived in Italy for a time, then in California. He had built a house next door to Irene's that showed a lot of California influence, and we liked both houses. I liked Frost, too. He was indeed a free spirit, but he felt strongly that a house should reflect the character of the people who were going to live in it. I especially liked his remark that "People got satisfactory houses in the days before architects stood between them and the contractor and prevented them from getting what they wanted."

Sadye and I spent a lot of time going over floor plans with Frost and discussing other aspects of his design, which we liked very much. One day I happened to notice that the old Methodist Church in Ann Arbor was being razed, and I mentioned this to Frost. "Let's go take a look at it," he said. We did, and his opinion was that "We could build your whole house out of this." So I bought the materials and excavation was begun a short time later—on January 2, 1941. I had the feeling that we were embarking on a whole new phase of our lives.

Chapter Six

War

Americans stood by and watched anxiously after Hitler invaded Poland on August 31, 1939. England and France immediately declared war on Germany, but there followed the "Phony War" that did not become a shooting war until the spring of 1940. In April of that year, Hitler invaded Norway. In May, Neville Chamberlain resigned and was succeeded as Britain's Prime Minister by Winston Churchill. Those of us who had been following newspaper accounts of the debates in the British House of Commons knew this meant that appeasement was at an end. It came as no surprise when, days later, the continent exploded in a series of battles that led to the British evacuation at Dunkirk.

My discussions with Vernon Tate and Bob Binkley about future issues of *The Journal of Documentary Reproduction* often touched on the concern we shared over the safety of books and manuscripts in European libraries. We agreed that something should be done to preserve the irreplaceable volumes in England, at least. It seemed that nothing could be done about library materials on the continent. The Nazis had the reputation of being book burners. I was shocked to learn that when they occupied Paris in mid-June, soldiers went into the Bibliothèque Nationale, grabbed my friend Jean Le Roy, and threw him bodily out the door. He later died from his injuries.

Meanwhile, during my regular visits with Randolph Adams at the Clements Library, he and I had come up with the idea of using the library's outstanding collection of Americana to make a microfilm history of eyewitness accounts of the discovery and exploration of our continent. Warner Rice suggested that we also do a series on American periodicals. These were exciting projects. I felt sure they would be of general interest to students of American history and culture, and they did prove to be so. In September 1940, I published another of my "advertisement articles" in the *Journal of Documentary Reproduction.* I wrote:

> Two invaluable microfilm collections of materials for the study of American culture are announced by University Microfilms for delivery commencing January 1941.
>
> The first of these, entitled the *American Periodical Series,* reproduces page by page all known extant magazines, as distinguished from newspapers, published in the continental United States between 1741 and 1799 inclusive.
>
> The second microfilm collection . . . consists of complete texts of the original editions of approximately 250 books of representative writings about America and Americans between 1493 and 1800, beginning with Christopher Columbus's *Epistola,* Rome, 1493, ending with *Washingtoniana,* Baltimore, 1800.

Randolph Adams prepared the bibliography for the second series, which we called *The American Culture Series,* and which comprised another 69,000 pages of microfilm materials.[1]

The war in Europe made me intensify my focus on American sources, and two others came up at the urging of

[1] Both the first and second series were successful and later were expanded.

118

Frederick Keppel of the Carnegie Corporation. The first was The Indian Art Exhibit that had been displayed at the San Francisco Exposition of 1939. The second was The Survey of American Painting. Both were black-and-white photographs of paintings and were designed to aid art students at the Carnegie Institute. In the program for the 1941 meeting of the Modern Language Association, I listed six UMI series:

1. English Books before 1600
2. American Periodicals before 1800
3. Selected Americana before 1800
4. Indian Art Exhibit
5. Survey of American Painting
6. Doctoral Dissertations

UMI sold the American Culture Series on the same subscription basis we used for STC books, and it went over quite well. Unfortunately, the records of sales figures for that period were accidentally destroyed, but I know the work was profitable, because the increase in our activities enabled me to purchase some additional camera equipment and expand our facilities, taking over the entire building. We used the office formerly occupied by Connie Wageman as a camera room.

Busy as I was at the office, though, I took an hour each day to drive out and check the progress on construction of our new home. I believe in the old Chinese saying, "The footprint of the owner is worth a thousand foremen." It was a rather unusual house for its time in that area because of the

119

wide overhang of its eaves, the curved walls in the living room, and the ceilings that follow the roof line. We used precast concrete joists and poured concrete floors on them. That was unusual, too. The living-room floor was recessed for a layer of common brick, which we treated with crank-case drainings from a gas station. After that heavy oil soaked in, we sealed the whole surface with tung oil and waxed it. It made a very satisfactory floor. The concrete floors were fine, too, except that those in the bedrooms were cold the first winter, before we got them carpeted. My mother was a frequent visitor to the construction site. She and Sadye spent hours chatting about how the various rooms would look. Mother liked the design of the place as much as Sadye and I did, but we may have been a minority; Sadye once bumped into a neighbor woman who said, "I was out looking at the house you are building last night."

"Oh, really," Sadye said. "And what did you think?"

"Well, I suppose it's all right—back in the woods like that where no one will see it."

In thirty or forty years, the design would not be considered unusual, but in 1940 it created some comment. The house has been very satisfactory, nonetheless, and we have been happy in it.

At that time, Frank and I owned a small sailboat, a twenty-five-foot sloop we had found on the beach at Old Mission Peninsula near Traverse City in the spring of 1936. We located the owner, and he was glad to get rid of the craft for a mere $500. We had never sailed anything larger than a canoe, so we were really babes in the woods that first year. Sadye and I slept in the bunks in the cabin and Frank stretched out in a sleeping bag in the cockpit. We had a gasoline stove with which we cooked on deck, and we always had great fun. One time we were in some dangerous waters where rocky reefs ran far out from shore. I contacted the Coast Guard, but could not seem to get a correct bearing. After several minutes the man I was talking to said, "Well, your compass must be off." I didn't understand how that could be. Neither did Frank. But he opened the binnacle, and sure enough, there was the source of our problem—a can opener Sadye had stored away in there!

We sold that boat to Bill Milliken, who was later to become Governor of Michigan. We had a series

Happy sailors Frank and Sadye

of cast-iron weights laid between the ribs, along the keel, as ballast, and the story I got is that Bill's mother was worried about them. She thought they'd make the boat sink if it filled with water, so she made him take them out. Trouble was, the boat was impossible to sail without them. I don't know exactly what happened, but the boat was wrecked in a storm.

Toward the end of the summer of 1940, Frank bought a sailboat from someone up on the Keweenaw Peninsula in Lake Superior; it was a beautiful thirty-one-foot Herreshoff racing sloop named *Renlu*. We did not have an opportunity to sail her that season, but we were looking forward to making some good trips the next summer. I loved being active, out in the open air, regardless of weather. So did Frank, and Sadye was a good sport about it. I suppose my impatience with indoor activities kept me from being more involved in literature. I read a lot, certainly, but I never developed a taste for serious fiction. That winter of 1940, for example, I spent much of my free time in Will Spooner's basement building a dinghy for *Renlu*. Will was a neighbor of ours and a fine sailor. He was a professor of marine engineering at U of M.

In the summer of 1940, Waldo Leland of the American Council of Learned Societies called a two-day conference to discuss possibilities for microfilming large blocks of European materials that were needed by American scholars and to protect them from war damage. I attended the conference and outlined what I knew about the European libraries, based on my trip two years earlier and my continuing correspondence with them.

At the conclusion of the conference, Archibald MacLeish, the poet, who was Librarian of Congress, moved that an advisory committee be appointed to make a selection of materials and that a Rockefeller grant be sought to support the work of photographing them. MacLeish recommended that the Biblio-Film Service Watson Davis was operating in the Department of Agriculture do the filming. I was disappointed. I felt I probably knew more about microfilming in Europe than anyone else in the country.

In November that year, Bob Binkley had the idea of sending ten cameras over to England and photographing all the books held by the British Museum in order to protect them from possible war damage. I did not realize it at the time, but Binkley was not well—he was suffering the onset of cancer of the throat, which would kill him within a few months. Perhaps the illness gave his proposal letter a more officious tone than he normally would have used. In any event, there was an unfortunate phrase in it alluding to "mopping up" the British Museum in a single year. Sir John Forsdyke, director of the institution, took offense at the suggestion and replied frostily, "Thank you very much, but the British Museum can take care of their own holdings."

On May 12, 1941, my mother died of a heart attack. We had seen her not long before; in fact she had been staying with Sadye and me and was happily following the construction of our house along with us. She was cheerful and full of vitality, and apart from being slightly overweight, seemed to be in the best of health. When she left to return to Traverse City, we all had every expectation that she would be back soon. So when my father telephoned me at two

My mother in Venice, 1935.

o'clock in the morning to tell me she was dead, it seemed impossible. Sadye and I had never made a sadder journey than that trip to Traverse City for her funeral. It was a large service, because mother had been very active in the church and the community. Our hearts were sad for a long time after that, though. Sadye and I missed her greatly.

A few months later, the start of summer vacation at the university gave me an opportunity to take care of a chore I had promised Frank I would tend to. He had been called up by the U.S. Army Medical Reserves that spring of 1941, and he asked me to go up and get *Renlu* out of the boatyard in Houghton and sail her back to Traverse City. Will Spooner and Ivan Walton, an English professor, agreed to help me. We had planned to go up July Fourth, but the boatyard didn't have *Renlu* ready. So it was the last weekend in August when my father and Sadye dropped us off with a load of equipment and the dinghy Will and I had built.

Our voyage turned into a true, storm-tossed epic. *Renlu,* we discovered, had been poorly rigged and equipped. During the three weeks it took us to sail back we had several misadventures that could have been serious. At one point after we had finally made it through the locks at Sault Ste. Marie and were turning south past Detour to enter Lake Huron, a sudden shift of wind tossed Will across the deck and into the water. He was wearing heavy clothing and rubber galoshes, so he would have had a bad time of it, but fortunately he was carried close by the stern, and I was able to reach out and grab an inch of his collar and pull him aboard. The trip also taught me never to sail on Lake Superior at the beginning of September without adequate equipment. We were lucky—and I guess the Lord must have been looking after us.

While I was away on that voyage, a letter arrived from my friend Arundel Esdaille, the secretary of the British Museum, informing me that, thanks to my recommendation, he had been invited by the University of Michigan to give a series of lectures on Samuel Johnson that fall. I was delighted. Sadye and I asked him to stay with us, even though we would barely be moved into our new house. He accepted, and I drove to New York and met him when he landed.

Esdaille was a charming man, and his stay with us most pleasant. Sadye was apologetic about the fact that, due to the confusion of moving into the house, she had not had time to get curtains up in the guest room. His gentle remonstrance—how could she even consider putting curtains on the windows of one who had come from London, where he was forced to live with blackout curtains drawn, unable to enjoy the pure light?— immediately made him at home amid our moving-in clutter.

Arundel Esdaille

Phil was three years old at that time, and we were reading *Winnie the Pooh* to him practically every night. He was so fascinated by the stories that he had designated one brush pile in our yard as Eeyore's house and another as Piglet's, and there was a tree where Owl lived. Sadye would take him out to visit these spots each day. At lunch, Phil would insist that places be set for the animals. So, of course, he was greatly impressed when he learned that Esdaille's house in Sussex backed up onto the Hundred-Acre Woods where all of Pooh's adventures took place. Phil promptly began calling Esdaille *Uncle Pooh.* The two of them got on very well, but Esdaille brooked no childish nonsense. If Phil would misbehave, our guest would tell him sternly, "Manners, boy. Manners."

Esdaille possessed that mixture of traits I have always considered typically British: being prompt and fastidious, yet with a capacity to dawdle lightheartedly. For example, his lectures were completely written out with notations for pauses and proper phrasing, like pieces of music. But one morning he became so involved in playing Uncle Pooh with Phil at breakfast that he went off with the wrong speech. He was to present an all-university lecture in the auditorium of the graduate school, and he didn't realize his mistake until we arrived at the auditorium. He was horrified, because the lecture was too complex to be delivered extemporaneously, and I broke all speed records driving the five or six miles out to Barton Hills and back to the campus with the right text. The lecture went off without a hitch.

We were sorry to see Esdaille leave.

Bob Binkley died that fall. His place on the advisory committee for microfilming European materials was taken by Herbert Keller, who had some difficulty making progress because it was a new field for him. He finally did get the group organized, though, and it began casting its net for suggestions on what collections needed to be preserved. There was no shortage of opinion on the subject: scholars suggested everything from Latin American manuscripts to

Our home in Barton Hills, winter 1942.

those in Greek monasteries. After creating a master card file of the suggestions and sifting through them, the committee's conclusion was that the holdings in British libraries had the greatest potential for use by scholars and stood most in need of protection and preservation. The Rockefeller Foundation granted $30,000 to initiate the work, but Watson Davis told the Council of Learned Societies that he would have to decline the assignment because he did not know how to operate such a service. I then received a letter from Keller asking if UMI could do the filming and, of course, I accepted.

Fortunately, since the British Museum management had their noses out of joint over my late friend Binkley's letter, I had a friend in court in Esdaille. I sent him a long cable asking if, since he was retiring, he would take charge of the work in England and I outlined what I wanted. He accepted and put a letter in the *Times* of London announcing

127

that we wished to photograph portions of manuscript collections throughout the country, both public and private.

It became increasingly clear that mobilizing the microfilming project in England was going to require my presence on the scene. When I mentioned to William Warner Bishop that I thought I would be going over there soon, he asked if I could make copies of a collection of German scientific periodicals in London. He thought they would be of great value to American scientists, because the subscriptions of American libraries were held up by the war. In a similar vein, my contacts at the Library of Congress in Washington, D.C. advised me that General William Donovan, then U.S. Coordinator of Information (COI), was interested in obtaining microfilm of certain other German publications and other documents that had been acquired by British intelligence. I believed that such demands were likely to increase, so I made provisions for that eventuality by having three Kodak Model D Microfile cameras shipped to London. Unfortunately, the vessel carrying them was torpedoed by a German submarine, and the three cameras went to the bottom.

My proposed trip was given a heightened sense of urgency on December 7, 1941, when the Japanese bombed Pearl Harbor, plunging the United States into World War II. I was scheduled to leave by plane in January, but I got bumped from the flight by a general with a higher priority. I was rescheduled for February and arrived in New York only to be put off again. My disappointment evaporated when I learned that the connecting flight from Lisbon to Bristol, which I would have been on, cracked up on the coast of England and everybody aboard was killed.

Finally, with the help of some string-pulling by Verner Clapp, assistant to Luther Evans, the deputy librarian of the Library of Congress, I was booked onto a Pan Am flying boat that was scheduled to leave March 10.

My plans were now complicated by an administrative problem at UMI. My secretary was not working out and I felt I must replace her before I would be able to leave. Coincidentally, Sadye's cousin, Margaret Harwick, had just lost her job—her position at the Michigan Crippled Children's Society was eliminated. I hired her, and it was one of those workplace matches made in heaven.

Of course I had no idea then that Margaret would be with me for twenty-three years and become my chief financial officer as well as a first-rate office manager and personnel coordinator. Those were not her titles. They were just a few of the things she did at UMI.

Margaret Harwick

I will never forget the look on Margaret's face—she had been on the job all of one week—when I told her I was going to England on an important microfilming project and said, "You will be in charge." Her eyes grew round in disbelief, but she nodded acceptance, and that was it. UMI ran as smoothly while I was away as if I had been there the whole time.

If I were compiling a book of lessons for entrepreneurs based on my experience, a major point would be: Find someone like Margaret Harwick to be your right hand and hire her as soon as you can. I might have been able to build UMI into the company it became without Margaret's brains, hard work, and loyalty, but I doubt it. It certainly would have been vastly more difficult.

Transatlantic air travel was still a novel experience in 1942. After I returned from my trip, I wrote an article describing it and the conditions I observed in wartime England for the *Michigan Alumnus Quarterly Review.* [2] I titled the piece "South to England," because our Pan-American Atlantic Clipper went first to Miami, Puerto Rico, and Brazil before crossing to Africa.

I described my mixed feelings—"excitement, adventure, and some concern at leaving one's family"—as we boarded the flying boat. I mentioned my two previous disappointments in attempting to get aboard, asserting that: "Passage on an Atlantic Clipper is almost as difficult to obtain as a seat in Congress."

The takeoff, I thought, "was the most exciting time of the whole flight. The plane, heavily laden with mail, five thousand gallons of gasoline, and passengers, must make a long run before it leaves the water with a final surge of power . . . from its four 1,600-horsepower motors. The heavy sea wings which serve as gasoline tanks flatten out

---

[2] The text of this article is included in *Miscellaneous Articles by Eugene B. Power,* cf. note 2, Ch. Five.

the spray which flies in great clouds from the bows."

In addition to the flight crew, there were fifty-six passengers, many of them Navy boys who would be leaving us in Rio de Janeiro. Those crossing the Atlantic included:

One Naval courier; a Hindu sixty-five years of age, caught at Pearl Harbor during the Japanese attack and at present trying to reach India by way of Africa; two Pan American men going out to their posts; representatives from the foreign offices of the Netherlands government in London, of the Danish legation in Washington, and the Portuguese Foreign Office in Lisbon; a Norwegian cabinet minister; a prominent Norwegian industrialist; and two famous English engineers. I was destined to spend enough time with these people to feel I knew them and their views rather well. For after landing in Bolama, Portuguese Guinea—where I bought a pith helmet which made me the target of much good-natured ribbing—our 2200-mile flight to Lisbon, the longest leg of the journey, was aborted twice by engine trouble. The second time one engine caught fire and burned up, my fellow passengers blamed the whole thing on my sun helmet. But I had been wise to buy it, for now I had use for it—we were stranded in the tropical heat of Bolama for nine days, waiting for a new engine to arrive from New York. A derrick had to be brought in from Cape Town to install it.

I was concerned that Sadye would be worried since she had not heard from me, so I went to the telegraph office in Bolama. They charged $2.50 (U.S.) a word, including articles and address, so I kept my message short. I wrote: "OK."

Our group was put up on the second floor of a building that served as a hotel. It was adequate. Each of us had a room with a bed draped in a mosquito net and a chair. There was a shower from which water trickled from a tank on the roof.

It was a godsend, but when we showered, we had to put paper towels on the floor to guard against the microscopic larvae of parasitic worms, which would grow under one's toenails. During the days I walked through the countryside and took photographs. We were only forty miles from some of the best big-game hunting in the world, but it was impossible to get there because gasoline was so tightly rationed. At sunset we would gather on the second-floor balcony of the hotel in our underwear shorts and have cocktails and a general discussion of the world situation. "One dominant note" in these talks, I recalled, "was the necessity for some kind of world organization, some federation, which would guarantee the security and peace of the world after this war." I felt there were "certain rather terrifying opinions expressed—opinions which I later found echoed in England and other countries by sane, responsible, intelligent people—a conviction that Germany *must* be taught a vigorous disciplinary lesson . . . that the German nation must be subjected to the experience of arson, murder, rape, and all that goes with it." Another feeling that came through strong and clear in these talks was "a considerable respect for Russia and also a fear that Russia might reach Berlin first!"

When the engine was replaced and we prepared to leave Bolama, I heard that the censor in New York had killed my message to Sadye. He thought it was some sort of code. I sent another, more complete, cable. I later learned that Sadye, alarmed at my apparent disappearance, had called Pan American and was told, "We don't know what happens to our flights after they leave the country." She then phoned

Vernon Tate, who checked with the State Department and said he got a guarded message that I was all right. That was some relief, she said, but she had a turn each time Phil would call to her, "Here comes Daddy!" when any man walked by.

I wrote that "Lisbon is reputed to be a hotbed of espionage, shadowing, and intrigue. I must confess I saw none of it, and if I was shadowed, it was completely unknown to me. There were Germans who stayed at the same hotel in Estoril, where I spent two nights. One of them was said to be the head of the German Gestapo in Lisbon and certainly looked the part. Most of the other guests at the hotel were Americans trying to get back to the United States."

In London, my experience of riding in a cab through a blackout and seeing the shocking evidence of German bombing everywhere was sobering. But it took a while for the facts of wartime conditions to sink in. When I went down to breakfast in my hotel the first morning, I told the waitress I would like scrambled eggs and bacon, some orange juice, a glass of milk, and buttered toast. She eyed me carefully and said, "Wouldn't you, though!" What I got was a little fish, warmed dry bread, and tea.

I concluded my article with a variety of observations on life in London: how people maintained their sense of humor despite the hardships, and what seemed to me to be a fundamental change in the British personality. "There is a cheerfulness and willingness to get things done *today* which seems quite foreign to those who knew England before the war." I did not mention my purpose in going to England. My mission was not "top secret," but it did have classified intelligence ramifications and the watchword of the day, seen on posters everywhere, was "Loose lips sink ships."

The U.S. Embassy assigned me an office and we began a series of meetings with representatives of the British Foreign Office and the Ministry of Information. These sessions were held at a round table that must have been twenty feet in diameter. I thought it was a particularly good arrangement, because each person could have eye contact with everyone else around the table. British agents were gathering printed materials of all kinds in continental Europe and sending them back to the Foreign Office by various means. The materials were reviewed in London, then disbursed to appropriate officials around the country. Donovan wanted to get copies of all these materials for COI—books, periodicals, newspapers, commercial catalogs, underground newspapers—and I was granted twenty-four hours to photograph them for our use and for the British library organization Aslib, which wanted German scientific periodicals.

Three Microfile cameras had arrived safely in London to replace those that were lost on the torpedoed ship. But I soon realized I would need at least twice as many to do the COI work in the time allotted. Before I left, after two and a half months in England, I had six cameras doing this work and two others working on a separate project under a grant from the Rockefeller Foundation, photographing manuscripts at the British Museum and traveling to other locations such as Bath and Amherst (see Appendix C).

I am not sure what the COI did with the mass of microfilm our service sent to them, although I was told about some of its uses. For example, writers in the U.S. Office of War Information were delighted to get the newspapers. They had been basing text for propaganda broadcasts on information that was six weeks old. We were able to provide them with the news only six days after it was published in Germany and by the French Underground. The catalogs were used by our intelligence analysts as a guide to enemy supplies of various goods. For example, they determined that the Germans were running short of ball bearings, because a series of technical catalogs listed substitutes for ball bearings in their specifications. That information was the catalyst for the daring daylight bombing raid of October 14, 1943 in which our B-17s attacked the ball-bearing factories at Schweinfurt. This was a costly raid. It was deep in enemy territory, beyond the range of fighter escort, and 60 of our 291 flying fortresses were lost in action.[3] The loss of life in such raids was terrible, and of course it was not all on our side. I was saddened to see, in one of our microfilms of a German newspaper that had been "liberated" by a British agent, a story about bombing of Berlin by our B-17s. There was a picture of the wreckage of the Staatsbibliothek, and the caption noted that the director, Herr Dr. Kruse, had been killed at his desk.

My efforts in establishing our COI service were advanced considerably when I discovered Lucia Moholy was in London. She was a Czechoslovakian whom I had met in Bern in 1939, and she was versed in the techniques of microfilming. I hired her, and she recruited a crew of women to help her. At that time, of course, one saw women

[3] *Encyclopedia Brittanica,* 1973, Vol. 23, 794Nb. The entry concludes that these bombing raids were not effective: "Despite the fearful damage suffered, Germany maintained its national morale and kept up its war production. . . ."

doing all kinds of work in England, from driving buses to running drill presses. We had been assigned a space in the Victoria and Albert Museum for our camera room, and each morning a courier from the Foreign Office would deliver the previous day's collection from the British operatives on the continent. If there was a mistake made in filming, we had no second chance. The work had to be done in twenty-four hours—period. One negative of the periodicals stayed in England, and two negatives were sent to Ann Arbor daily by diplomatic pouch via Washington, D.C. At UMI, the negatives were inspected, cut into 100-foot lengths, and one negative and a positive were sent to COI headquarters in Washington. At first, Colonel Donovan did not want us to keep a copy of the periodical negatives in Ann Arbor. I went to talk to him about it, but he said, "No, I simply cannot allow that." However, several heads of important libraries around the country, including Archibald MacLeish, the Librarian of Congress, who was one of Donovan's trusted advisers, [4] managed to get him to change his mind.

During my stay in London, I spent considerable time with Sir John Forsdyke, who was then living alone in the director's quarters of the British Museum, because his wife had taken their two children to the country to avoid the Nazi air raids. Sir John's response to Bob Binkley's *mopping-up* letter had seemed to validate his reputation for icy reserve, but I found him an engaging conversationalist. I would go over to the Museum in the evenings and we would sit in front of a small coal fire, slumped down into overstuffed chairs to

[4] *Donovan: America's Master Spy* by Richard Dunlop, Rand McNally & Company, 1982, pp. 274-275.

keep our backs warm, and smoke our pipes as we discussed the problems of the world. We became fast friends, and Sir John became a convert to the idea of using microfilm in libraries.

I returned to the U.S. at the end of May 1942. The following month, the COI was reorganized and Colonel Donovan was promoted to the rank of general and made director of the new Office of Strategic Services (OSS). The Research and Analysis or R&A branch of COI for which I worked as a civilian with the military

Sir John Forsdyke

equivalent rank of colonel was brought into OSS entire. This was due in part, I am sure, to our success in working with the British.[5] Dr. James Phinney Baxter III, a historian and former president of Williams College, was made chief of R&A. He brought my friend and riding companion from Ann Arbor, Joseph Hayden, into OSS and made him a

---

[5]*Donovan: America's Master Spy* op. cit., p. 290. Report in the *New York Times* quoted the White House announcement as stating: "In his capacity as coordinator, Mr. Donovan will collect and assemble information and data bearing on national security from the various departments and agencies of the government and will analyze and collate such materials for the use of the President. . . . Mr. Donovan's task will be to coordinate and correlate defense information, but his work is not intended to supersede or duplicate or to involve any direction of or interference with activities of the General Staff, the regular intelligence services, the Federal Bureau of Investigation, or of other existing departments and agencies.

member of the R&A Board of Analysts. According to Yale historian Robin W. Winks, this board was dubbed the College of Cardinals; Joe Hayden's work with it was more in the nature of a cover. He was an active OSS field operative. He was a former vice governor of the Philippines and he was responsible for sending submarines to the Philippines to supply agents who worked there behind Japanese lines.

In about July 1942, General Donovan sent word that he wanted me to place a photographer in Stockholm to work with the Norwegian Underground, which was intercepting sacks of German mail between Berlin and Oslo. Thinking of someone to send to Stockholm was not easy, but I finally came up with a person who seemed just right: Adele Kibre, whom I had met in Rome in 1939. I recalled that she liked to talk about international intrigue and espionage. She had lived in Berlin for a time before the war with Fritz Wolbach, who later became head of the Christian Museum in Rome. She had gone to Oslo, then to Copenhagen, The Hague, and Paris, leaving each city a step ahead of the German invasion. Earlier, I had wanted to send Adele to Lisbon, but the Portuguese refused to let her into the country. They must have looked at her record and concluded she would be bad luck. In any event. I contacted Adele at the University of Chicago, and she jumped at the assignment.

She was a real Mata Hari type. I arranged a briefing for her at the British Museum. Then, armed with an Eastman Kodak Microfile Camera, she left Scotland by dark of night in an American bomber and landed in neutral Stockholm. I knew that Adele was supposed to be terrific at her paleographic specialty, translating ancient inscriptions; what I did not know was that she was all thumbs mechanically. She simply could not operate the camera. Finally, I had to arrange for David Wilson, a young photographer from the British Museum, to go to Stockholm and give her a crash course in photography. He was supposed to stay for three months, but Adele somehow managed to keep him for the duration of the war. He didn't complain. He met his future wife, Dorothy, in Stockholm, where she was with the British Embassy.

M icrofilm really proved its usefulness during the war. It was far from the first time it had been employed for combat intelligence—a French photographer named René Dagron had employed it as early as 1870, during the siege of Paris in the Franco-German War. He reduced pages of manuscript to a film negative 1/4-inch wide. He stripped the collodian film off the glass, rolled it up, placed it inside a feather quill, and fastened it to the tail feather of a carrier pigeon that winged its way over the enemy lines to friendly troops inside the city. Thereafter, however, microfilm was forgotten.

The revival of microfilm during World War II was not restricted to intelligence or the kind of scholarly work we were doing with Esdaille's help under the Rockefeller grant, which, by the way, had been increased from $30,000 to $150,000. Russian composer Dmitri Shostakovich wrote his Seventh Symphony, the *Leningrad,* during the seige of Leningrad in 1941. Getting the complete orchestral score out of the country was deemed impossible until someone thought of putting it on microfilm. The negatives were sent to the U.S., where the premiere of the work outside the U.S.S.R. was a great propaganda triumph.

One of the most celebrated uses of microfilm during World War II, though UMI was not involved in it, was V-Mail, the brainchild of my friend Charlie Case of Kodak. It was a correspondence service for soldiers. V-Mail letters were written on prepared forms, which then were censored and microfilmed on 16mm film to be processed and forwarded by air to a central point. Each reel of the film contained about four thousand letters. At the central point, enlargement prints on paper were made, trimmed, placed in envelopes, and sent on to the men on the front lines or from them back to the States.

UMI added another specialty to its work in the summer of 1942 when the U.S. Justice Department asked for bids on the work of microfilming a collection of ship manifests it had been accumulating for many years. The original specifications were clearly biased, because they called for use of a particular type of microfilm reader of which there was only one brand, manufactured by Graphic Microfilm Corporation, a company based in New York. I knew it would be a valuable contract, because Vernon Tate had examined the material to be microfilmed and told me it was an enormous job, about eight million pages. I did not want to waste time preparing a fruitless bid, so instead, I protested the apparent rigging in favor of Graphic Microfilm in a letter to Michigan Senator Arthur Vandenberg. He managed to have all bids thrown out and new specifications drafted. The next time it came around, I bid a figure I thought would cover our costs and provide a reasonable profit. It turned out to be twenty cents less per thousand exposures than a competing bid by Recordak, a subsidiary of Kodak, so UMI got the job. Kodak and others in the industry expected us to fall on our faces on this job because of the volume of work required. To do it, I knew we would need a continuous developing machine, a new piece of equipment that was under strict war priority. I knew of only two such machines in existence— one in the National Archives, and one at the Library of Congress. But thanks to UMI's work for the OSS and the Justice Department, we had the priority rating to get the next machine off the assembly line, although we had great trouble getting it released. Until the machine arrived, we worked two shifts and subcontracted developing to a friend of mine in Detroit. I had three cameras on the job at the Justice Department records facility on the West Side of Manhattan, and I put the operation in charge of Alexander McDermott, who had been a movie actor in the days of silent films.

McDermott telephoned one day and said, "Gene, a funny thing happened today. A lens dropped out of one of our cameras."

"Oh-oh," I thought. "What's going on?" The type of camera we were using had a self-focusing arrangement. The lens mechanism had worked loose during the raising and lowering of the camera, and probably had been out of focus for some time before it finally dropped out. We checked over the recent batches of ship-manifest film and, sure enough, three hundred rolls of it were out of focus! That meant we had to work even harder. But we got the job done.

The benefits of the Justice Department contract to UMI were great, both subjective—in the boost it gave employee morale to tackle such an ambitious project and master it—and objective—in the revenue it produced, of course, but more importantly in the fact that the mechanized equipment we acquired to do it allowed us to bid on even larger jobs. One of these was making positives for the U.S. Air Force.

In retrospect, I suppose that our Air Force work was one of UMI's important contributions to the war effort. For example, some fifty thousand drawings were used in the design and construction of the P-51 fighter plane, and many of these had to be used for reference by the mechanics who maintained the aircraft. The Air Force would microfilm these blueprints and other drawings by the thousands and send the negatives to us. We would make quantities of positives of each to be sent to aircraft-maintenance facilities around the world. They would project the image on a wall with a special projector developed by Kodak. This obviated voluminous shipments of paper, of course.

Those were hectic days! The Air Force work continued through the end of the war, as did the OSS work and the manuscript filming under the Rockefeller grant. I estimated we photographed some 13 million pages of enemy materials for the OSS and about 6 million pages of manuscript materials. And, of course, we were continuing our civilian work on the American Culture Series, doctoral dissertations, and all the rest. Like a lot of boys who saw combat, World War II forced my little company to grow up fast. But it put us in a much better position to deal with the business boom that came with the end of the war.

Chapter Seven

Peace

After D-Day, June 6, 1944, when the Allies invaded
northern France and the war in Europe entered its
final stages, American libraries showed increasing interest
in purchasing our microfilm of German publications, which
General Donovan had finally given me permission to distribute.

I had been concerned about copyright ownership of these
materials from the outset, because even though they had
been acquired as enemy property in time of war, that
circumstance might not give us the right to sell them to
libraries. This was because, although few Americans were
aware of it, many of these German periodicals were copy-
righted in the United States. There was a German Property
Branch in our State Department, and the Alien Property
Custodian of that branch had taken over the granting of
permissions from German publishers during the war. For
example, Edwards Brothers had worked through the branch
in aquiring permission to reprint a series from a German
chemical journal.

With this in mind, after I returned from England in 1942,
I had set up a separate company to handle the photography,
duplication, and billing of all German periodicals sold by us in the United States. I called the new
company Microfilms, Incorporated. My theory was that

143

having a separate entity handle the foreign work would limit our liability. I was not interested in risking everything I owned in a suit over copyright, even though we might have won easily.

Warner Rice, who had replaced William Warner Bishop as librarian of the University of Michigan,[1] helped catalog all the German materials. This was a major undertaking in itself and was extremely helpful to everyone concerned, including the OSS, and eventually even to German libraries whose collections were destroyed in the war.

One interesting, though unintended, result of the formation of Microfilms, Incorporated was that any firm wishing to incorporate in the State of Michigan using a name that contained the word *microfilm* had to get our permission. This kept me abreast of competitive moves.

Another new company I founded in 1942 was Projected Books, a not-for-profit organization. The idea for it came to me while visiting hospitals in England and seeing wounded soldiers who were immobilized in traction or body casts. I asked myself, "How could they read?" Well, obviously, they couldn't. Even if they could use their arms, holding a book up while supine is most uncomfortable. Having someone hold a book in front of their face wasn't practical, either. Realizing that there were a lot of civilian patients in the same fix—accident and polio victims, people in iron lungs—I had a flash of inspiration: if I could project film of a book's pages onto the ceiling in an image large enough, the bedridden person could read it easily.

[1] Warner Rice was appointed on December 8, 1941, the day after the Japanese attack on Pearl Harbor.

144

After some discussion with the owner of a machine shop in Ann Arbor, he put together a prototype projector. It was a very crude machine, but it demonstrated that the idea could work. I took it to my friend Bob Howse, president of Argus, Inc. and he thought his staff could design a projector that would be attractive, compact, and functional. The trick was not only to make a device that would project a readable image on the ceiling but to have a switch that would advance or reverse the film, in effect, "turn the pages," by means of slight pressure of a patient's chin, fingers, elbow, or foot— whatever worked. My former employee Jan Vandenbrock, who was then working for Argus, designed an effective piece of equipment.

I contacted all the important publishers in the country, explaining what we wanted to do. Along with my letter I sent a form contract that gave us the right to reproduce a particular title on a royalty-free basis for this specific purpose. Every single one of them granted us this permission. I did a modest public-relations campaign for the enterprise, which resulted in articles in two or three national magazines, and this in turn helped enlist the support of Lions International. The Lions developed a national service project in which its clubs across the country could place our projectors in hospitals in their communities.

Neil Staebler mentions my enthusiam for this project in his tape-recorded recollections:

> Gene was always bristling with ideas. I was stationed in Washington, D.C. early in World War II, and one day he called and said he was coming by for a visit. "I have a surprise for you," he

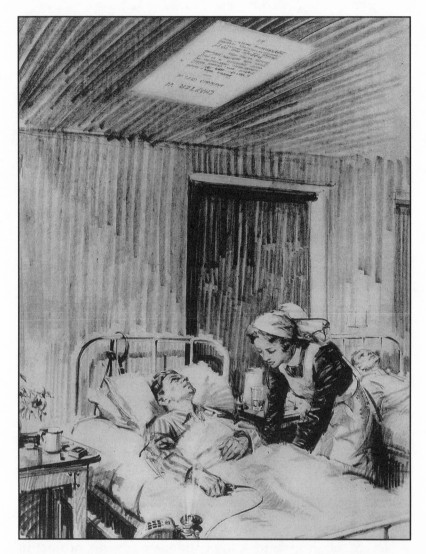

This sketch by Terence Cuneo appeared in the Illustrated London News *in 1945 under the heading "Those Who Cannot Run May Read: The 'Ceiling Book' System." The accompanying story tells how the projected-book reader was invented by Eugene B. Power of University Microfilms, Inc. and was introduced to Great Britain in a demonstration at the Victoria and Albert Museum arranged by Sir John Forsdyke of the British Museum.*

146

said. When he walked in the door of our apartment, his first words to Burnette and me were, "Now lie down on the floor." We did so. "Now keep looking up; pay no attention to what I'm doing," he said, and he proceeded to project pages of a book onto our ceiling. Well, you couldn't help getting excited about it—Gene's enthusiasm was contagious.

We distributed about four thousand of the machines, and they were well used. One of my friends had a daughter who was recovering from an operation and could not sit upright. She was concerned about missing practice on her flute. I filmed her flute music, set it up in one of our ceiling projectors by her bed, and she practiced her flute to her heart's content. My friend Sir John Forsdyke came to visit us in 1946, accompanied by Sir Henry Thomas, Keeper of Printed Books for the British Museum. They stayed at our house for a few days while observing UMI's operations, and Sir John became convinced that the Museum should have its own microfilm laboratory. He received a Rockefeller Foundation grant for this purpose, and we planned the laboratory for him, purchased the equipment, and sent it all to England. Sir John also was fascinated by our Projected Books program. When he returned to London, he set up a similar program, using a special British piece of equipment. The advent of television in the 1950s eliminated demand for Projected Books, although I am sure there must be some of those readers still in use somewhere in the country.

In 1944, the American Council of Learned Societies gave the University of Michigan a $3,200 grant to catalog the six million pages of manuscripts that we had microfilmed in England under the Rockefeller Foundation grant. Warner

Rice directed this work.[2] UMI supplied one positive copy of each document to the University of Michigan library and sent the negative to the Library of Congress, which supplies copies to scholars and to other libraries.

I expressed hope in an article I wrote for *The American Archivist* [3] that "the work can be continued and expanded after the war to include not only English libraries but libraries of other countries as well—Europe, Asia, and South America. In this way we will gradually assemble the materials for research and make them available to American scholars." Actually, as one of my researchers for this book noted, UMI returned largely to photographing books after the war, "partly because books are more available (libraries and collectors are not so possessive of them as they are of manuscripts) and more in demand; and partly because many manuscripts are in Medieval or Renaissance Latin, and Americans are poor linguists."

I went back to England shortly after the war in Europe officially ended on May 8, 1945. The push for microfilming of enemy records had dropped dramatically after D-Day and I had to oversee the dismantling of our OSS operation and reassign the cameras to scholarly undertakings in the

---

[2] The manuscripts included papers from the Public Record Office in London relating to England's North American Colonies; the British Museum's Cottonian and Harleian collections and its Thomas Collection of pamphlets published during the Civil War and the Commonwealth; and from the Bodleian and the libraries of the Oxford Colleges 1,500 manuscripts and more than 3,000 volumes in Arabic, Persian, Turkish, and Urdu.

[3] *The American Archivist*, January 1944, pp. 28-32, reprinted in *Miscellaneous Articles by Eugene B. Power*, as an "Edition of One," available from University Microfilms, Inc.

British Museum, Cambridge and Oxford universities, the Bibliothèque Nationale in Paris, and the Vatican. The years 1945 and '46 were probably the bleakest of all in London. The supply of consumer goods had dwindled to almost nothing, and what little food was available in restaurants was bland. However, the officers' mess at Grosvenor House had good meals. You could get all you wanted for three shillings (about 75 cents). I used to take my friend Arthur Cain, the Scotland Yard man, over there for lunch from time to time, and he would have double servings of everything.

One day in late June 1945, a U.S. Army officer came to see me in my office in the American Embassy in London and asked if I would serve as a consultant on microfilming a vast collection of captured German documents. He said these documents were measured not in number of exposures but in tons and, "We have tons and tons of them to photograph." I agreed, and early in July I flew to Frankfurt in a military transport. I was shocked by the scene of total devastation in Frankfurt. Factory chimneys seemed to be the only structures standing above the rubble.

The photography was being done in the small town of Herbst, which had not been bombed. When I toured the operation, I found three men doing a job normally handled by a single operator. One man would pick up a document and place it in front of the camera, another would push the button, and the third would take the document away. I later realized that this was simply "make work" in order to keep the boys busy. I made a few observations on things they might do to increase the possibility of getting more of those tons of materials onto film, but I never learned what became of that job or how successful it was.

From Frankfurt I made my way to Paris, and ran into none other than Adele Kibre, my former employee from Stockholm. She told me all about the exciting times she'd had working with the Norwegian Underground. Of course, the end of the war finished that episode. Yes, David Wilson, the young photographer from the British Museum, had finally gotten back home. Adele was headed home herself, but she wanted to be in Paris for the Bastille Day celebration, which was the following day, July 14. I thought that was a great idea, and we met the next morning and walked all over the city as the Parisians toasted the holiday, their liberation from the Nazis, and the end of the war, all in one enormous blowout. I remember smelling a new perfume on a girl who passed me and saying to Adele, "I must have some of that for Sadye!" I followed the girl and her scent down the street for several blocks. Then I went to a perfume shop, Guerlaine's in Place Vendrome, where they had hundreds of sample bottles of fragrances. I sniffed and sniffed until I thought my olfactory senses would go numb from exhaustion. But I finally found the right one, *Femme,* and bought a vial of it.

The next night I managed to get a lift to Rome on a bomber. I sat in the copilot's seat. There was a full moon, and it was an enchanting midnight flight out across the Ligurian Sea, over Corsica, where every feature of the ancient landscape seemed frozen in the pale lunar glow, and then over the Pyrrherian Sea. At the Vatican library I was greeted with open arms by Father Alberada, who had taken over as librarian when Father Tisserant was made a cardinal. Fr. Alberada assured me that he was anxious to get a new camera and resume microfilming.

Italy was in bad shape economically, of course, and anyone with American money could get some real bargains. I bought a length of beautiful silk cloth in Rome, white with big flowers; I knew it would make a terrific dress for Sadye. I also got her some other clothes, including a black wool dress and a pillbox hat with a veil, and a turquoise jacket trimmed in black Persian lamb. Italy's railroads were out of commission (railroad locomotives had been favorite targets of our pilots during the war; they loved to find an enemy train and strafe it, to see the boiler blow up in a spectacular burst of steam). Consequently, I took a bus from Rome to Milan. It was a real adventure. All the highway bridges had been blown up, too; the U.S. Army Corps of Engineers had built temporary pontoon bridges, but there were several spots where it seemed the bus was not going to make it. However, make it we did, finally, and I went on to Switzerland to pay a call on my old friend Pierre Bourgeois at the Swiss National Library. Then it was back to Paris. The French customs officers gave me a bad time about my Italian purchases at the border, and they made me pay what I considered an exorbitant duty. At the Bibliothèque Nationale, I renewed my acquaintance with the director, Julien Cain, and we mourned the death of Jean LeRoy. Cain, being Jewish, had spent most of the war in a concentration camp. In fact, he had just returned to Paris a few weeks before I arrived. He, too, was willing to accept a UMI camera and operate it for us, thus opening the vast holdings of the Bibliothèque Nationale to American scholars.

I was to return to the United States by way of London, but

not without another confrontation with French customs over the Italian silk cloth and Sadye's clothes. They did their best to make me pay duty on these things again, but this time I won out.

In London I managed to save two complete sets of the Office of War Information propaganda posters that were dropped on Europe during the course of the war. They may be the only ones in existence, because the rest went up in smoke, as did masses of other documents that military commanders did not want to take the trouble to send back to the States. I gave one set of the posters to the Library of Congress, the other to the University of Michigan Library.

T he end of the war was a blessing. Everyone was glad to see it, of course, but like many other businesses that had developed a significant volume of work linked to the war effort, UMI found itself in a new and difficult period. I had the feeling of starting all over again. But it was quite different now from the days when I did everything myself. The company had grown to fifteen employees during the war and I had an obligation to them and their dependents to keep the business operating as fully as possible. We muddled through, although our profits were flat during the last half of 1945 and all of the following year.

Sadye also had some adjusting to do. During the war she had been very active in the local Civil Defense Women's Auxiliary headed by Ted Raphael's wife, Mary. Sadye was in charge of personnel and worked on all sorts of emergency-aid programs. In addition, to keep her hand in her profession, she continued to spend one day a week at

Kingswood School in Bloomfield Hills.

We also returned to a more active social life, which the war had put a damper on. Sadye had the silk cloth I brought her from Italy made up into a stunning dress. But the smash hit was her black dress, pillbox hat, and turquoise jacket. Every time she wore it, women would come up to her and ask, "Where did you get that outfit?" Of course, that made it worth all the problems I'd had getting it back. Sadye also liked the "Bastille Day" perfume and wore it regularly for a long time.

Phil had entered University Elementary School and was doing well. We had been worried about his health when he was five years old—he seemed to have a constant cold that winter—and it got so bad that Sadye had taken him to Florida in February 1943. They spent six weeks there, living in a boarding house in Naples, which was then a small crossroads village with a drugstore, hardware store, grocery store, and a movie theater. I went down and stayed with them for two weeks. One day, just for the heck of it, I decided to try my hand at fishing off the pier. I was casting a plug in a rather perfunctory fashion when suddenly a huge silver tarpon rolled on the surface. Instinctively I tossed my lure toward him. He struck, and we engaged in a fierce struggle that lasted more than an hour. Time after time I worked him back into shallow water, only to have him speed off into the depths again. Each time he came back, I had to climb over a bait shack in the middle of the pier. He finally broke my line, having weakened it by repeatedly hitting it with his tail.

My big fish got away, but Sadye had better results with

Phil's health—he gained eight pounds during the stay in Florida and came back to Ann Arbor looking quite husky. This prompted Sadye to repeat the trip the following two years. After that, Phil's schoolwork prevented any further February excursions. He liked school, and he was a leader, but so were most of his classmates, which created conflicts. He played sports and enjoyed the other activities boys his age took part in, which as far as I could see consisted mostly of shouting at the top of their lungs and hurling themselves about. Phil was a good, though not exceptional, student at that age. It was not until his college years that he began to shine scholastically.

When Sir John Forsdyke came to visit in 1946, as I mentioned, he had become a staunch advocate of microfilm. He built the facility I had sketched for him for the British Museum's newspaper collection in Collingdale, and then sent a few technicians to UMI for training.

In 1947, after months of looking for ways to increase UMI's post-war sales volume, I came up with an idea I thought would be a genuine breakthrough—a service that would allow libraries to keep periodicals on microfilm instead of storing the original copies in bound volumes.

The idea surfaced through repeatedly asking myself the question, "What are the problems of libraries?" One answer that came immediately to anyone who spent much time chatting with librarians and reading their journals, as I did, was: raising funds for expansion. Why did they need to expand? Because of the ever-growing flood of periodicals that had to be bound and shelved. I knew that the average library was doubling in size every sixteen years, mostly to house periodicals.

My notion of microfilming periodicals, however, was like Edison's idea for the light bulb. One could readily see its possibilities, but the technology was not at hand. One had to invent a way to make it work.

My first approach was unproductive. It involved using a reduction ratio high enough to allow us to get a row of ten magazine pages across the width of 35mm unperforated film and ten pages down on a 1-7/8-inch frame. This could make it possible to obtain copies at very low cost, using the diazo process, enabling a library to provide copies to patrons free of charge. But how could we achieve a 50-to-1 reduction ratio? I took the idea to Eastman Kodak, who worked with the possibility of a two-stage reduction system, to no avail. The materials and lenses available at the time were simply not up to the task.

I then experimented with a 17-to-1 reduction, which was higher than reductions then being used for most microfilming. I found that by enlarging such positives on the reader twenty-one times, one could achieve a satisfactory substitute for the original, providing the film work was carefully done. We could get approximately thirty-six magazine pages per foot of film, which, at the going rate of six cents per foot for positive, would cost slightly under one-sixth of a cent per page. At this rate, I concluded, the microfilm could be sold for less than the cost of binding the periodicals.

Heartened by that finding, I intensified my concentration on the problem. I did a study of a large number of call slips for periodicals at the general library of the University of

Michigan and found that in many fields the major use of periodicals decreased markedly between one and three years after publication. Periodicals older than three years were unarguably essential to research, but it was equally clear that they occupied an inordinate amount of space in proportion to their use.

Now the rationale I had been seeking began to emerge. Why not have the library continue to subscribe to paper copies, but instead of sending them off to be bound—which invariably occurred during the period of their greatest use—keep them in circulation and, at the same time, purchase copies on microfilm with the money that would have been spent for binding? When demand for an issue tapered off, the library could substitute the film copy and discard the originals. I figured that film periodical files would require so little space that libraries could save 90 percent of their storage costs. These costs are cumulative. For example, if a library's storage costs for a given number of periodicals are $2,500 in the first year, that amount will be added to the cost of the next year's issues; if no new titles are added, that would make the second year's cost $5,000. The curve goes up exponentially (see Appendix D). And ironically, after fifty years, the entire expenditure is wasted because the paper in the bound volumes will have deteriorated to the point of uselessness.

In January 1948, I went to New York and explained my idea to my friend Fred Melcher, president of *Publishers Weekly*. He recommended that I call first on McGraw-Hill, which published a number of magazines. It was good advice. I obtained an agreement that gave UMI exclusive rights to copy all McGraw-Hill magazines and duplicate them as positive microfilm copies. In return, we would pay McGraw-Hill a 10 percent royalty based on sales. That contract was useful in approaching other magazine publishers. I was generally successful in selling them, too, and our first catalog for the service listed seventy-five titles.

It was slow going, because every magazine publisher I talked into joining the service, and every librarian I persuaded to use it, had to be given an education in the advantages of microfilm. Moreover, I was doing it all myself. My employees were mostly production workers; I was a one-man band in sales, and it was becoming more apparent every day that I needed help.

Then, as I struggled to come up with a way to stretch myself a little further and build some momentum, I got a lucky break. Chester Lewis, the librarian of *The New York Times,* whom I had met at ALA conferences, called up and said he had not been pleased with the quality of microfilming Recordak was doing for them. "Would UMI be interested in filming the *Times's* current and back files?" he asked. I said, "Sure." I went to New York and worked out the details of what turned out to be a very nice contract—doing the current issues for distribution to libraries as well as the back files. We filmed each day's newspaper and made four hundred positive copies every two weeks for library subscribers. That was a lot of volume, and I had to buy another processing machine to handle it.

On one of my trips to Washington in connection with the periodicals project I sat next to my long-time friend, Joe Hayden. We reminisced about the days when he and his wife, Betty, and Sadye and I stabled our horses at the same farm and would ride through the fields together. Joe had subsequently gone to the Philippines to serve as vice governor general under Frank Murphy. Then, during the war, he had been recruited by Donovan into the OSS and was put in charge of delivering supplies to the underground in the Philippines by submarine. He was on General Douglas MacArthur's staff, but as an Army man, not OSS, because MacArthur did not like the OSS, would not have them in his operations. Now, Joe told me in strictest confidence, he was going to Washington to be appointed Governor General of the Philippines. The next day, I was shocked and surprised to learn that Joe Hayden had dropped dead on a Washington street of a heart attack!

Shortly after I had signed *The New York Times* agreement, Warner Rice mentioned that his brother Stevens E. "Steve" Rice wanted to make a career change. Steve was then assistant to Dean Ralph A. Sawyer of the U of M's Horace H. Rackham School of Graduate Studies and was the principal counselor to doctoral candidates who were writing their theses, so naturally he was familiar with UMI's dissertation work. I had Steve talk to Helen Shell, a longtime friend of Sadye's and an expert on personnel. Helen liked him, and she and I spent much of a weekend late in January discussing how I might fit him into the organization without creating friction among the other employees. Helen was a great help to me. She understood the psychology of the workplace and how certain individuals would react to my plans. Steve joined UMI in February 1950 as head of our "Editorial Department," charged with overseeing product development and helping me in sales.

Steve Rice also dictated some of his recollections of our association, and here is how he remembers his introduction to selling periodicals on microfilm:

> I went with Gene to an American Library Association conference and helped him set up a little booth to display UMI's wares. But the real purpose of the booth seemed to be to serve as a message center and meeting place for most of the top librarians of the country. I discovered that they were all Gene's friends as well as his customers.
>
> At that first conference I was introduced to a tradition that endured for many years—Gene's poker party. He sent me around to inform eight or ten people that "tonight is the night—room such and such." It was a wonderful time, with the librarians of Princeton, Yale, the Library of Congress, and other prestigious institutions sitting around in their shirtsleeves playing cards and talking. Gene kept a bottle of Old Granddad on the sideboard, but it rarely was touched. Conversation about library affairs was the main focus, and it was all off the record, so there was a mixture of political gossip and frank talk about problems.
>
> I remember Gene asking offhandedly what they thought about his idea of putting periodicals on microfilm. With only one or two exceptions, these top librarians said, "No, that will never work." They reasoned that they had already bought the periodicals. They owned them. How could they expect their boards to approve of buying them again? They all agreed that space was no problem for them. Besides, patrons don't like to use microfilm, they said.
>
> Being new to the firm, these reactions convinced me that the idea of microfilming periodicals was a bad one. But Gene told me, "Listen, don't worry about it. The customers are not always right. In fact, they are hardly ever right. They cannot see what is coming in the future. I am glad to know their objections,

though, because when I know what's bothering them, I will know how to sell them."

I gave my periodicals idea a hard push in a series of articles published in *American Documentation*, successor to *The Journal of Documentary Reproduction*, which had been suspended during the war. Vernon Tate continued as editor of the renamed publication. I think he expected some controversy over the articles, but I doubt that he was prepared for the storm they stirred up. Librarians were horrified. There were howls of outrage from one end of the country to the other, because I actually advocated throwing away printed materials!

Over time, however, the value of our service began to sink in and the logic of disposing of paper copies in favor of microfilm files became obvious. To my surprise, the first users of the service were mostly smaller libraries. The big ones took longer to come around. There were some hold-outs, too, among the larger magazine publishers, notably Time and Life who, because their attorneys could not agree on the effect microfilm would have on their copyrights, took five years to decide that their publications should be included. I knew what I wanted and felt no need to consult a lawyer about it. I wrote a simple, one-page contract[5] that gave us the exclusive right to reproduce the particular publication in miniature form, which included microcard, microprint, and microfiche as well as microfilm.

It was gratifying to see people who had scoffed at the idea

[5] At the outset, we were permitted to supply microfilm only to customers who were on the magazines' lists as current subscribers. This was later modified to allow anyone to purchase the microfilm version.

160

in the beginning gradually become advocates. A couple of competing firms tried to break into the field after they realized that we must be doing pretty well at it, but they ran into problems. Our contract established a royalty of 10 percent, which to my mind was a fair price, and the competitors were offering 15 percent. This put them at a disadvantage from the start. Our real competitive edge, though, was the breadth of our agreement in the words *in miniature form*. Had I written microfilm instead, the competitors might have been able to get around it by using microfiche or one of the other forms. Another problem they had was that by the time they got started in the business, most of the important publications had signed with us and were tied up by our exclusive contract. When the competition could not make any headway in the field, most gave it up. Our original list of seventy-five titles grew by the late1980s to more than sixteen thousand, and there were about four thousand libraries using the service. By 1980 some individual publishers were collecting royalties from us of $100,000 a year. One of the things I liked best about the service, however, was the way in which it bore out our basic idea of publication on demand. If a library wanted a back file of a given periodical, we could produce the entire file or any segment of it as ordered. In this way, a new library or an existing collection that needed to expand could immediately obtain a representative collection of periodical materials at a reasonable cost. Accumulating a comparable file in paper copies would be an extremely slow and expensive process.

Lest I sound like my business acumen was allowing me to walk on water, I should point out that not every project worked out as well as our periodicals program. One that seemed filled with promise but gave me nothing but frustration for many years was an idea that was brought to me in 1947 by George Hammond, librarian of the Bancroft Library at the University of California at Berkeley. Hammond was interested in the Archives of the Indies, in Seville, Spain, which are the records of Spain's exploration, conquest, and colonization of about half of the New World. The Spaniards were good at keeping and preserving records; each officer in distant posts would correspond regularly with his superiors back home, where the letters were annotated for reply. All correspondence dealing with a given topic—the governor of Cuba's complaints about Dutch pirates and mosquitoes, for example—was folded inside the original letter and tied in a bundle. Hammond told me that in Seville there were eighty-five thousand such bundles. Scholars had not worked with them much, he said, because they are hard to get to. Some of them were stuck together; of one such bundle, a Spanish archivist explained to Hammond, "When Napoleon took these up to Paris they got rained on. . . ."

Hammond was eager to have UMI put these records on microfilm, and after much negotiation between the U.S. State Department and the Spanish government, he had reached an agreement. I was excited about the prospect and arranged for the necessary equipment to be sent to Madrid. When I got there, however, I discovered that the archivist in Seville had not been consulted on the matter. When that gentleman finally gave his permission, and I had my equipment sent on to Seville, I found that the conditions were too primitive to permit the work to be carried out. The electrical age was represented in the Archives of the Indies by a single light bulb. The director had workmen chisel a hole through a stone wall four feet thick to bring in power cables, but when the local engineer saw my equipment, he declared that there was not enough power in all of Seville to operate it. So I had to give up on the Archives of the Indies, at least for the time being. I made another try in 1967, but nothing came of it.

In any event, my experience in Spain made for interesting conversation at home. Sadye and I entertained a good deal, and I think the main reason our house was so popular was the cooking of Margaret Runge, who had come with us in September 1941, when we moved to Barton Hills. Sadye had found new outlets for social service as a member of the Family Service board and worked hard for the local Planned Parenthood affiliate, which became a favorite cause for both of us. In 1949, Sadye returned to U of M as a psychological counselor to students.

We had many visitors in connection with my business and Sadye's work, but there was a regular group, a circle of special friends who came often and invariably filled the house with laughter and lively conversation. This circle included Neil and Burnette Staebler, Arthur and Mary Bromage, Jack and Emma Dawson, Al and Dorothy Connable, and Ted and Mary Raphael. The women were all strong personalities, and they asserted themselves so vigorously that we men began calling ourselves the RAMS, an acronym for Revolt Against Male Servitude. The ladies responded by forming the LAMS—Lesbians Against Male

Supremacy. All in the spirit of fun, of course, but a stranger who was unaware of that fact might well have concluded that blood would be shed before the evening was over.

Margaret Runge always had the last say, however, and her provincial form of debate unfailingly disarmed both sides. She usually infuriated the LAMS by insisting that the RAMS take extra helpings of her marvelous desserts.

We entertained at least twice a week at home, and some of the parties, especially the theatrical cast parties, would have fifty or sixty people. Margaret took them in stride, though, and I think she enjoyed them as much as we did. The one she invariably mentions whenever we see her (she's retired now and lives in Lake Leelanau in Northern Michigan) was the cast party attended by Jimmy Stewart and Helen Hayes.

I like to participate in planning dinners, and Margaret and Sadye and I enjoyed experimenting on new dishes. We also collaborated on keeping vases of fresh flowers throughout the house. Sadye and I grew many of the flowers, and Margaret made the floral arrangements with a true artist's touch. I have a greenhouse off our cellar where I raise orchids, and I found that taking care of fifty or sixty orchids, which includes talking to them each morning before going to the office, put me in a proper frame of mind to confront the problems of the day's business. Margaret was just twenty-one when she came to work for us, Phil was just three and a half, and she was with us for forty-three years.

While I was working on getting our periodicals business started, UMI's "bread and butter" remained in the STC book service, the American Culture Series, newspapers, and filming doctoral dissertations. The latter got a terrific boost in 1951 when Ralph Ellsworth, then librarian at the University of Iowa and president of the Association of Research Libraries (ARL), was named chairman of a special committee of the ARL to examine the whole subject of publication of doctoral dissertations.The findings of the committee were that UMI's service was the best way to publish theses. Librarians representing one hundred twenty-five of the leading educational institutions campaigned with deans of graduate schools to persuade their schools to accept microfilm as the medium of dissertation publication. Getting the committee to back UMI was not easily accomplished, however, as Ralph Ellsworth recalls in this excerpt from his engaging 1980 memoir, *Ellsworth on Ellsworth:*

One of the gaps in the distribution of the literature of scholarship opened about the time of World War II because by then most American universities had stopped requiring graduate students to publish their dissertations in book form. They were available only on interlibrary loan. European universities, however, continued the old practices and their dissertations continued to arrive on an exchange basis. Many wanted something in return. Also, although some of the information in the best of our dissertations eventually found its way into the stream of scholarship in the form of journal articles and even printed books, much valuable information was lost; and even when the dissertation information became available, the delay was always long.

The Association of Research Libraries created a committee, of which I was chairman, to study this gap and find ways of closing it. Naturally, we turned to microfilming as the best solution. There was already an ongoing publishing project through whose service we thought we could publish our dissertations. I refer to the *Microfilm Abstracts* publication program run by University Microfilms, Inc. The essence of their program was to publish theses and dissertation abstracts in *Microfilm Abstracts*, and the making of positives of the dissertations for sale upon demand.

This program seemed appropriate for expansion at the national and international level. I began discussions with Eugene Power, then president of University Microfilms, Inc. There was a sharp difference of opinion within the committee (later reflected in ARL), not about the nature of the program but over who should control it. One member wanted the Library of Congress to do it; one member objected to having a commercial company control it. My point of view was that the service would have to be fast and accurate and responsive to changing demand and I did not see that the Library of Congress at that time could be sure of meeting those conditions. As a devout New Deal Democrat I believed that one should use the private sector as long as it could deliver the goods efficiently, promptly, and at a reasonable price—which of course included the possibility of making a reasonable profit. Besides, since University Microfilms, Inc. had developed the plan, it seemed ungracious, if not illegal, to take the program away from them. It also seemed wrong to use tax-free university laboratories to compete on equal terms with commercial laboratories that had to pay taxes and also to make a profit.

The final program the committee brought for approval to the 1951 annual session of the Association of Research Libraries, meeting in Iowa City, insisted that there be only one publication in which dissertation abstracts would be published, and that University Microfilms, Inc. should manage it. Dissertations would be mailed by the sponsoring university to Ann Arbor, where they would be microfilmed by University Microfilms, Inc., thus guaranteeing high quality. Positives of the dissertations would be sold by University Microfilms, Inc., but the authors could, if they wished, publish the dissertations later as books or journal articles. The film negatives would be considered as the archival copy and would be kept in the vaults of University Microfilms, Inc.

One of the reasons we wanted University Microfilms, Inc. to manage the projects was that they were in a position to make the financial investment in storage vaults, filming equipment, and personnel that would be constantly expanding, whereas we couldn't be sure that a university or the Library of Congress would have access to the money when it would be needed.

Discussion at the Iowa City 1951 sessions of ARL was heated and bitter. I was accused on the floor of the meeting of having accepted bribes from University Microfilms, Inc., or at least of being in their secret employment. Arguments were put forward for placing the service at the Library of Congress or in a university photo laboratory. Our reply to the charge that a commercial company like University Microfilms, Inc. could take advantage of the participating universities was twofold: one, that it would not be to their advantage to do so; and two, that ARL could stop using the service and set up its own any time it wanted to.

But as I said, the plan was bitterly debated and feelings ran high. Finally the meeting adjourned at 4:30 and the members boarded university buses to go to my house for cocktails.

Our neighbors, for years after, loved to tell about some fifty rather tall men stalking out of the buses and into our house, wordless. Professor Stow Persons, who served as barman, told me later that the group consumed an average of four martinis apiece. The noise level rose to the point where the immediate neighbors became concerned, and I glanced out the windows nervously, looking for the cops.

Finally, after an hour or so of drinking, all the members but one rolled out of the house into the bus: everyone by that time was in a jovial and rosy mood. Our neighbors noticed the difference and

167

marveled greatly.

The chairman called for a vote on the committee plan first thing in the evening session and the plan was approved with no dissent, thus reaffirming the value of the martini to civilize the human beast. The one member who chose to walk to the dinner, rather than ride the bus, never made it. I think he decided to take a nap in a ditch between our house and the dormitory. He was all right the next day, but slightly subdued.

The committee had much work to do during the next five years in working with Eugene Power and Stevens Rice of University Microfilms, Inc. to solve the problems that arose. One of the hardest problems was to get the participating universities to send in the dissertations and abstracts for filming on time. . . .[6]

As a result of the ARL decision, our dissertation business really began to boom. Today nearly every degree-granting university in the United States uses the service. Even the exceptions, those that have their own microfilm labs—MIT, the University of Chicago, the University of Southern California, and Harvard—participate to some extent, because their Ph.D's wish to be listed in *Dissertation Abstracts*.

One measure of our increase in business, in addition to steadily growing sales and profits, was the fact that after three additions to our offices, we were still cramped for room. The third addition had included two small offices for Steve Rice and the staff he had hired, as well as two dark rooms, larger cutting rooms, and more vault space. Our fourth expansion included a larger shipping room and camera room, for by 1950 we had twenty cameras. Our fifth

[6] Excerpted with permission from *Ellsworth on Ellsworth*, copyright © 1980 by Ralph E. Ellsworth, published by The Scarecrow Press, Inc., Metuchen, N.J.

and final addition virtually doubled our space. I bought a barn next door to our property and converted it into office space, work rooms, and a cafeteria. The latter was the best builder of good employee relations I ever had at UMI. We kept the prices low, charging only for the cost of the raw food and subsidizing the preparation. Consequently, many employees had their main meal of the day there, and they usually showed their appreciation by going the extra mile on their jobs.

Chapter Eight

Eskimo Art

I awoke with a sinking sensation. Something was wrong. It was too dark in the boat's cramped cabin to make out more than the dark shape of Sadye in her sleeping bag. But I could feel an ominous tilt to the bench on which I'd been sleeping.

It was September 1959, and Sadye, Phil, and I were aboard a picket boat operated by our host, Jim Houston, and two Eskimos. We had been caught by a storm the night before as our twenty-four-foot craft chugged along the barren coast of Baffin Island from Cape Dorset near the Arctic Circle. The Eskimos pulled into a small harbor, taking soundings with a line to be sure the water was deep enough, and we anchored there for the night, protected from wind and the crashing waves. Phil and Jim and the two Eskimos had bedded down in the hold with our cargo of green soapstone.

Now I realized the reason we were listing: the wind had changed during the night, swinging our boat into more shallow water. The tide was going out—which in this region meant a swift drop of forty feet—and we were about to be left high and dry.

The two Eskimos hit the deck running at the same time I did, and I was amazed to see them disappear over the side,

171

jumping into the icy water! I watched them begin shoving planks under the hull of the boat in an attempt to keep it from being punctured by rocks as the tide went out. Fortunately, the bottom of the cove turned out to be sandy in that spot. If the boat had been damaged, it might have been days or weeks before we were found. As it was, all we had to do was wait eight hours for the tide to come back in.

The delay gave me ample opportunity to reflect on the events that had led us here—beginning eleven years earlier when I was shooting skeet with Clay Bedford at his farm near Ann Arbor. Clay was CEO of Kaiser-Frazer Corporation, and he had moved to our area to direct the automobile plant Henry Kaiser established at Willow Run at the end of World War II. Clay shared my enthusiasm for hunting and fishing, and we had become good friends. Between our rounds of shooting that day, he asked me if I would like to accompany him and his wife, Kit, on a fishing trip to an exclusive club in central Quebec. It sounded interesting, and I accepted.

The trip was our introduction to Jim Houston, a club member who accompanied us. He was extremely interesting and likable, in addition to being a first-class fisherman. We were kindred spirits, and we hit it off immediately.

One still night while paddling our canoe down a lake, Houston told me the story of his life. Born in Toronto in 1921, he had studied at the Ontario College of Art and served with the Toronto Scottish Regiment during World War II. He spent some time studying life drawing at the Ecole Grande Chaumiere in Paris after the war, but returned to Canada to please his widowed mother. He soon grew

172

restive, though, and thinking that a change of pace from the urban scene would help him settle on what to do with his life, he headed north by train to the end of the line at Moosonee, and then by canoe and float plane into the land of the Inuit.

"I looked out at that stripped-down country and saw the ice floes floating out into Hudson Bay, and I knew I had arrived in the place I'd been looking for all my life," Jim told me. "I'm going back up there as soon as possible—to stay."

Three years elapsed before I heard from Jim Houston again. He telephoned from Chicago one day in 1952 and told me about his adventures up north. He said, "I had not known that the Eskimos are artists, but in fact they make wonderful carvings of soapstone and ivory. I have some samples I brought down to show to the director of the Art Institute in Chicago. Would you like to see them?"

I was interested, of course, and invited Jim to visit us in Ann Arbor. He arrived at our house with a huge, heavy leather bag full of soapstone carvings, which he proceeded to place on tables and bookcases for Sadye and me to examine. I am not an art critic, but I know what I like, and I liked those carvings instantly. They exuded vitality.

Most of them were representations of seal, walrus, polar bear, and other animals common in the Arctic. They were shown in action, often with Eskimos in hunting scenes. There were some creatures from Eskimo mythology, too, and every piece showed care in composition in addition to a powerful, primitive sense of design and great skill in carving. Sadye and I were surprised when Jim said that the Art Institute in Chicago had refused to exhibit them, explaining: "They consider them to be handicrafts, not art."

173

Jim's selfless interest in helping the Eskimos earn some money from the carvings was admirable. His goal was to help the Eskimos break free of the Arctic's relentless natural round of feast and famine based on the lemming population cycle. Lemmings burrow in the Arctic grass and increase in number for seven years. As they proliferate, so do the weasels, foxes, otters, owls, bears, and other lemming eaters. Consequently, hunting and trapping are increasingly good during this period, and the Eskimos prosper. In the seventh year, however, the lemmings migrate in great hordes across the land, running and swimming in what looks like panic flight. During the year after the lemming migration, hunting and trapping are especially good because the predators are hungry. The year after that, however, the Eskimos start being hungry.

The key to Jim's idea was that sales of Eskimo carvings would give the people enough money to buy cartridges, matches, and tea so they could survive the lean years. It stood to reason that they could do more carving during the bad years. I liked his approach, and I decided I would do everything I could to help him. My first move was to contact my friend Bob Hatt, director of the Cranbrook Science Museum in Bloomfield Hills, and show him the carvings. He was immediately taken with them. Sadye and Phil and I set up a nonprofit organization, Eskimo Art, Inc., whose purpose was "to distribute and develop public appreciation for Eskimo art in the United States."

Jim Houston sent down forty or fifty pieces for display at Cranbrook. The exhibit was so enthusiastically received that we thought it would be of interest to the rest of the

174

country. Bob Hatt con-
tacted Anna Marie Pope,
who was in charge of the
Smithsonian Institution's
traveling-exhibition service, and she agreed to put
the exhibit on the road. Bob
had his Cranbrook staff
build specially padded
traveling cases, and we sent
the exhibit off under the
aegis of the Smithsonian.
We didn't see it again for
eight years.

Jim Houston in 1952

The exhibit clearly fulfilled its function, because every
museum that displayed it asked for pieces to sell in its gift
shop. Such sales really established the market, and interest
has grown year by year.

Filling the orders became difficult, however, when U.S.
Customs officials decided that since the carvings were made
of stone, they should be imported as minerals. Customs
agents would scrape the bottom of each sculpture and
charge duty according to the type of stone. When I asked
why the carvings could not be classified as art objects, the
official answer was that "the sculptors were not graduates of
a recognized art school"! Obviously, this was an intolerable
situation. I protested, and U.S. Customs in Washington
finally changed its ruling relating to Eskimo art objects,
allowing them to enter the country duty-free. Strangely
enough, Detroit customs officials would not comply com-

pletely, although they finally compromised by saying that human figures could be brought in duty-free; we still had to pay a slight duty on animal figures. At present no duty is charged.

For several years, Eskimo Art, Inc. was the sole source for the carvings in the United States. Then, as Eskimo art became more popular, other importers came on the scene. I was happy to see that development, even though it had the effect of inflating the prices.

In 1959, Jim invited Phil, Sadye, and me to come up and see the area firsthand. We made our way to Moosenee and took a seaplane, an old Navy PBY, from there to Cape Dorset. On Jim's advice we brought an outboard motor for the Eskimos. We also had a beef roast, a lamb roast, a case of whiskey, fishing gear, and two rifles. When we landed in Cape Dorset Harbor, all the Eskimos were lined up on the shore to greet us. It was a touching ceremony, although we were aware of their strange and pervasive seal odor and their decidedly different ideas of hygiene. (The Eskimos did not have handkerchiefs, so they blew their noses in their hands. After doing so, the polite Eskimo would rub his palm on his pants before shaking hands with you.) They didn't bathe very often, if ever, but their body odor was masked by the perfume of seal. Our sensitivity to this smell lasted only two days. After that, I suppose *we* smelled the same way.

We stayed among the Eskimos for a month and learned to admire them a great deal. They were intelligent and seemed to have an intuitive grasp of how mechanical devices work. If an outboard motor broke down at sea, for example, they would set to work repairing it with makeshift parts, including bits of bone and rawhide, and almost invariably got the thing going. They used the outboards on square-sterned canoes about eighteen feet long.

It was the height of the Arctic summer, and a large group of Eskimos had gathered to await the arrival of the Hudson's Bay trading ship. They were living in tents pitched on the tops of hills where the wind would blow away the omnipresent clouds of mosquitoes. The only permanent buildings in the camp were a small nursing station, a Hudson's Bay post, Jim Houston's home and office, and a small church. Jim and his family and the couple who ran the Hudson's Bay post were the only white residents of the community.

Religion for the Eskimos appeared to be a veneer of Christian beliefs laid over their native polytheism. We attended their church, and the services consisted mainly of interminable readings from the Bible which missionaries had translated into a syllabic script originally created for the Cree Indians. The reader was the oldest man in the village. He would read a sentence, then spend about ten minutes explaining it. As he droned on, small children ran up and down the aisles wearing parkas but no pants, and every once in a while a mother would grab one of these youngsters and sit it on a No. 10 tomato can pulled from under her bench. After about three hours of this, the congregation would sing a hymn at one-quarter speed, and that concluded the service.

I found the Eskimos to be singularly unaggressive, considering the harshness of their environment. They appeared to have deep respect for the wildlife they killed in order to survive. Their attitude toward children, I thought, was more enlightened than most in our more heavily populated parts of the planet, though we regard ourselves as being more civilized. The knife-edged balance on which life progresses from day to day for the Eskimos makes children very important to continuity of their culture. They don't discipline children; they indulge them. If you were to strike a child in an Eskimo village, even giving it a gentle spanking, the villagers might think you were crazy and do away with you; after all, to their way of thinking, no one in his right mind would strike a child.

Our trip down the coast in the picket boat was to see the place where the Eskimos quarried the special green soapstone characteristic of Cape Dorset carving and bring back a load of it. By the time the tide came back in and floated our boat, the storm had died down and we continued our journey. One morning we were having breakfast after spending the night in another cove, when a narwhale showed up in the harbor. The Eskimos piled into the boat and we took off through the fog in pursuit. It was an exciting though unsuccessful trip, and also kind of scary because—though I pride myself on having a keen sense of direction—I had no idea where the devil we were. We were completely enveloped by mist. The Eskimos were unconcerned. They laid their compass on a thwart, placed a rifle on either side of it, and headed full speed into the fog banks. After traveling a considerable distance, they came out exactly where they wanted to, at a passage between two islands.

On our return trip, with a load of stone we had quarried from a vein of green rock, the Eskimos shot some eider ducks. This occasioned a happy shore lunch. I entertained some doubts as I watched the birds being cleaned and

178

skinned on the rocks and boiled in seawater, but they were delicious. The water added just the right touch of salt, and itself became a tasty sort of duck soup.

The Eskimos are excellent marksmen, as they demonstrated in bagging the ducks and proved again when they took us on seal hunts. We went far out to sea in one of their square-sterned canoes, searching the waves for sight of our quarry. The Eskimos explained their technique: when the black dot of a seal's head was sighted, usually at a considerable distance, they would shoot at it with a .22 caliber

The Eskimos gave me this fur-seal coat. My setter, Buck, approved.

179

rifle, for which shells were relatively inexpensive. This would frighten the animal into diving. Then they would head for the area where they thought it would surface and try to get a clear shot with a heavy rifle when it rolled its back out of the water. After being wounded, the seal could be harpooned and dispatched. Not a pretty method, but certainly effective.

We'd been out for about an hour when an Eskimo suddenly grabbed Phil by the arm and pointed toward the horizon. A black dot was bobbing in the swells nearly one hundred yards away. Phil made an excellent shot with the .22—he actually hit the seal. The animal was soon dispatched and towed to a nearby island, where our companions gleefully cut it up and cached it for the winter ahead. The pure, cold air would keep the meat from spoiling, and the Eskimos protected the cache against polar bears by urinating on the rocks with which they had covered it. The hunters were overjoyed at Phil's success. He had just turned twenty-one, and a young man's first seal is a great occasion—he is subject to his mother's direction until then. That evening there was a dance in tribute to Phil, in which all of the Eskimos in the camp took part.

Earlier, on our way to Dorset, we had made an overnight stop at the village of Povungnituk, where a priest named Father Steinman had a Catholic mission; the first missionaries there had been Anglican, and he was seeking converts to Catholicism. He was a kind and earnest man, but his work was not going well; he had not had a convert in the two years he had been there. He had established a social center for the Eskimos, which was a help to them, but I do not believe he was a good influence on native carving. He operated on the theory that the bigger the carving, the higher the price. This was bad policy, of course, because size is no measure of artistic merit. Father Steinman also had the Eskimos carving crucifixes and statues of the Virgin Mary, which I thought was unfortunate because the pieces were completely foreign to the native culture.

Jim Houston was careful not to introduce the influence of white artists to the Eskimos, but he did help create a new form of Eskimo art by teaching them printmaking, which they were just beginning to do at the time of our visit. This proved to be a real boon to the Eskimos.

A few months before we were to depart on our family trip to Dorset, I had received a telephone call from Arthur A. Houghton, Jr., the president of both the Metropolitan Museum of Art in New York City and the Steuben Glass Company. I knew him through his reputation as a collector of STC books — a library at Harvard is named after him. We had not met, though we later became friends, after we received honorary degrees together from St. John's University. Houghton said Prime Minister Lester Pearson of Canada had told him about Eskimo art and he wanted to learn more about it. In the course of conversation he mentioned that he had been in Africa several times and was looking for a change of pace, so I told him about our planned trip to the Arctic and told him how to contact Jim Houston. As it turned out, Houghton visited Dorset with a group of friends shortly before we went up. He was so impressed with Jim that he offered him a job as custodian of the Corning Glass Museum. Jim declined, but later Houghton offered him the design job at Steuben Glass, which he accepted and moved to New York.

Before leaving the Arctic, Jim fulfilled his promise to his Eskimo friends that he would supervise the start-up of the West Baffin Eskimo Cooperative. When he left, after fourteen years among them, he told the Eskimos, "I don't believe you should have any civil servant over you. I want you to hire someone to support your work, not to tell you how to live." The cooperative hired a man named Terrance Ryan, also an artist, to consult with them and help them in printmaking. Ryan has an outlet, Dorset Fine Arts in Toronto, for which he goes to the Arctic and selects the best carvings. Our Eskimo Art, Inc. representatives buy from Dorset Fine Arts, but we also get carvings from other Eskimo communities.

The members of the West Baffin Cooperative usually take their carvings to Ryan first for evaluation. They also may take them to the Hudson's Bay post, where, in effect, they get payment up front in the form of credit. Canadian law is very good about regulating the transactions to prevent exploitation. In other Arctic communities, Eskimos may take their carvings to Canadian Arctic Producers (CAP), which is a government organization authorized to mark the price of carvings up 12 percent. CAP has a wholesale office in Winnipeg to supply retailers. Print sales are controlled by a commission that reviews them and sets prices for them. The sale of Eskimo art has had a tremendous impact on the people of the Hudson Bay region. There are about twelve thousand Eskimos living there, and the art has brought in some $15 million (U.S.) a year. This has contributed greatly to a rapid change in the whole culture. Eskimos now have prefabricated houses, electricity, television, and stereos. Snowmobiles have largely replaced sled dogs. Most Baffin Island Eskimo families today will keep just one or two dogs to smell out seal holes in the ice.

Not all these changes have been for the better. The early prefabs, designed by someone who had never been in the Arctic, were too hot and were poorly ventilated, so for the first time, the Eskimos were subject to colds. Still, the prefabs probably are better than the traditional igloos, whose damp, chilly interiors, Jim said, caused countless

The carvings I am examining here are typical Eskimo Art, Inc. pieces.

Eskimo babies to die of pneumonia.

I felt obligated to help minimize the adverse effects of the cultural change as much as possible; after all, I was partly responsible, due to my part in forming Eskimo Art, Inc. So I got together with Arthur Houghton and we proposed to raise money to expand the nursing station at Cape Dorset. Our private actions apparently spurred the Canadian government into doing more for the Eskimos, and they built a fine modern infirmary.

Eskimo Art, Inc. is now housed in a handsome new gallery at Domino's Farms, the headquarters of Domino's Pizza, Inc. in Ann Arbor. Sadye and I have many pieces we treasure; some of them are valued for personal experiences we've had—for example, the carvings of Kiawak, a small Eskimo man who contracted tuberculosis and had to leave Cape Dorset to spend more than a year in a hospital in Ontario. The stay in the south seemed to rob Kiawak of his hunting skills, so that when he returned to Baffin Island, he was not much of a success in the field. He was a gifted artist, however, and he was able to survive and prosper on the strength of his carving.

I deplore the cheap imitations of Eskimo art that are found in souvenir shops—in response, I suppose, to the higher prices that the real thing is now able to command. But Jim Houston is not upset by it. He says, "Imitation is the sincerest form of flattery."

Jim has put his knowledge of Inuit culture and his talent for storytelling into writing prizewinning stories. He is the only triple winner of the Canadian Library Association's Book of the Year for Children Award.[1] His writing has helped him maintain his contacts in the north, and I'm happy about his assessment of Eskimo art today and his optimism

---

[1] The Book of the Year for Children Award was won by Houston for *Tikta 'liktak* (1966), *The White Archer* (1968), and *River Runners* (1980). His novel *White Dawn* (1973) was made into a movie.

about its future.

"It's very much the liveliest art around in Canada now," he says. "Certainly it has been a huge financial success, enabling the Inuits to support themselves. I used to have the feeling that when the [older] generation of Eskimos died or stopped working, we would see the end of genuine Inuit art. I was wrong. The works of the children, and even the grandchildren, have been equally good. In fact, Inuit art has never been better."

For me, it has been gratifying to see Eskimo Art, Inc. be instrumental in developing appreciation for the art and establishing a market for it when Jim Houston and the Canadian Handicraft Guild were ready to give up and all hope for such aid to the Eskimos seemed lost.

Chapter Nine

Politics

N eil Staebler likes to claim that he showed me the error of my Republican views in 1939, while we were traveling together in Europe. He takes credit for my conversion to the Democratic party. It is a nice story but, unfortunately, it is not completely accurate.

True, Neil may have perceived a change in me after that trip. Possibly he found me more reasonable, more liberal, more like his idea of a proper Democrat. But in fact, my actual split with the Republican party did not come until 1952, after Dwight D. Eisenhower, the Republican candidate for President, put his arm around Senator Joseph R. McCarthy and told him, in effect, "My boy, we're all for you."

McCarthy had been using Congressional hearings to pursue "Communists and fellow travelers" he claimed had infiltrated the U.S. State Department and other government offices. He painted these people as being part of an evil conspiracy to undermine the American way of life. His hearings were nothing but witch-hunts, and they had caused innocent people to lose their jobs simply because they were accused. McCarthy seldom had any actual proof of wrongdoing; he did not need it. His use of what pundits called the "Multiple Untruth," cloaked in his Senatorial immunity, made facts irrelevant. I despised McCarthy's demagoguery, and when Eisenhower embraced him, I fired off an angry telegram saying I resigned from the Republican party.

Sadye was pleased with my political switch, since for some years she had been a Democrat, as were many of our friends. Neil Staebler was by this time state chairman of the party. He had played a major role in getting G. Mennen Williams elected governor of Michigan in 1949, and through Neil I got to know Mennen personally, and I liked him. So I suppose friendship, as much as conscience, made me feel comfortable as a Democrat.

There were other motivations. At that time, I was undergoing psychoanalysis with Ted Raphael, and it made me realize how much one's attitude toward life influences one's choice of political affiliation. Sadye was also in analysis with Ted, and we both found it enormously helpful. Another strong influence on my political thinking was Jack Dawson, a law professor and former Rhodes scholar, whose wife, Emma, and Sadye were close friends. When I switched parties, Jack reminded me that he would be running for the House of Representatives on the Democratic ticket in the 1952 election. Would I help him? he asked.

I assured him I would, though my time would be limited, because I was immersed in the process of reactivating the National Microfilm Association (NMA). This latter undertaking started with the announcement earlier that year that Watson Davis, whom I mentioned earlier in connection with his Science Service, would have a display of microfilm equipment at a meeting of the American Documentation Institute at the Library of Congress. This served to spur me into action on the NMA, whose dormant status had been nagging at my conscience for some time. When the NMA was founded in 1943, I thought it had great potential. I envisioned it providing a forum for exchange of information about microfilm and stimulating contact among members that would advance the state of the art. But the young organization was paralyzed almost at birth by financial mismanagement. Its executive secretary spent the entire year's budget in three months and then resigned. The president then submitted his resignation. As vice president, I automatically became president, with Vernon Tate remaining as secretary. But by that time there was only $352 left in the bank account. Vernon and I decided that, given the continuing demands of the war effort, it was not a good time to attempt to rejuvenate the organization. So we closed it down and kept it alive but inactive. Now, eight years later, I felt it was time to either reactivate the NMA or give it a decent burial, donating its bank balance to some worthy cause. I talked this idea over with Vernon, who would be attending the American Documentation Institute (ADI) in his capacity of Director of Libraries at MIT.[1]

[1] Vernon Tate received a BA degree from UCLA in 1929, followed by an MA in 1930 and Ph.D. in 1934 from UC Berkeley. His first contact with microfilm came in 1928, when he saw a demonstration of an early Recordak bank-check machine, which coincided with some work he was doing with a Leica camera in copying books and manuscripts for research. In 1932-35 he was sent to Mexico by the Library of Congress to photograph historical manuscripts in the Mexican Archives (he was assisted by his wife, Kathrine, who became an expert photographer). In 1935, he was appointed director of photography at the National Archives, where he helped form the photoduplication service of the Library of Congress. During WWII he served as a U.S. Navy lieutenant assigned to the OSS. From 1946 to 1956, he was director of libraries at MIT. After 1956 he was archivist of the Naval Academy and executive secretary of NMA. He died September 30, 1989.

189

Vernon and I had always worked well together, and ever since his days with the Department of Agriculture, when he showed me the Draeger camera, I had had great respect for his knowledge and insight. I told him I did not want to be a president of nothing or act as custodian of an entity that was falling on its face. "It's high time we get the NMA back into action," I said. "If we don't, the British will do it and call it the Royal Microfilm Association." He agreed and suggested we act immediately and call a meeting to discuss it when we were in Washington for the ADI meeting.

Vernon Tate

We reserved the Coolidge Auditorium for the day after the American Documentation Institute. Watson Davis agreed to leave his microfilm exhibit on display and gave me time on his program to announce our proposed meeting. We had no inkling of what the response would be. I figured there was a good chance that only two people would show up—Vernon Tate and me. However, my doubts were banished at 9:30 A.M. the following day when no fewer than forty people were seated in the auditorium. I called the meeting to order, and we plunged into a discussion that continued with increasing intensity throughout the day. By the time we adjourned at 10:30 that night I was exhausted, having chaired the entire session with scarcely a break. I cannot remember being so tired before or since. But

I felt we had accomplished a great deal: (1) the group decided to reactivate the association; (2) I agreed to continue as president; (3) Vernon would be executive secretary; (4) a board of directors was elected; (5) a program of activities was proposed; and (6) a date was set for our first annual meeting.

The organizational concept that emerged from that meeting was very close to the original idea Vernon and I had for what a national association for the field of microfilm should be: a combination of scientific and professional interests, as opposed to the commercial interests that characterize most trade associations. We established various types of awards, as academic societies do. For example, the Award of Merit was created as the highest honor the association could give. It was to go to individuals who had made major contributions to the industry.[2] We also formed the rank of Fellow of the Association, to be given to those who contributed to the advancement and development of the industry through their activities in, and service to, the association. Other awards, such as the Pioneer Award, were established later.

[2] Those who have received the Award of Merit are: George P. McCarthy, Recordak Corp. (1954); Ray M. Hessert, Remington Rand, Inc. (1955); Charles Z. Case, Eastman Kodak (1956); Eugene B. Power, University Microfilms (1957); Verneur E. Pratt and George Francis Gray, Pratt & Gray (1958); John K. Boeing, Recordak Corp. (1960); Vernon D. Tate, NMA (1963); John H. Dessauer, Xerox Corp., and Marshall R. Hatfield, 3M Co. (1964); Sir Frank Francis, British Museum (1966); Carl E. Nelson, IBM Corp. (1967); Richard W. Batchelder (1972); Joseph Curtin [posthumous] (1974); Van B. Phillips, Eastman Kodak Co. (1975); D. W. McArthur, 3M Company and Loretta J. Kiersky, Airco Company (1977); Karl Adams, Jr. (1978); John R. Robertson, Microseal Corp. (1980); Henry C. Frey, Bell Telephone Labs (1981); Harold J. Fromm, Eastman Kodak Co. (1982); Earl P. Bassett, Jr., 3M Co. (1985); Don M. Avedon, director of International Information Management Congress (1987); and Thomas C. Bagg, National Bureau of Standards (1988).

Breaking ground for an organization like NMA is much like plowing a boulder-strewn field for the first time. One proceeds in fits and starts, struggling to clear problem rocks out of the way.

One of the larger problems we came upon and had to work around for several years was the reluctance of big companies such as Kodak and Bell & Howell to join the association. Kodak made the excuse that it could not join an association with its competitors because of antitrust problems. I considered this stuff and nonsense, but Kodak clung to it bullheadedly. Bell & Howell took much the same position. It was not until after the association had become an important forum for the industry and no longer really needed them that first Bell & Howell, then Kodak, changed their policy and applied for membership. Thanks to Scotty McArthur of 3M, that company joined early on and was an important help to the organization.

The value of the organization is reflected in the steady growth of its membership over the years, during which it has changed names three times. In 1975, it became the National Micrographics Association; in 1980, that name was expanded with the addition of the phrase *The Image Processing People;* in 1983, it became the Association of Information and Image Management (AIIM). The 1988 roster of AIIM listed six thousand members, with another three hundred and fifteen "trade" members, and its annual convention that year had an attendance of 17,500. The commercial atmosphere that Vernon Tate and I tried to avoid has gradually gained ascendance, and AIIM is today a fairly typical trade association. That outcome would not have

192

been my choice, yet I believe in the organization and am glad that it serves its members well. I am proud to hold the rank of Fellow No. 1 and to have been presented the Award of Merit in 1957. I have gained a great deal from the association. In addition to many business and personal contacts and the wealth of technical information to which it gave me access, it provided an outlet for articles I wrote. I would send reprints of these articles to customers and prospective customers of UMI and, as I mentioned in a previous chapter in connection with other publications, I found this to be the best advertising I could do.

The view from behind my desk at UMI was quite rosy all the while I was working with Vernon Tate and the others to reactivate the NMA. I was eager to capitalize on the marketing momentum UMI had going, and thought it was time for us to expand further in microfilming abroad.

I had my eye on England, which was beginning to emerge from the economic pall of World War II, although rationing would continue there until 1953. I knew the country contained rich troves of material for microfilming, and I wanted a branch there to provide UMI with a steady supply of negatives. The person I had in mind to run an operation in London was Phyllis Cain, wife of Arthur Cain, my old friend from Scotland Yard. They had been married in 1947, and she struck me as being a very practical and energetic lady with rather good administrative experience. So I formed University Microfilms Ltd., putting Phyllis in charge. Margaret Harwick went over and set up the office along the administrative lines we were using at UMI. Arthur Cain served on the board of directors.

We already had a number of cameras in England, of course. One of Phyllis Cain's first commissions was from the Colonial Williamsburg Foundation, which wanted her to track down and microfilm all documents in England relating to the Virginia colony. It was a satisfactory job. But overall, the progress of University Microfilms Ltd. was exasperatingly slow. Phyllis Cain gives her own view of it in the following tape-recorded commentary:

Gene Power felt there was great promise for microfilming here in England, but he insisted that our office had to earn its own way. We had very little money—I think our total capital was 300 pounds. Our equipment was all used, and we did none of our own processing—that was hired out to Recordak in Fulham.

We simply did not get a lot of support from British organizations. They were quite pleasant and willing to allow us to microfilm their materials, but they could not pay for it. I think it was simply too soon after the war. Nobody here had money.

One of my more interesting jobs was from the French government, who hired me to go to Paris and stay in the home of a prominent communist and photograph all his papers.

Scholars would sometimes hire me to microfilm *Case Books,* which is the British Museum's designation for pornographic materials. I had a nice, rather naive young girl working for me, and one day I thoughtlessly handed her a packet of these *Case Book* materials to check for film quality. When she returned them, she told me, "My education has been completed."

I stayed with the job for twelve years, two years after Gene sold the company to the Rank organization—Rank-Xerox—when the whole scale of things changed; we were given new equipment and moved into larger premises. I don't think University Microfilms Ltd. ever quite lived up to Gene's expectations, but it was a noble effort and there was never a dull moment when you had Gene Power for a boss.

POLITICS

While our London office was sputtering like a damp fuse, our operations in Ann Arbor were exploding with a firecracker string of new services, posting increased profits in every quarter. Morale was high, and new ideas were percolating all over the place. I made certain my associates in UMI understood my business philosophy: that one must know the cost of doing business and set prices so as to make a reasonable profit. A business must make a profit or it cannot survive and grow. At the same time, the profit motive does not justify maximizing one's return in a given situation just because circumstances permit you to do so. We sold many products that were unique, on which I could have placed a substantial premium and received a high rate of profit. But I would not do so. I believe that if one operates his business effectively, aims at realizing a reasonable return, and concentrates on being of service to the customers, keeping their needs in mind and producing the best possible product, then profits will come to him automatically. This philosophy was one I developed early, in part because I disagreed with some of the policies Edwards Brothers followed when I worked for them, and I have followed the same principles throughout my life. I think they were responsible for the high regard our customers had for us, and also for the high morale at UMI. No one was ever *forced* to work overtime or to come in on a Saturday, but almost everyone did so routinely. In fact, the regular morning meetings I had with Margaret Harwick, Steve Rice, and Bob Holliday were usually most productive on Saturdays. We could let our hair down then and do some truly creative thinking without interruption by telephones and other business.

Bob Holliday was in charge of production. He lacked the formal training to make the most of his intuitive engineering ability, yet he developed several original designs. Bob's ignorance of the rules of engineering tended to work to his benefit. Since he didn't know a certain approach was not supposed to work, he went ahead and tried it. The results were often successful, and sometimes unique. I often joined Bob in tinkering with cameras and various types of engines and equipment—I have always been keenly interested in how things work—and we collaborated very well. Bob was also in charge of construction for UMI; he handled the continuing program of expansion of our facilities, which involved some unusual challenges, such as installing air-conditioning in those old buildings. This required installation of a large system that we discovered would be extremely expensive to operate using city water. So we decided to dig our own well. After one hundred and fifty feet, the driller gave up. We had a dry hole that cost us $10,000. I recall being pretty disgusted about that.

One of my farmer friends in the area said he knew a "dowser" who could find water every time. I had heard about such individuals since I was a boy up north, but stories of their feats always sounded like snake oil to me. So I asked a professor in the geology department about it.

"I can't say," he answered. "Water-witching is not a scientific method, but to my knowledge it has never been disproved. What have you got to lose?"

I might have said, "Nothing but another ten thousand dollars." Yet something told me to give the divining rod a try, so I got in touch with the "dowser."

He was a stooped old man in bib overalls who wandered around our property holding a forked branch from a peach tree in front of him with both hands. Finally he stopped, straightened and, pointing a gnarled finger toward the ground at his feet, announced, "Dig here!"

At ninety feet, the second hole was just as dry as the first. Bob Holliday was crestfallen.

"Gene, this has cost us another nine thousand dollars, and I'm afraid we're thowing good money after bad," he said. Do you think we ought to go on?"

"Do you doubt the power of the divining rod?" I asked, trying hard to keep a tone of humor in my voice. "Keep digging."

About an hour later, Bob yelled for me to come outside and see the flood. The streets were running with water from our new artesian well. It was wonderfully cold, clear water, excellent for drinking, in addition to running our air-conditioners.

The early '50s also were a time when my interest in local theater was rekindled. As usual, Sadye was the spark. She and I had supported Ann Arbor's old Drama Season, beginning in the mid-'30s. Its plays were directed by Valentine Windt, a member of the University of Michigan faculty, who cast them in New York with well-known actors. There were five productions each spring, immediately after the university's traditional May Festival. The Drama Season contributed a great deal to the community, but World War II put a stop to it. I made an attempt to revive it shortly after

the war, when Roger Stevens, the famous theatrical producer and real-estate magnate who lived in Ann Arbor [3]
mentioned casually at a cocktail party that if the Drama
Season were revived, he would underwrite any financial
losses incurred. I telephoned him the next day and asked if,
in the sober light of morning, he still felt that way. He did,
so I set to work contacting potential board members who
went on to reactivate the program. Fortunately, we were
able to persuade Valentine Windt to get back in harness.
One of the plays we produced that first year—1946—was
Twelfth Night, and Roger Stevens liked it so much he took
it to New York, where it enjoyed a modest success. We
discovered, however, that the time was out of joint for the
Drama Season; it was difficult to engage good actors for
such a limited engagement. Then Windt died. We were
unable to find a successor so, after two more seasons, we let

[3] Roger L. Stevens was honored in a nationally televised performance on December 4, 1988, for his contributions as a theatrical producer and as the guiding
force behind the establishment of the Kennedy Center for the Performing Arts. He
was born in Detroit in 1910 and raised in Ann Arbor, where his father was in the real-
estate business. Financial reverses suffered by his father made it necessary for him
to leave the University of Michigan in 1930, after one year, and work on auto
assembly lines in Detroit. He joined the Hannan Real Estate Company in Detroit
in 1935 and was extremely successful. He became interested in theater while
serving as a Navy lieutenant during WWII. Upon returning to civilian life, he
embarked on his dual career: forming a real-estate corporation in New York to buy
and sell major properties such as hotels and skyscrapers; and financing several
plays, including Molnar's *The Play's the Thing* and *Right You Are If You Think You
Are.* He continued pursuing both business and theater with dramatic flair, and
maintained his house in Ann Arbor and apartment in New York City. Perhaps his
best-known endeavor in real estate was the formation in 1951 of a syndicate which
purchased the Empire State Building for $51,600,000, then the highest price ever
paid for a single building. He served as head of the Fine Arts Commission for
President Lyndon Johnson. Beginning in 1978, as Chairman of the Kennedy
Center, he presided over the annual presentation of the Kennedy Center Honors.

the Drama Season go to the grave with him.

At roughly the same time, in 1948, Sadye joined the board of the Arts Theater, a repertory group of young professional actors, most of them from New York City. I admired their dedication and hard work, but I did not pay much attention to them until 1951, when I accompanied Sadye to one of their performances. The theater was inauspicious; it was on the third floor of a commercial building in downtown Ann Arbor, and I remember thinking it was a firetrap because only one staircase led to it. But the play was good. It was my first experience of theater-in-the-round, and I enjoyed it. I thought the Arts Theater had potential as a replacement for the Drama Season in the community.

The Arts Theater's chief problem was the unrealistic idealism of the actors and actresses. They believed the play was the thing; attracting a paying audience was not high on their list of priorities. I liked these young people very much. One of them, Jimmy Coco, went on to a career in television, and Bob Kingston later became deputy director of the National Endowment for the Humanities. But I despaired at their attitude toward financing the theater. The thing that broke them was a grand scheme to mount a production of *Noah* in the Lydia Mendelssohn Theater. It might have worked if only they hadn't chosen to schedule it during Thanksgiving vacation. You could have fired a cannon into that theater without hitting a ticket holder.

In the wake of the *Noah* debacle, I got together with a law professor and helped the Arts Theater close its operations. Then, with a group of friends—the Staeblers, the Dawsons, Phyllis and Hart Wright, and a few others—we donated enough money to send the young actors back to their cold-water flats in New York. We also bought their assets—costumes, chairs, and sets—for five hundred dollars. There wasn't much to this theatrical paraphernalia, but in considering what to do with it, we began talking about forming a new repertory theater.

On May 3, 1954, I composed a letter proposing establishment of a Dramatic Arts Center as "a focal point for all organizations interested in dramatic arts." It was signed by a number of us and mailed to one hundred citizens of Ann Arbor. After several organizational meetings, we established the Dramatic Arts Center as a nonprofit operation and acquired the use of the ballroom of the old Masonic Temple. We had enough chairs from the Arts Theater to arrange in-the-round seating, and all of us rolled up our sleeves and went to work nights and weekends building seating platforms, a lighting grid suspended from the ceiling, and a light board. My friend Warner Rice, by then the distinguished chairman of the University of Michigan's English department, donned blue jeans and wielded hammer and saw with the rest of us. He also lubricated our labors with his humorous asides. For example, one night during a break in which the hot dogs we had sent out for arrived *sans* catsup, Warner told about his difficulty in adapting to bland English breakfasts in 1926 when he was sent to Oxford by Harvard College, to study the tutorial system and make recommendations on how it might be adopted by Harvard.

"After a few months, I was perishing for a taste of American breakfast cereal," Warner said. "One day I noticed a box of Shredded Wheat in the window of a shop near our lodgings, and at breakfast next morning I asked the waiter if he could get me some. He said he would, and after a considerable wait, while he went to the shop and made the purchase, he came in bearing a Shredded Wheat biscuit in the center of a dinner plate, flanked by knife and fork, with salt and pepper on the side."

We finally got the Dramatic Arts Center going. We hired a director and staff, which included some of the former members of the Arts Theater from New York, and we opened the 1954 season with a production of *Arms and the Man*. It was a reasonably

Jane Rice-LaRue
Warner Rice

successful season, but only because it was subsidized, principally by Neil Staebler and me. I doubt that it would have lasted long, even if I had stayed with it. But I did not stay with it, because I decided late in 1954 to run for the office of Regent of the University of Michigan. I knew this would leave me no time for the theater group, so I resigned as its president, and Burnette Staebler took my place. The Dramatic Arts Center continued for three more years before it, too, closed. The lesson I learned from that experience was that a professional theatrical program can be successful in Ann Arbor only if the university participates; the Ann Arbor Summer Festival, which I will discuss in Chapter Fifteen, is a good example.

M y liberal sensitivities were offended by discrimination against minorities. The problem was most apparent in Detroit, but access to employment and housing were being denied to blacks in the Ann Arbor area, too. UMI had one black employee, an automatic developing machine operator named Dick Jewett. Dick had had a hard time finding a place to live, and I thought it would be good if he could get a piece of land where he could build a house. It happened that I owned several residential lots on the west side of Ann Arbor, in the triangle between Dexter and Jackson Roads. I had bought them at a tax sale shortly after World War II for $60 apiece. I told Dick I would sell them to him for what I paid for them and he could resell them to his black friends. However, the neighbors objected and put so much pressure on Dick that he gave up the idea.

Another situation involving discrimination came about when Ted Raphael asked me to propose him and his second wife, Louise, for membership in the Barton Hills Country Club. I was glad to do so. Ted was one of my best friends and neighbors in Barton Hills, in addition to being my psychoanalyst, and Louise was from the socially prominent Earhart family. I met with the board of the club, and they took the nomination under advisement.

Dr. Theophile "Ted" Raphael

202

Then they called me back for a second meeting and said Ted would not be eligible, because he was 50 percent Jewish. I couldn't believe my ears. I had a third meeting with them to try and get them to change their views. They refused, so I resigned. I would not belong to an organization so biased.

It later developed that the bylaws of the club stated that any resident of Barton Hills was automatically a member. But by the time we found out about it, neither Ted nor I had any desire to belong. I was so annoyed that I retaliated by donating to the club some of the squirrels and gophers that were attracted to our bird feeders. I would live trap the animals and carry them down to the golf course, which was distant enough to prevent their return. I'd walk past the greens and wave to the groundskeeper, "Hi, Tony. How's everything?" He'd wave back and say something like, "Just fine, Mr. Power. We sure have a lot of squirrels and gophers again this year, though."

My father, whom our family called Gov, died on April 13, 1954. I had grown closer to him in the years after my mother's death. Part of this was due to the fact that he finally was able to view me as a person in my own right, no longer as a son in need of direction. Another factor was my improved understanding of him and my ability to be more patient with him as a result of my two years of psychoanalysis.

About 1951, Gov had met a woman from Chicago who spent summers in Traverse City. This turn of events caused some lively discussions among the rest of the family. Gov was then seventy-five years old, and she was about ten years younger. I was pleased to see them getting on so well together. They were considering marriage, but in the end they decided it was not a good idea.

If they had married, they would have settled in Traverse City, because that's where all Gov's business contacts were. He never retired, you see. He was Chairman of the First National Bank and went into his office every day, and he also remained active in his insurance agency until the day he died at age seventy-eight.

A woman who had worked closely with him for many years bought the agency, Hastings Santo, from the estate. She later sold it to two young men who also had worked there a long while. My brother, Frank, said he would like to have our father's bank stock, and I was happy to let him take it.

Somehow, Father's death brought Frank and me even closer than we had been. There was more affection and respect between us. Another legacy from my father was a minority interest in the old Park Place Hotel in Traverse City, which he left to Frank and me. I did not pay much attention to it at first. The business was not making any money, it had an adverse union contract, and its prospects looked glum because the whole community seemed discouraged.

I threw myself back into work at UMI. That summer we built another addition to our office. Our staff was up to two hundred people, and we had to have more room. The land our original building was on was owned by the Ann Arbor Railroad; we had it on lease, and the railroad did not want to sell. Fortunately, adjacent to the property, and also on railroad land, but under a long-term lease, was a stable owned by the Ann Arbor Dairy; we bought that and remodeled it. This doubled our space, to about thirty-five thousand square feet.

Later that summer of 1954, Sadye and Phil and I took a trip to Europe. I was not pleased with the developments, or the lack of them, I observed in our London operation, but as a family excursion, the trip was a success. I was proud of the way Phil conducted himself; he seemed—in my admittedly prejudiced, fatherly view—to possess a poise and understanding far greater than his sixteen years.

After our return to Ann Arbor, I once again helped Jack Dawson campaign for the House of Representatives. It was a repeat of his effort in 1952: he lost. But the campaign further strengthened our relation-

Phil at age sixteen.

ship, and it was Jack Dawson who suggested a few weeks later that I run for Regent of the University of Michigan. Jack had popped over to our house that day in December 1954 for a neighborly visit, I thought. His suggestion was a bolt out of the blue to me. I was familiar with the position of regent—my great-uncle, the father of my Traverse City physician uncle, Dr. Percy Lawton, had been a regent, and in 1948, when Governor Kim Sigler was making an appointment to the board of regents, Sadye's name was one he considered before awarding the post to Roscoe Bonisteel. The idea that I should be a regent had never occurred to me.

I protested that I had never run for political office and I knew nothing about the Democratic party machinery in the county or state. At that time, regents were elected statewide along with judges, in the spring of every odd-numbered year to the governing boards of the University of Michigan, Michigan State University, and Wayne State University. The timing took these races out of the political jousting of regular elections and, therefore, voters paid more attention to them. Jack said not to worry; he and Arthur Eastman, a professor of English at the U of M, would be my campaign managers; he would introduce me to all the right people and guide me through the nomination process. I talked it over with Sadye, and together we gave it considerable thought. Finally, I told Jack Dawson I would run.

Looking back on it now, I marvel at how naive I was. Even though I had known academic people and worked closely with them ever since my graduation from business school, I had no clear-cut ideas about what the problems of higher education were or what should be done to solve them. After formally announcing to a county Democratic meeting in December that I would be seeking nomination at the party's convention in February, I simply went along with Jack and Art, who put together statements of my positions on several issues and had them printed up on posters. I also visited various district meetings and asked district chairmen for their support.

One day I called on the state council of the AFL-CIO for

an interview. It went very well until Bill Marshall, vice-chairman of the state organization, asked me what my attitude would be toward having communist speakers come to speak on the University campus.

"I think it would be a good thing," I said. I added that I thought students should be exposed to all points of view. I had confidence that they would be able to think for themselves, and if there were free-and-open discussion, they would see the fallacy of the communist position.

The state vice-chairman was alarmed. His union was a hotbed of anxieties about Communism at that time. Its leadership was trying to purge Communists from its ranks. And although Senator Joseph McCarthy's red-baiting had been largely discredited by then,[4] the unreasoning fear of Communism he had generated was still abroad in the land.

Bill Marshall told me he considered my position unacceptable and he could not support me.

I also had an interview with Gus Scholle, head of the UAW. He seemed more reasonable and more favorably disposed toward my nomination; I think this was because he respected Jack Dawson.

The convention was held in Grand Rapids. Sadye and I took a small suite at the Pantlind Hotel, and I began making my rounds to chat with the various delegations. In the course of this, I heard that the AFL-CIO intended to oppose me from the floor the next morning after Jack made his

[4] The U.S. Senate voted, 67 to 22, on December 2, 1954, to condemn the highly improper conduct of Senator McCarthy. Richard H. Rovere writes that with this vote "McCarthy had not been lynched but he was finished. He was no longer a threat to anything, no longer a serious force in American politics." *Senator Joe McCarthy* copyright ©1959 by Richard H. Rovere; Harcourt, Brace and Company, New York.

207

speech nominating me. So I arranged a meeting with Bill Marshall and some of his people. They arrived at our suite about one A.M. and I launched an impassioned speech about intellectual freedom and why Michigan could not continue to be a great university without it. "After all," I said, "Communism is not a contagious disease that infects people on exposure. It is a political idea that thrives on ignorance, which is precisely what you would promote in denying Communists the right to speak. Your denial would strengthen their cause. . . ." I don't know what more I said—there was a lot of talk by everyone in the room—but when we concluded the meeting at three A.M., Bill Marshall said he had changed his mind. He would second my nomination.

Paul Adams, a lawyer from Sault Ste. Marie, was the other Democratic candidate. I had a meeting with him the day after we were nominated to discuss campaign strategy. I had to confess I had only a vague notion of what I was talking about. Then Sadye and I went home so I could prepare to go off on the campaign trail. I picked up some posters Jack and his group had prepared for me, put them in my Ford Thunderbird—a racy little convertible the Ford Motor Company had just introduced—donned my beret and trench-coat, kissed Sadye good-bye, and headed for Traverse City. There weren't many Democrats in the Traverse City area, so I figured it was a good place to start. I could lose fewer votes there than anyplace else.

I received a nice reception at the Park Place from a small group organized by Alex Wunche, a local apple grower. Then I set off to tour the northern part of the Lower Peninsula. I thought things were going rather well. People seemed very friendly. But before long I got a call from an agitated Neil Staebler. He said he'd had complaints about "some character who looks like a French movie director zooming around in a hot sports car, claiming to be a Democratic candidate for regent." Neil paused, then ordered, "Come home and change cars, and leave the beret behind." I did so, switching to my Buick sedan, and there were no further problems. People in small towns across the state were good about letting me put my posters in store windows. I would visit the local radio station, where someone was always eager to have me on the air, a break from watching the record player spin; the newspapers usually ran interviews with me, too. I enjoyed sharing views with people in coffee klatches and evening meetings. They were a cross section of our citizenry, and I felt rubbing elbows with them made the whole experience worthwhile, even if I lost the election.

The pace of campaigning accelerated as election day neared. I was called to appear in various parts of the state with Mennen Williams, who was very active in helping the party ticket. We would meet at six A.M. at the gates of a factory and shake hands with people changing shifts. During the last two weeks of the campaign, Sadye went along with me, which was very helpful. Routinely, we would get home after midnight from a rally and get up at 4:30 or 5:00 A.M. to drive to another session.

When election day finally arrived that April, all I could think of was getting some sleep. After the polls closed, a group of friends gathered at our house to see the returns come in on television. Everyone was excited because the voting for me seemed strong. Phil kept busy posting the numbers and calculating percentages. It was intriguing, but about nine o'clock I said, "I don't care who is elected. I am going to bed."

They woke me shortly after midnight to tell me that Paul and I were the winners—the first Democratic regents to be elected since 1933. I grinned and waved and fell back to sleep.

As it turned out, the results of the election were not final for three more days. Paul Adams was in for certain, but my Republican opponent, Bill Cudlip, would not concede. In the end, I won by nearly nine thousand votes, which was close.

I was elated, proud, and eager to get started on this distinctive new service the citizens of Michigan had elected me to fulfill.

Chapter Ten

Regent

M y first lesson in my new role as regent was patience. I had to restrain my eagerness to get started, for although I was elected in April 1955 and was sworn in six weeks later, I would not actually take office until January 1956.

There were numerous other lessons to be learned. One was how to deal with the obsequious behavior my new position seemed to bring out in other people.

On December 10, 1955, I attended a meeting called by Harlan Hatcher, president of the university, to present his proposal for a major building program. The presentation was good, but I was put off by the kowtowing of staff at the luncheon afterwards. It tended to inhibit my conversation with some of the alumni—perhaps unintentionally, because the alumni were talking frankly about problems with the university's image. I noted in my diary:

> They were trying to let us know that we are considered highbrow, unapproachable, and uncooperative; that we do not respond favorably to requests for speakers; [why] we have an unfavorable press and the Detroit newspapers miss no opportunity to kick us in the pants. . . . If a business institution were faced with this problem, [its management] would first find out the attitudes of its clients, hire skilled public-relations counsel, and make a real attempt to tell its story to the people.

As the date for my taking office approached, people I knew only slightly became effusively friendly. During the first week of January 1956 I had three dinner invitations from such people. I mentioned this to Jack Dawson, who said, "They're just brownnoses. Avoid them." He cautioned that these people carry a virus that is the bane of every public servant. It causes the ego to inflate and creates an exaggerated sense of one's own importance. "You have to examine every contact and consider the reason or motive behind it," he added. "View every relationship as suspect until it is proven sound.

I believed that if I were to be effective as a regent, I needed to know much more about the university. So I planned to take one afternoon off each week to visit a different department and have lunch with its chairman. This approach proved very enlightening, both as to the academic challenges faced by the various departments and the political currents running between the department heads and the administration.

One pet idea I mentioned in some of my departmental visits was establishing a cooperative program between the University of Michigan and some institution in the Orient, such as the University of Taiwan, to study Chinese herbal medicine. I had read reports of remarkable cures, both by Chinese and Russian physicians, based on centuries of experience with herbal medicine. There was some enthusiasm for such a project, and some work was done on feasibility by Dean Albert C. Furstenburg of the medical school, but the idea never got beyond proposal form.

Another concern I had was the pressure being placed on

the university to expand its adult-education services into labor education. I felt this was somewhat at variance with the institution's basic purpose, yet perhaps it was a case of new wine requiring new bottles, if indeed there was a need for such a program. Competition between Michigan and our sister institution at Lansing, Michigan State University, came into play here. There was a fear that labor unions would support Michigan State's request for budget increases because it did more extension training around the state. Jack Dawson arranged a dinner at his home for me to meet with Brenden Sexton, an influential representative of organized labor, and Sexton convinced me that there was a need to train union leaders to apply good, responsible management practices and bargaining techniques. Lack of training, from local leadership up, was one reason union bosses like Jimmy Hoffa and Dave Beck could get away with gross misconduct.

I was uncomfortable in dealing with unions. As a businessman, I disliked their excesses, although it seemed to me that, at bottom, management was responsible for making labor unions necessary. Moreover, I could sympathize with labor's point of view in many instances. I feel obliged to point out here that UMI had never had a union, because our workers saw nothing to be gained from organizing. I also admired certain labor leaders such as Walter Reuther, the head of UAW, who was a man of integrity, vision, and broad social interests despite his reputation as a troublemaker. In fact, my regard for Reuther was one reason my first meeting as a member of the board of regents, on February 9, 1956, turned out to be explosive.

The January meeting had been called off because Harlan Hatcher had been delayed in returning from a trip to the Far East. This put a severe strain on my patience, because one of the items on the agenda was the question of the university's continuing to do business with University Microfilms. I assumed this was a matter of protocol, but I was anxious to deal with it and put it behind me. When the question came up at the meeting, however, action on it was tabled due to the fact that someone had discovered the existence of a state law preventing any regent from having a financial tie with the institution he serves. I was stunned and embarrassed.

As the meeting broke up for lunch, I rushed over to Roscoe Bonisteel, a Republican regent, and said, "As my attorney, why the hell didn't you let me know about this law?" He did not answer directly, but said he had advised me against any attempt to use my position for personal gain. He thought that should have been sufficient. Perhaps so, but I still felt ill-served.

When the meeting resumed, we approved a Workers Education program as an extension service, incorporating some of the points I had discussed with Brenden Sexton. Then came a discussion of who should be awarded honorary degrees at commencement that spring. President Hatcher explained that the Honorary Degree Committee of the faculty proposed two or three names and that the regents themselves usually nominated one or two.

"Very good," I said. "I would like to propose the name of Walter Reuther."

Jaws dropped and eyebrows elevated in surprise all around

214

the table, but I plunged ahead with my explanation of why Reuther should be so honored. Roscoe Bonisteel promptly chimed in with the name of a man in the Philippines; he then offered another man in Detroit. I thought my candidate would be lost in the shuffle, but Al Connable quickly made a motion to approve all three nominations. This parliamentary ploy stymied any objections, and the motion passed. My brashness ruffled some feathers on the board. Certainly it was a case of a fool rushing in where angels feared to tread, although President Hatcher later told me he approved. He could hardly have disliked the favorable coverage the announcement stirred in the press.

That evening, I went to my office and dictated a memo informing the executive staff of UMI that because I was a regent, state law prohibited us from having business dealings with the University of Michigan. This caused some cries of dismay at our meeting the next morning. No one was in favor of suspending our services, because this would have worked a hardship on the university. So we agreed to continue the services—free of charge. A system was devised to allow the university library to do its own microfilming of the theses. We would process the film free and give the positives to the library, which would ship them to customers and do the billing. We would publish the abstracts of U of M theses in *Dissertation Abstracts* as a gift to the university. I wrote to Attorney General Horace Gilmore and requested an opinion on this method of proceeding. To my relief, he responded that he could see absolutely no conflict of interest.

Yet another lesson I learned in my first few months as a

regent was restraint.

Running my own business for nearly twenty years had conditioned me to take immediate action on any problem. I shunned the type of indirection and routing of matters through channels that is the hallmark of the bureaucratic process. For example, when I first became a regent and got a complaint from the parent of a prospective student, my reaction was to pick up the phone and call the Admissions Office. That, apparently, was regarded as throwing my weight around, as were my personal meetings with department heads. After about three months, my friend and fellow regent Al Connable invited me to his home in Kalamazoo for a talk. He told me, "Gene, you are scaring these people to death!" He explained that while ultimate authority at the university rests with the regents as a whole, individual regents cannot act directly in administrative affairs without snarling the control wires of the system. Sometimes the most effective use of authority is in not exercising it. "To subtly suggest the possibility of using authority, but refraining from doing so, usually gets the best result," Al said. I appreciated his advice very much and thereafter was more discreet in my approach. However, I did not let this deter me from continuing to learn everything I could about the workings of the university.

I was criticized, too, for attempting to polarize the board of regents along political lines because Paul Adams would come down from Sault Ste. Marie and stay at our home the evening before the regents' meetings. We would have a "homework" session, going through the next day's agenda, which usually was an inch and a half thick. After Paul resigned in December 1957 to take the post of attorney general, I continued to hold "homework" meetings with Donald Thurber, a Grosse Pointe Democrat who was appointed to replace him. Roscoe Bonisteel disapproved. He called our meetings a "Democratic caucus." He seemed to feel these meetings might be politically oriented. This was ridiculous. I never had a single suggestion from the governor, the Democratic party, or from organized labor as to how the university should be run. In fact, I had long thought that one of the great strengths of the University of Michigan board was that once a regent was elected, party politics were thrown out the window. It should be a truly nonpartisan group.

Roscoe's opinion of me was not improved when I made a motion at one meeting that Eleanor Roosevelt be given an honorary degree. In response to his indignant objection, I said I thought it rather close-minded to allow a political prejudice from twenty years ago to influence one's judgment of a person who in her own right is one of the outstanding citizens of the world. Roscoe's view may have stemmed from the fact that two more Democrats, Carl Brablec and Irene Murphy, had been elected to the board in January 1958 (thus making the board split 4-4). But it was more likely part of a general outlook I noted in my diary in March 1959:

> The older members of the board do not seem to realize there is a new breed of dog in the kennel. The younger regents want to know more and ask more questions. For some time I have been complaining about the brevity of our meetings—only about four hours in length once a month. Consequently we are arranging to

217

meet Thursday night before the meeting for any regents who wish to ask questions and for a give-and-take discussion. Nothing official. The president can be there if he wishes. I have also suggested that for an hour during this evening the senior members of the Faculty Senate Advisory Committee be welcomed to come and discuss anything they wish.

One of my major concerns during my first few years as a regent was the lack of a congenial, cooperative relationship between the University of Michigan and Michigan State University. I thought rivalry between the schools should be confined to athletics, because a contentious approach in educational programs seemed to me wasteful of public funds and counterproductive for all parties concerned. It also affected other institutions. For example, the head of MSU's extension service reportedly announced at a meeting of his peers from other schools in the state, in effect, "Get out of the way, boys, because we are moving in!" [1]

One day in the spring of 1958 I happened to be in Lansing on business and took the occasion to pay a call on John Hannah, president of Michigan State. It was my first opportunity to sit down and talk with him, and it was an interesting experience, because I heard from him the same complaints about us that we had been making about them.

I proposed to Hannah that the state be considered as an educational region with one unified extension service to which the various educational institutions would contribute according to their abilities. The concept of an educational region would help reduce cost. For example, I felt it would

---

[1] This quote is from my diary entry of April 5, 1958. The source is unknown.

be wasteful for Michigan State to pour money into building a nuclear reactor and assembling the highly skilled faculty to operate it, when the U of M already had such a facility and could make use of it available to Michigan State. Hannah mellowed considerably during our meeting, and he was more cordial to officials from the U of M thereafter.

Gradually, relations between the U of M and MSU improved during my tenure as a regent, and the idea of a unified extension service was developed in a way that I think serves communities throughout the state very well.

In retrospect, it took me about three years to become effective as a regent. By the end of my fifth year, I thought I was fairly good at the job. In my sixth year, I became senior regent when Roscoe Bonisteel retired. By this time I knew a good deal about the problems of higher education and was vitally interested in helping solve them. One problem in Michigan and several other states was that the legislatures were attempting to reduce financial support to education. They believed that students should be made to pay a greater share of the cost through increased tuition. In 1959 I noted in my diary:

> The problems facing the university are increasing in complexity. The legislature has thus far failed to agree on any kind of tax program, or for that matter on any source of income that will make it possible for us to meet our payrolls next month. This is the greatest example of legislative irresponsibility that I have seen. Part of this stems from an attempt on the part of the Republican section of the Senate to discredit Soapy [Williams] on a nationwide basis. They want things to get worse rather than better, and in this they seem to be succeeding. . . . We have borrowed all the money possible, about $4 million. We have

used up our working capital, and have received no money since we got part of the January allotment.

In 1961, the appropriations committee of the legislature recommended that the U of M be given an increase for the next year of only $147,000. I noted that this was not enough to extend our enrollment or even to keep pace with increases in faculty salaries "if we are to preserve our faculty." I was the author of the education plank in the Michigan Democratic platform that year, calling for continued state subsidy of education. I repeated the same refrain in two articles I wrote, "Public Education and the Low-Tuition Principle" and "Who Killed Higher Education?", which received wide circulation. However, when the legislature again failed to appropriate adequate funds for the U of M in 1964, I voted with the Republican regents to raise tuition fees. It was the only way to maintain quality. I insisted, though, that

A reelection campaign photo, 1964.

a rider be added to the tuition increase, granting an additional $150,000 to student aid.

Al Connable introduced Sadye and me to the Association of Governing Boards of Universities and Colleges (AGB), a national organization which I found to be invaluable in forming an intelligent and ethical approach to my role as regent. I became active in the AGB and ultimately served as its president. This provided me with a number of opportunities to speak before groups. I agreed with Winston Churchill when he said, "The three most difficult things a man can attempt are climbing a wall that's leaning toward him, kissing a girl who's leaning away from him, and making an after-dinner speech." But I found that public speaking came easier with practice. My main role model as a speaker was Harlan Hatcher. A handsome man of dignified presence, even during informal discussion, he spoke beautifully and persuasively. Harlan and I had our differences at first, but I came to believe he was the right man in the right place at the right time.

In that vein, I have often marveled at how fortunate the University of Michigan has been, in recent years at least, in having leaders who are in tune with the times. During Harlan Hatcher's tenure, when the student body comprised representatives of the post-World War II "baby boom" and returning veterans of the Korean War, it was a period of serious attention to studies. Harlan was a very good president in this climate. Under his administration budgets increased, enrollment and staff grew, and an ambitious building progam flourished. Bob Fleming was the perfect leader for the difficult period of student unrest in the late sixties. By the same token, Harold Shapiro's temperament was just right for the economic challenges of the early 1980s, and the tradition continued with the selection of James J. Duderstadt, who was sworn in October 8, 1988. He was Dean of Engineering before he became provost, and his orientation toward technology seems exactly what is needed

221

as the U of M moves into the twenty-first century.

I have often thought, too, what a good thing it is that the governing boards of the three state universities in Michigan were mandated by the state's constitution and, therefore, are autonomous in their decisions on expenditures of state appropriations and other finances under their control. This has been a great source of strength for them.

Our family life became more closely intertwined with the U of M than ever before in 1958, when Phil transferred there from Harvard. He loved his freshman year at Harvard and would have gone back were it not for an unfortunate accident that fractured two vertebrae and left him in constant pain. Surgery was recommended to fuse three vertebrae, and he came home to have the operation performed in the University Hospital during the summer. He planned to live with us while recuperating—he would have to wear a body cast and corset for a year—and he decided to transfer so he could continue his studies. By the time he shucked off the cast, he was enjoying the U of M so much that he stayed on.

Phil proved to be an excellent writer. He became editorial director of *The Michigan Daily,* where he wrote an outstanding series of articles on problems facing the university, and also contributed to national magazines. Incidentally, Phil's close colleague at the *Daily* was a young man named Tom Hayden, who became a leader of the "New Left" during the late sixties, married the political activist and actress Jane Fonda, and went into politics in California.

I was proud but not at all surprised when Phil was named

to Phi Beta Kappa. I was hoping that he might go to business school after his graduation and then join UMI and eventually become my successor. I put it to him directly, saying I needed to make plans for the future of the company and that I would very much like for him to join it.

He said he appreciated my feelings, "But my answer is that I don't want to join the company because it's both too hard and too easy."

"What do you mean by that?" I asked.

"It's too easy because it would mean joining a company that had already been created and developed by you. That wouldn't be a good thing for me, because I would have attained a substantial position of business success without having earned it by my own capability."

"I understand that," I said, "but why too hard?"

"Well, it would be too hard, because for us to work together under the circumstances—that is, with the problems of too easy—would very probably destroy our relationship, and that is too hard a burden for me to accept."

I did not like his decision, but I accepted it. He made it clear that he wanted to do something on his own, although he wasn't sure what it would be. He entered graduate school and investigated several fields, including medicine—he was fascinated by a premed course in neuromuscular physiology—but his choices finally narrowed down to politics and journalism. He studied political theory with Professor James Meisel for a time, then went to Fairbanks, Alaska, to work on the *Fairbanks News Miner* as sports editor.

The Alaska experience was salutary for Phil, because except for the one year at Harvard and sharing an apartment in Ann Arbor with Peter Dawson during his last two years at Michigan, he had never lived away from home. He enjoyed his work and the outdoor life in Fairbanks, but socially, he said, he might as well have been living on the moon. Sadye and I visited him during Christmas of 1961. In January 1962 he applied for a Marshall Scholarship to study at Oxford and won it. That May, my brother Frank and I drove up to Alaska in a van and brought Phil back home.

Going from Alaska to the intense intellectual environment at Oxford must have been a bit of a culture shock, but Phil seemed to thrive on it. He spent two years at University College, Oxford, reading P.P.E.—Politics, Philosophy, and Economics—and took a high second (he was viva'd for a first, the highest rank in honors examinations, and missed it). While at Oxford, he kept his hand in journalism by contributing occasional pieces to the *Chicago Daily News,* and he returned home looking for a newspaper position that would fit his goals. One of his goals was to enter politics, for Oxford had given him a keen appreciation of the public-service component of politics as a profession.

During the ten years I was a regent, of course, the day-to-day concerns of running UMI were steaming along on a parallel track. It was a period of great growth for the company, as I'll describe in the next chapter, but I could devote to it only two-thirds of the time I would normally have spent on business. The other third was given over to my duties as regent. This was a large investment, but I think that anyone who runs for regent should be prepared to give the post at least that much time and attention.

I like to think my efforts as regent made a difference for

the U of M and its student body. It is difficult to assess such things. But there is no question whatever about what my service to the university did for me. It was a tremendously enlarging experience personally.

Although I am not a scholar myself, I am committed to the idea of education as a solution to the problems that face our country. Education often makes the difference between one who can be effective in managing his or her own life and one who cannot.

Being on the board of regents was an ego bath in some respects. The board reviews important functions of the university, including financial (technically the board controls all the assets of the university), faculty hiring, and curriculum and admissions policies. Consequently, the community treats regents as wielders of great power and influence, and holding the office is a heady experience. I also found it intensely stimulating. Ours was a cohesive board; we all worked hard and respected each other's opinions. We got things done, and in what we did I experienced something that comes to a person all too infrequently in this life: a feeling of participating in an extremely important aspect of the evolution of our culture.

Chapter Eleven

Merger

P hil's decision to pursue journalism rather than follow me at the helm of UMI presented me with a rather disturbing question: what would happen to Sadye and my business if something happened to me?

Since I had plowed virtually everything back into the business, most of my estate was tied up in brick, mortar, and machines. Consequently, if I died, the inheritance taxes could leave Sadye in an extremely difficult situation.

I wasn't planning to step out of the picture any time soon. In fact, I had never felt healthier. At age 55, I was playing squash regularly with Warner Rice, and with Phil whenever he was at home. I also played water polo three days a week with The Flounders,[1] a game in which, as the *Ann Arbor News* declared in an article about our group, "only the fittest survive."

---

[1] The Flounders were formed in 1926 by my former swim coach and summer-camp employer Matt Mann, who had developed a roughhouse style of water polo a few years earlier, when he was with the Detroit Athletic Club. An informal history edited by Richard W. Bailey was printed by UMI to celebrate the group's fiftieth anniversary. It noted that "The only fixed rule is that a married man may not be held under water for more than five minutes," and "The remarkable feature is that members with such differences in skills of swimming, passing, team play, and wrestling can join in . . . and enjoy it so thoroughly." At this writing, I am eighty-four and continue to play regularly, although I am absent more often than in the past and have to wear flippers. The latter are allowed to be used by any player over age seventy.

However, my experience at UMI since 1954, the first year in which our revenues exceeded half a million dollars, had made me sensitive to the need for considering the tax consequences of any business strategy. We had an after-tax profit that year of $50,909.98. Revenues continued to grow each year; they reached nearly $600,000 in 1956. But our taxes grew even faster, and cut into our profits in an alarming fashion.

At the same time, our sales projections were climbing sharply. A big surge in sales was predicted for 1957—the result of my idea for producing single copies of bound books on demand—so it was imperative that we find some legal means of reducing the tax bite.

The solution Al Connable came up with was for Sadye and me to form a holding company, E & S Realty, Inc., to which ownership of the UMI buildings was transferred. E & S also owned 100 percent of the stock in UMI and Microfilms, Inc. This sort of approach was fairly common under the tax laws at the time. I paid rent to E & S Realty. This effectively reduced our personal taxable income, and E & S was able to invest some of its income in common stocks. The holding company could convert some of my assets to cash, perhaps through a public stock offering or by merging with another company, if that became necessary to make Sadye's future more secure financially.

Meanwhile, there were a lot of other things demanding attention, such as making certain our new book product—actual paper copies produced from microfilm—got launched properly. Ironically enough, considering later developments, the idea for producing books occurred to me while watching a Xerox Copyflo II machine in operation. I had followed the progress of this machine since it first went on the market in 1956. It would enlarge 35mm microfilm and print it electrostatically onto a paper web eleven inches wide at a speed of twenty feet per minute. Salesmen from Haloid Xerox, as the company was then called, had been trying for some time to sell me a Copyflo machine. But it was a big unit that cost seventy-two thousand dollars, and we had no work to justify such an expenditure. That picture changed, however, when one of our sales representatives, Fred Bertsch, learned that the Register of Deeds in Muskegon, Michigan had seven hundred rolls of negatives, each one hundred feet long, that he wanted enlarged and printed on paper. Fred proposed that we do the job with a Copyflo machine. His presentation of costs based on the time savings afforded by the machine was persuasive. The Haloid Xerox salesman was delighted, of course, at my request to rent one of his machines for a three-month trial.

I was impressed with the speed and quality of work done by the Copyflo machine, and one day while watching it disgorge its paper web of enlargements of the negatives of the Muskegon Register of Deeds, the thought flashed into my mind: "My gosh, we have thousands of negatives in our vaults—we could use this system to produce books!"

For a moment I stood transfixed, feeling the same sensation I experienced in that hotel room back in 1934, when I watched Ted Schellenberg project the images of his agricultural records and the idea for microfilm publishing had flashed into my mind full-blown. That original idea was completely fulfilled by this new concept. At last I could truly publish a single copy of a work "on demand" without compromise. I needed no market surveys to tell me it would sell. It was obvious, for example, there would be great demand for doctoral dissertations as bound books, which would be so much easier to use than microfilm.

By the end of that day I had worked out a system for handling the continuous web of paper, printed on one side, as it came out of the Copyflo machine, cutting and folding it into pages that could be trimmed and bound to make a book.[2] Our production people picked up on the idea immediately and the various parts of the operation fell into place like dominoes. It was not long before we owned two Copyflo machines and had a hand assembly line trimming and binding the books. We used sixteen-pound, acid-free paper, and this produced books that were limp and easy to hold open, yet strong enough to stand up to use in libraries.

I realized immediately that our new approach made it unnecessary to allow any book to go out of print. This thought opened a vision of a whole new field of service we could perform: helping publishers eliminate inventories of books for which demand was not great enough to justify conventional reprinting. Once again I headed for New York

---

[2] Our first approach to the problem of making a book from the long sheet of paper with pages printed side-by-side on only one side of the sheet was to cut from the roll two facing pages. These were then run through a folder, bringing them together, back to back, with the former center of the pages forming a hinged outer edge. This meant that when the book was collated, trimmed, and perfect-bound, it was like an early-printed, uncut book. Of course, the pages were not meant to be cut. This was not an entirely satisfactory approach, since all the left-hand pages in the original book became right-hand pages in our copies. We later devised a means of cutting individual pages and collating them so that all pages were right-hand pages, and this, though it added bulk to the final product, was much better.

City to sell my idea. I first went to Fred Melcher at R. R. Bowker Company, publisher of *Publishers Weekly,* just as I had in 1948 when I wanted to arrange for microfilming of periodicals. Melcher again gave me invaluable tips on whom to talk to—the people who made the decisions—at the various publishing houses.

The major publishers sold themselves on the idea without much work on my part. I contacted twelve of them on that trip, and all contracted to turn over to us their out-of-print books. We would list the titles in a catalog and sell copies one (or more) at a time for three and a half cents a page plus seventy cents for binding. The publisher would receive a royalty of 10 percent of our sale price.

Within two years UMI became the largest reprint publisher in the world. By 1968 the number of publishers under contract for our service had grown to 240, and our O-P Catalog listed 45,000 titles.

Meanwhile, our collection of early printed books on microfilm was expanded through the work of Donald Wing, a librarian at Yale, who extended the Pollard and Redgrave STC by cataloging "English Books 1641-1700." We arranged with Wing to eliminate duplications.

The service started what was dubbed by one enthusiastic reporter "The O-P Revolution," a movement lauded by no less an authority than Sir Frank Francis, director of the British Museum. "It was Mr. Eugene Power, president of University Microfilms of Ann Arbor, Michigan, who first grasped the enormous possibilities of applying the xerographic process to microfilm of books," Sir Frank wrote in the *Times Literary Supplement* in December 1958. "As a result of it, no book ever *need* go out of print."

Newsweek magazine wrote that UMI was "prepared to deliver copies of the first book printed in English, Caxton's *Recuyell of the Histories of Troy,* any one of the first folios of Shakespeare, the sermons of John Donne, *Dictas and Sayings of the Philosophers,* or a 1914 copy of *The Saturday Evening Post.*"

An unidentified writer noted that "almost always it would be cheaper and easier for the librarian to order a Xerox edition from University Microfilms than to find a copy of the book through secondhand book dealers."

Such commentary in the press was so effective in stimulating orders that I began thinking I should hire a public-relations firm to spread the word about UMI around the country. Don Thurber, who had replaced Paul Adams on the U of M board of regents, agreed to have his PR firm in Detroit represent UMI. His partner, Ray Chapman, contacted *Business Week* magazine in our behalf, and in due course they sent a writer and photographer out to interview me. The article appeared in the April 22, 1961 issue and began with this tongue-in-cheek paragraph:

> By conscious design or not, Eugene Power over the years has transformed the interior of his modern office building into a labyrinth of narrow passageways, winding stone staircases, monkish work cells, and dimly lighted vaults containing much of the world's great and not-so-great literature. The building resembles a modern version of a medieval monastery, but in actual fact it is the headquarters of a $1.2 million-a-year business.

It went on to describe the "treasures" contained in our vaults, "thousands of small spools of microfilm," and how, through the use of Xerox printers, we were bringing "printed-on-paper copies [of these treasures] well within the reach of the general public."

The writer noted that I felt I was engaged in a fight,

at some odds, to prevent the records of our civilization from deteriorating. It has long been known that the wood-pulp paper in general use since about 1870 doesn't have the lasting quality of rag paper.

Experts estimate that anything printed on wood-pulp paper is doomed to extinction within two hundred years. Already newspapers of only fifty years ago, stacked in University Microfilm's storage rooms, are so brittle they fall apart upon touch.

Many micro-reproduction companies have jumped into the breach, building on Power's pioneer work, and now there are many more 'copyists' than there were printers five centuries ago. . . .

The main emphasis of the story, though, was on our production of books. It described the Xerox process of "dry printing based on electrostatic rather than light-sensitive chemical principles. The copies . . . look more like printed documents than photostats," and noted that "University libraries have placed some big orders for Xerox copies. A few weeks ago, for example, University Microfilms turned out sixteen thousand pages of Wordsworth's original, handwritten manuscripts for Cornell University at a cost of five hundred and sixty dollars."

I was pleased with the article. Naturally enough though, it omitted some things I believed were unique about UMI and which contributed to our success, such as the employee cafeteria. We kept the cost low, charging only enough to cover the cost of the raw food. When we set out to hire a cook, the guidelines I gave Bob Holliday were that the person must be at least fifty years old and live on the West Side of Ann Arbor (the old German community). He found a Mrs. Charlotte Knoedler, who met those requirements and turned out to be an outstanding cook. The cafeteria was responsible, I am sure, for the high level of employee loyalty at UMI. I wanted to install a day-care center and a recreation center for employees, too, but subsequent events prevented those moves. At any rate, the *Business Week* story provided exactly the type of public reaction I had hoped for when I engaged Don Thurber's company. It also stimulated some overtures from other companies who wanted to buy us, which I had not anticipated.

The first of these calls came on April 26, 1961, only a few days after the article appeared, from a Mr. Adams at Itek Corporation, a publicly held communications company based in Boston. We had a long conversation about the possibility of my selling UMI. I noted in my diary that Adams said, "I believe Itek would be willing to pay you ten times earnings."

"That's very interesting," I replied, "but your corporation's stock is selling for about fifty times earnings, and I think our rate of growth is just as great as yours. There is also the consideration that our ratio of earnings to sales is better than Itek's."

"Well, of course, this is all very preliminary," he said. "We don't have any specific figures on your operations. We just want to start a dialogue here and come up with a mutually satisfactory offer. Obviously, you have done an outstanding

234

job and we would want you to stay on, perhaps as a senior adviser. You could continue doing the creative work you love but be free of the kind of daily pressure you now have."

I must say I found his comments about relief from some of the pressure I had been under somewhat appealing. There were days when I felt like Atlas supporting the world on his shoulders, as I am certain is true of any entrepreneur. But I gave him no particular encouragement, just some general figures, which he was to take back to Boston for review. He said he would get in touch with me again soon.

Another approach was from Leonard Glueck and Sam Freedman who owned Microphoto, Inc., a Cleveland-based competitor specializing in newspaper filming and some periodical work. An idea that occurred to me was that UMI should take over Microphoto on a stock-exchange basis and then take the combined company public.

Microphoto's 1961 sales would be somewhere around $600,000 compared to our $1.2 million, with about the same rate of profit. Len Glueck had reached the age when he no longer wished to work, and like me, his assets were tied up in brick and mortar.

There were some real advantages to such a deal. Sam Freedman was an able and competent executive who had been in the business a long time. He could be a good backstop for me. Representatives from Hayden, Stone, the New York brokers, talked to both of us and were eager to initiate a public offering if we were to buy Microphoto. They said we could bring Microphoto in as a division of UMI and offer about 20 percent of our stock at around twenty times earnings. After the stock adjusted itself and found its level in the market, I could sell more if I wanted to, up to 45 percent and still retain complete control of the corporation. The proposed basis of an agreement with Glueck and Freedman was one-third of UMI's stock in exchange for all of theirs. It seemed like a good thing, but I was uncertain whether I wanted to go through the difficulty and expense of a public offering and doubtful that I wanted to have outside stockholders.

Yet another company that expressed interest in merging with UMI was General Precision Corporation, whose courtship came about as a result of my interest in the development of teaching machines. Many educators viewed teaching machines as the wave of the future in their field. As an article in *Barron's* put it: "Major book companies have plunged into automated teaching on a big scale, making flash cards and devising various systems for programmed learning. Perhaps never before in the annals of finance have so many competitors jumped into an industry in which nobody at the moment is making any money."

I felt that if there was a future in teaching machines, UMI should have a stake in it, so I devoted considerable time during the spring of 1961 to studying the field and working out a system of our own using microfilm, of course, instead of flash cards. Early in May I traveled to Rochester to show our idea to Graflex Corporation. G. C. "Gee" Whitaker, the president of Graflex, invited me to sit in on a meeting with a representative from Link Trainers, who demonstrated a Link teaching machine. It was quite good, but its selling price was $600, which was too high to make it practical for use in high schools and colleges. I then presented our

236

proposal for use of a small viewer on a microfilm reader with questions and answers contained in quarter-inch frames on microfilm. A masking arrangement made it possible to program the questions and answers.

The Graflex executives were excited about our approach. Their consultant on programmed learning, a Professor Hall from Southern Illinois University, declared, "This is the first real, practical, down-to-earth teaching-machine program we have seen." Gee Whitaker agreed that Graflex would go ahead and design equipment to use the material which we would program and produce. I would approach publishers and try to work out an arrangement for putting their programs on microfilm. Gee also broached the possibility that General Precision, which owned Graflex, might acquire us in somewhat the same way Itek had suggested the previous week. The result of these various proposals was a summer of intense activity, meeting with bankers and brokers and with the various companies who were hoping to merge with UMI or acquire us. Such sessions were followed by considerable discussion with Sadye and Phil, since they were on the UMI board and we were dealing with their future as well as mine. Al Connable was a key person in these meetings and our planning, too.

Phil was getting ready to go up to Alaska to work on the Fairbanks paper, and Sadye and I were planning a trip that would begin with visiting Phil in Fairbanks at Christmastime, then going on to Japan, then to Saigon and Singapore to visit friends, going with them to Bali, Indonesia, and possibly the interior of Borneo. We discussed making it an around-the-world trip, going on to India and then heading

237

west. But Sadye was inclined to come back by way of Fairbanks so she could see Phil again, and I liked that idea, too.

Another project I got under way that summer was the organization of the nonprofit Microfilm Research Foundation. We had our first trustees' meeting [3] and decided that one of the first projects we should address was to establish a system to preserve deteriorating books, which meant most of the books printed since 1870. We drafted a proposal to the Council on Library Resources asking for funds to do a test of methodology for this project. My hope in establishing the MRF was that it could create a national microfilm library of the most important books published since 1870. The MRF would pay developing and storage costs and make the microfilm available free to member libraries. Unfortunately, we could never get the Council on Library Resources or other foundations to join in our efforts, and the idea and MRF died for lack of interest.[4]

[3] The trustees of the Microfilm Research Foundation were: Luther Evans, Keyes Metcalf, Curtis Benjamin, Ralph Ellsworth, Don Thurber, Vernon Tate, Stevens Rice, and Eugene Power.

[4] Preserving the knowledge in books printed since 1870 had become a subject of wide interest by 1989, when UMI instituted a program to preserve deteriorating books. Beginning in 1987, a steady stream of articles along the lines of the *New York Times Book Review*'s "Millions of Books Are Turning to Dust — Can They Be Saved?" appeared in printing trade magazines and scientific journals. A videotape, *Slow Fires*, documented the problem of deterioration caused by acid paper. In 1988, acccording to *Science* magazine (Vol. 240, pp. 598-600), the Library of Congress launched an experiment at Texas Alkyls, Inc., in Houston to "develop a reliable method for removing chemicals that are slowly eating away the printed knowledge of the world." *Science* quotes Tamara Swora, who helps direct microfilming at the Library of Congress, as saying, "We're only chipping away at the brittle book problem." She "notes that 11,000 volumes at the Library are photographed annually although an additional 77,000 start to disintigrate during the same period."

Back on the business front, Graflex came up with a good device for utilizing our teaching-machine idea. It used reflection optics and required no electricity. It would sell for about twenty dollars. We showed it to two publishers, Grolier and McGraw-Hill, both of whom wanted to buy world distribution rights to it. The sales projections they made would have increased UMI's film production by twenty-five million feet a year, which was exciting to me. This would mean we would have to add more staff and probably more space. We were already so busy and crowded that we had to put on a night shift of a dozen people.

In mid-September I made another trip to Rochester, this time to meet with Peter McColough of Xerox Corporation regarding our participation in the exhibit to be sponsored by the American Library Association at the World's Fair, The Century 21 Exposition, in Seattle the following year. I agreed that UMI would provide microfilm equipment to be photographed for the slide-show presentation Xerox was contributing to the exhibit, which was to be called "Libraries of the Future." In the course of our conversation I mentioned to Peter that I was going to Cleveland to talk to Len Glueck and Sam Freedman at Microphoto about our proposed merger. Peter was extremely interested, so I told him about Itek's offer also, and he said, "Before you do anything else, Gene, I wish you would talk to our president, Joe Wilson."

I had not met Wilson, though I knew his reputation as a dynamic and farsighted executive from reading the business press. Just a little more than a year earlier he had invaded the general-office copying-machine market, then dominated by

239

Mimeograph, Ditto, and Thermofax, with the astonishingly successful Xerox 914, a desk-size machine that would produce at the touch of a button seven dry copies per minute, on ordinary paper, anything printed, written, or drawn. The name *Xerox,* taken from the Greek for "dry writing," soon became part of the language of American business. In its first full year on the market, the Xerox 914 propelled Wilson's company's annual sales from $33 million to $61 million!

What many people did not know, but I had reason to find out after I met him, was that Wilson, who grew up in the family business of making photographic paper and photo-copying products, had taken an enormous risk in 1948. He literally mortgaged everything he owned in order to develop an electrophotographic process that had been invented in 1938 by a patent lawyer named Chester Carlson. The Battelle Memorial Institute of Columbus, Ohio had funded Carlson's research, and in 1947 Wilson bought commercial rights to the invention from Battelle. In negotiating this, Wilson had the assistance of his longtime friend Sol M. Linowitz, a brilliant young lawyer who had just left the Navy, where he had served on the staff of the Secretary of the Navy. Linowitz was beginning his civilian practice— prior to his Naval service he had been an assistant general counsel in the Office of Price Administration—but he was a cultivated man and a global thinker, president of the Rochester Institute of International Affairs and the Roches-ter Association for the United Nations. In addition, Linow-itz was an accomplished violinist and linguist; he paid his way through Hamilton College and Cornell Law School by playing in orchestras, and upon graduating *summa cum laude* from Hamilton in 1935, he delivered the salutatorian's address in Latin.

When Linowitz drafted the option for the Haloid Company to obtain the rights to the experimental process of electrophotography from Battelle, both he and Wilson considered it a "one-shot" deal. But the chemistry of their relationship was such that Linowitz played an increasingly important role in the management of the company. By the time Peter McColough introduced me to Wilson, Linowitz was chairman of the board.

I suspect that Linowitz had had a lot to do with changing the name of the dry-copying process from electrophotography to xerography, and probably with the 1961 change in the corporate name by lopping off the prefix *Haloid,* making it simply Xerox Corporation. In any event, Linowitz was the conscience of Xerox, and he had a great influence on Wilson. They would take long walks in the woods on Sundays and discuss the philosophy of business they wanted to instill in Xerox. This became significant to me because their philosophy paralleled mine. Their approach to such things as service, pricing, and personnel policies was identical to those I had developed at UMI.

Given this background, I suppose it was natural that Joe Wilson and I should hit it off immediately, as indeed we did. It turned out that he had read the *Business Week* article about me and UMI. In fact, unbeknown to me, he had ordered thirty thousand reprints of the piece and sent them out to prospective customers.

Joe understood what we were trying to do at UMI. Of all

the people with whom I had discussed the possibility of acquisition or merger—and Joe and I had not talked long before he brought up this subject—I think he had the most ready grasp of why I priced our work so low. Many of my business acquaintances thought UMI was some type of nonprofit organization, that we couldn't show a profit because we kept our rates comparable to the charges libraries made. We did profit, of course, because we were efficient and knew how to cut costs. Joe understood that—he followed my explanation of it by quoting one of my favorite mottoes, a Rotary Club slogan: "He profits most who serves the best." He also shared my view of executive responsibility toward employees. If employees fail to do a job, it is as much my fault as theirs, because I have not provided proper training instructions or have misjudged their ability or something. Another belief Joe and I shared was in the value of taking the long view and persevering in a service even though the return on it cannot be realized immediately. Joe told me that in the five years after he acquired the rights to the xerographic process he invested twice the amount of his company's profits in research and development annually before the Copyflo II was brought to market.

Joe said he would send Jim Wainger, who was in charge of development and acquisition for Xerox, to Ann Arbor to look over our operation. I agreed.

In the days that followed, I did a very thorough check on Joe Wilson and Sol Linowitz and Xerox Corporation. After all, if I merged with Xerox, I would be turning over control of a business I had spent my lifetime building. As I have indicated above, I was impressed with them.

Joe Wilson and I—kindred spirits—confer about our impending merger.

Having assured myself I was dealing with honorable men, I welcomed Jim Wainger and disclosed everything about UMI's business and finances. He went back to Rochester with a great quantity of information. I proceeded to conduct a study of Xerox stock as an investment by talking to a number of bankers. Al Connable and his associate Mike Hindert also did an evaluation of Xerox on my behalf.

Jim Wainger returned to Ann Arbor in late October with a few other questions. When I had answered them, he said

243

Xerox would like to acquire UMI on a stock-for-stock basis. In other words, they would take all the stock of E & S Realty, including the listed stock I had put into it as an investment, which amounted to about $250,000. I said it was an offer worth careful consideration and that I would be in touch with him about it soon.

All of my advisers and my own research indicated that Xerox was a sound investment. I talked to Wainger and told him we were ready to make a deal, but I did not know what the basis would be for striking an agreement, because Xerox stock was jumping all over the place, moving up or down three or four points every day. He said he thought I ought to talk to Joe Wilson about that.

I thought about it for a time. Then one day in the first week of November 1961, I telephoned Joe.

"You have seen our financial records and our plans, and I think you would agree that UMI's prospects are as good as those of Xerox," I said. "Therefore, it seems to me that, since your stock is selling at forty times earnings, ours should be worth an equal amount."

"Gene, that sounds reasonable to me," Joe replied.

Our attorneys began working out the legal arrangements on that basis. And I must say that at 40:1 the Xerox offer was very attractive. I was pleased with this result. So was Joe Wilson.

In view of the negotiations with Xerox, Sadye and I decided against making our planned trip to the Far East. But Ben and Madeline Gilbert had been entreating us to spend the month of January with them, cruising from Trinidad to the Virgin Islands on her Uncle David Rockefeller's yacht.

I talked this over with Joe Wilson and he saw no problem, as long as I was back in time for the signing of documents of sale to Xerox, which was scheduled for early February 1962. Accordingly, Sadye and I went to Fairbanks to spend Christmas with Phil as planned. It was mighty cold, but we wore the Eskimo clothing we had acquired on Baffin Island (see Chapter Eight) and were quite comfortable. We returned to Ann Arbor and left almost immediately for Port of Spain, Trinidad, where we joined the Gilberts, Ben's mother, and another couple, Red and Nancy Fairchild, who would be accompanying us.

The *Wayfarer* was a beautiful boat, I think the finest I have ever seen. She was a 95-foot, steel-hulled sloop with a 103-foot main mast and a crew of seven. She was outfitted with automatic pilot, ship-to-shore telephone, supplementary diesel power, and air-conditioning. There were four staterooms; the aft one, the owner's cabin, was luxurious. Our cabin, though small, was entirely satisfactory.

We stayed in Port of Spain the first day, simply enjoying the warm sun, lush vegetation, and brilliant colors of the island. I made copious notes in my journal concerning the truly excellent orchid collection of a Dr. Gillette. I was struck by the fact that all their Vanda orchids were planted in charcoal. I thought I would try that with mine when I got home. I also would have some pots made like those used by the Gillette horticulturist. They had slits and holes in the bottom, and I thought this would be a great help in getting adequate air to the roots. I also noted how they used mosses —tree fern is best for Cattleyas—and that Dendrobia like quite a lot of water. In fact I was struck by the frequency with which they watered all their orchids despite the humid climate.

The carefree days we spent sailing from island to island were absolutely idyllic. Red Fairchild was a good swimmer, and he and I did a great deal of snorkeling, skin diving, and some spear fishing. I took a lot of photographs, too—each port we visited had some unique and interesting vistas. We had dinners in some wonderful restaurants in these places, but none could top the cuisine offered by the boat's own French chef. My favorite times aboard were when we would go for a late-afternoon swim before dinner with a good wine. Then we would sit out in the cockpit afterward conversing and enjoying the wonderfully soft evening air as the sun set and the stars came out like a gigantic tray of jewels on black velvet.

Occasionally we would have visitors aboard or go ourselves to visit other boats. One was the *Harbinger,* which had come out of Antigua and anchored next to us at Tobago Cay. Its passengers included Thomas Hart Benton, the painter, and we had an interesting time chatting with him and listening to one of his friends, a lawyer from Kansas City, read the poetry of Edna St. Vincent Millay.

When we got to St. John in the Virgin Islands, we found the hotel alive with excitement about the presence of Princess Margaret and Lord Anthony Snowdon. We were invited to a formal dinner for them, and I felt rather sorry for her because I did not see a single change of expression on her face the entire evening. It was as if she were wearing a mask and simply enduring the dinner, which for her was probably just one of a succession of such events. Her job seemed to me monumentally dull and fatiguing.

Only once during the entire trip did business intrude: I got a call from Alan Stillwagon, whom I had hired four months earlier. It was some question I was able to answer with a phone call.

The only other communication from "the real world" was a most welcome one: a cablegram from Phil telling us that he had won a Marshall Scholarship to Oxford. Naturally, this called for a toast by our entire party.

Sadye and I flew home from St. Thomas on Monday, February 4, and I found that my attorneys, Roscoe Bonisteel and his son, Roscoe, Jr., and the legal staff of Xerox had completed all their work. They had an imposing pile of documents for me to sign, and I spent an entire half day doing nothing but writing my signature.

Having signed away my creation, I faced the future with ambivalent feelings. I was not sure how to act, now that I was no longer in control of UMI. The sense of loss could not be denied. At the same time, however, under the terms of our agreement, I was a member of the Xerox board of directors, which pleased me. I thought Joe Wilson's initiative in putting me on his board was very generous.

I probably should have felt wealthy, since I had just closed a deal that brought me more money than I had ever dreamed of having. But I did not feel any different.

Since the Xerox stock I acquired was unregistered, SEC rules prevented me from selling any of it for almost a year and a half. So I had no idea what was in store for me.

It is probably well that we cannot predict the future, for if

I had been able to foresee the period of conflict I was about to enter, I might have considered entering a monastery instead.

Chapter Twelve

Conflict

T here was little outward change at UMI after the sale to
Xerox. Our employees soon grew accustomed to the
new tagline on our signs and letterhead, "A Subsidiary of
Xerox Corporation," and it was back to business as usual.
The big difference was hard to see, because it was subjec-
tive, and primarily—at least initially—it affected only me.
It was the subtle but complete infusion of the immediate-
profit motive into all major decision making.

My practice when I owned UMI was that if I thought a
product would fill a need, profit would ultimately come
from it, and I would go ahead and develop it without
insisting on an immediate profit. Oddly enough, some of our
most satisfying and profitable ventures— dissertations, periodicals, out-of-print books, and series of early printed
books—were undertaken in precisely this way.

Now I began to experience the "paralysis from analysis"
that sometimes makes larger corporations bog down. A
proposed product had to be supported by all kinds of
projections indicating the profit it would make. Small
margins were not acceptable. If a product could not be
expected to show a very sizable profit in the first year, there
was no use discussing it, no matter how beneficial it might
be.

At my initial meeting with the Xerox staff, I was

somewhat taken aback at the reaction to my estimate that UMI's sales would be "three and a half million dollars" at the end of three years. That was not what they had expected. They thought I should be predicting sales of around $6 or $7 million.

However, although both Xerox and I had some adjusting to do, there was no real friction. Certainly not between Joe Wilson and me. We were able to keep things moving ahead satisfactorily through regular telephone conferences. My rapport with Joe made it easier for me to deal with the new obsession with the bottom line.

I did not enjoy the process of relinquishing control at UMI. However, I made good use of the time it afforded me by branching out into other ventures: radio broadcasting and the hotel business.

Sadye did not have much enthusiasm at first for my idea of going into radio. She thought it would be a dissipation of my energies in a field far removed from my real interests. Then she began to see it as a substitute for the ownership I had given up in the merger with Xerox.

Actually there was no single motive behind the idea. It had come to me over time, mostly through discussions with Jim Vinall, who had been doing an outstanding job as public-relations director for the Democratic party in the state of Michigan. Jim had helped Don Thurber and me in our tandem campaign for reelection as regents in 1963. He also had handled Neil Staebler's 1962 campaign for congressman- at-large. Neil won in a landslide; the party swept every office in the election except that of governor, where George Romney proved to be too tough an opponent.

CONFLICT

I was impressed by Jim Vinall. He had been a popular newscaster in Detroit and was director of the news department of WJR before the Democratic party hired him. He was very professional, and I admired his ideas about the potential of radio, both as a business and as a means of developing a more-informed public.

One day not long after our merger with Xerox, Jim came to see me and said he wanted to make a career switch and get out of the public-relations business. He was hoping to become manager of a radio station. I had a penchant for wanting to help young men get started in business, thinking that if a person has a good idea and strong desire, all he needs to succeed is some guidance, an opportunity, and sufficient capital. Subsequent experience has taught me that it is not quite that simple. But I thought Jim would be a winner, so I told him to look around and find a station we might buy together.

Jim contacted an old acquaintance of his, a radio-station broker from Texas named Landis, whom everyone called "Judge," and after looking over several facilities in different parts of the country, they settled on Station KVOR in Colorado Springs. KVOR-AM was a CBS affiliate along with KSPC-FM. It had once been a strong enterprise—its call letters stood for "Voice of the Rockies"—but it had lost a lot of business due to increased competition after World War II, and it was losing money.

I liked the situation of KVOR as Jim described it. I thought we had a chance to turn the business around and also make a difference in the cultural life of the community. With that goal in mind, Jim and I formed Wolverine Broadcasting

251

Company in September 1963 (Sadye and Phil were on the board with Mike Hindert and me) and we bought KVOR and KSPC for $250,000.

Jim moved his family to Colorado Springs. We had to go through the customary waiting period for FCC approvals, but once the license was transferred, we wasted no time launching our campaign to make the station profitable. It was an uphill battle. Sales were no more than $15,000 a month in the first few months, and we had to support a staff of twelve.

Our studios were in the Broadmoor Hotel, which added a touch of class, since the Broadmoor was arguably among the top-ten hostelries in the world. Later, as Jim's efforts in building public-spirited and sometimes controversial programming paid off in advertising revenues, we decided to build our own studios on land the station owned near its AM transmitter building. FM was beginning to become popular across the country at that time, and we began operating our FM facilities on a round-the-clock basis with programming separate from that of the AM station. Our sales increased to about $60,000 a month during the peak tourist season, yet we had difficulty showing a profit.

I realized, finally, that numbers did not mean as much to Jim as they did to me, and for this reason we would never quite see eye-to-eye in management terms. His business proposals were logical and persuasive, though, and he was extremely creative. A good example of his approach was an idea he had for setting up a separate corporation to sell a program he had worked out with a local computer firm to handle all the paperwork for any radio station, including the accounting, sales records, billing, and log maintenance. Jim knew little about computers and I knew less, but in blind confidence we plunged ahead and established Broadcasting Computer Services, Inc.

A number of stations bought the system, but it proved to be a constant drain on us. There was no limit to the changes and additions required to support the program, and each, of course, demanded further financing. We finally sold the unit to a computer-service company in Colorado Springs, which did quite well with it. So the idea was sound; we had simply plunged into it too early with too little knowledge of what it would take to make the service viable.

I was disappointed but not discouraged by the venture into radio. KVOR was a good investment despite the fact that I had to repeatedly give it infusions of cash in order to keep it going. When we sold it to Sunbelt Broadcasting of California in January 1979—fifteen years to the day after our purchase—I had approximately $400,000 invested in it and the sale price was $1.7 million. I gave Jim Vinall 25 percent of the capital gain for his efforts in building the station. He and his wife went into ranching in New Mexico. We hear from them from time to time, and they seem to be quite happy.

The experience with KVOR was the first of a two-part lesson I learned about the difficulties of managing a growing enterprise from a distance. I found that it is exceedingly hard for someone with my hands-on approach to make such an operation work. Part two of that lesson was my venture into the hotel business with the Park Place Motor Inn in Traverse City.

As I mentioned earlier, I did not pay much attention to the Park Place after Frank and I inherited our father's minority interest in it in 1954. I did not think it was worth much, and neither, apparently, did its management. The structure was allowed to run down until by 1960 it looked far older than its thirty years. In 1962, the management had to pay the price for years of treating its help shabbily by being saddled with a costly union contract. In 1963, the place was closed.

I thought it a great shame to see this good-sized, ten-story building standing vacant and forlorn right in the heart of my hometown. The problem was more than just an appearance of failure, because the hotel accounted for nearly 14 percent of the tax base of the whole downtown area. So its closing cast a pall on other businesses. The whole community seemed discouraged and going downhill.

Meanwhile, my newly acquired stock in Xerox had been on something of a roller coaster. Soon after the sale, it took a nosedive, gradually recovered, then rocketed upward. After that, it was split twice—five for one and three for one—so by the end of the eighteen months during which I was restricted from selling the stock, my financial position turned out to be far better than I had imagined.

Prudence suggested that I sell some of the Xerox stock to provide cash for investments. I decided to make gifts to the University of Michigan and my family. I also gave a total of three thousand shares to my full-time employees at UMI. Those who held onto them did very well indeed.

I don't believe any reasonable man can experience such a dramatic change in personal wealth without a concommitant change in attitude toward certain things. My attitude toward the Park Place certainly changed. I later said my decision to purchase it came in a moment of weakness, but that probably slights the effect of my shift in attitude. Now, instead of viewing the place as a cup half empty, as the old saw has it, I saw it as a cup half full—and I decided I would not allow it to continue to be a drag on the community. I offered to buy the assets of the old corporation, and the owners were delighted to get rid of their obligation. The sale was accomplished without a hitch. I paid $250,000 for the building, its contents, and surrounding real estate.

With Mike Hindert's help I structured a financial arrangement that was simple and straightforward: I was the sole owner of the hotel; the Park Place Motor Inn Corporation, which we formed with Sadye as one of the stockholders, rented all the facilities from me. The corporation was to operate the hotel and pay me an annual rent of 6 percent of my investment.

Now, of course, we faced the problem of how to get the place open and running again. Sadye was full of ideas, and together we planned a complete refurbishing. We hired a manager named Ralph Gillam, at the recommendation of the Michigan Hotel Association, and put him in charge of day-to-day supervision of reconstruction. We installed a new heating and air-conditioning system, new wall coverings in all the rooms, new carpeting, new furniture and bathroom fixtures. We redecorated most of the rooms with framed Eskimo prints.

We completely remodeled the lobby, changing its orientation from north to west, and built a new kitchen. We also built a swimming pool under a plastic dome, with a sauna and treatment rooms adjacent. But our most innovative addition was a convention building under a dome of Styrofoam, one hundred feet in diameter, that had been developed by Dow Chemical Company. I thought the dome was a good idea, but evidently not enough other people did, because Dow discontinued making the structures.

We gave our refurbished hotel its crowning glory by remodeling the tenth floor, which had been largely given over to elevator machinery and water tanks, transforming it into a restaurant, the Top of the Park, enclosed by glass on three sides. The room provided a superb view of the surrounding countryside and Grand Traverse Bay to the north.

Sadye and I were delighted with what we had wrought and could hardly wait to hold our grand opening in June 1965. It was a gratifying occasion. The Traverse City Chamber of Commerce gave a luncheon in our honor and presented us with a certificate attesting to the contribution we were making to the city's business renaissance. They were so anxious to have the hotel in operation that they would have agreed to virtually anything we requested at that point. I was too naive to take advantage of this and insist that they create a convention bureau within the chamber of commerce and hire a person to work full time at promoting the city. Such a development would have helped everyone, and probably would have lessened some of the problems we later experienced with the hotel. But the ancient adage, "Live and learn," never seems to go out of fashion.

One of our first business callers after the grand opening was a representative of the Restaurant and Barkeepers Union, who said that since we bought the building, we also bought his union's contract. I said the contract went with the old corporation, not the new owners, and the union responded by filing suit against us. We went to court, and the case was decided in our favor. This did not prevent the union from continuing an "informational picketing" in front of the hotel for the next two years. If anything could harden my heart against the union that did, and I filed a suit against them. They continued to attempt to organize our employees until, finally, I agreed to drop the suit if they would desist in their attempts to organize us for two years. Soon after that, they withdrew their pickets and we heard no more from unions from then on.

I favor the philosophy of organized labor and have been on the side of the workingman when employers were guilty of taking unfair advantage. I feel strongly, however, that good management, by which I mean management with enlightened personnel policies, can make unions unnecessary.

We encountered some notable cost overruns during the remodeling due to changes I made while the work was in progress. I expected that. What I had not expected were the losses which began after the success of our first summer of operation. Ralph Gillam believed the losses were due to the fact that we did not have enough guest rooms in proportion to the amount of public space we had. The public space included the dome, which was used for conventions and dinners as well as for productions by the Cherry County Playhouse, a summer stock company; the swimming pool; and two meeting rooms in the basement and one on the first floor. Sadye and I were reluctant to sink any more money into the place, but our other advisers agreed with the manager's thinking; besides, the sixty-room addition he proposed was really quite handsome. So we finally agreed and construction was started. Of course, I kept a closer eye on expenses while this work was going on; the final cost of the addition came to about $650,000.

The predicted change in our financial picture based on our sixty additional rooms did not happen. Instead, at the end of our first fiscal year in October 1966, we showed a loss of $275,000. I was baffled. The only remedy I could think of was to make a management change.

I went to the well-known executive-search firm of Hydrick & Struggles in Chicago, and they came up with a candidate, Theodore "Ted" Okerstrom, who impressed me immediately. He came from a hotel family in Big Bay, Wisconsin, and he had run hotels in Madison and other places. At that time, he was working as a consultant to hotel operators in various locations. My first impression of Ted was reinforced in subsequent discussions: he was clean-cut and solid looking, and had extensive experience in hotels. But I was determined not to allow some unfortunate and undetected quirk of character to emerge and trip us up after we had an agreement, so I asked Ted to submit to an examination by a psychiatrist. He assented, cheerfully, and was approved without reservation.

I was glad to get the change over with, but the departure of Gillam distressed me very much, because I dislike failure and I knew the failure was mostly on my part.

Ted Okerstrom took hold of the Park Place, and slowly but steadily improved the operation. He knew the value of being accepted into the community in an area like Traverse City

258

and he worked hard at it. He bought a house there and joined the Traverse City Chamber of Commerce and the Rotary Club. His efforts in promoting the area soon got him elected to the board of the Chamber of Commerce, which pleased me very much. The Park Place began getting more convention trade, and our facilities, particularly the rooftop restaurant, enjoyed increased popularity.

A few years later, a dude ranch along the Boardman River, owned by a man named Rudolph, came up for sale. It was unique, since dude ranches are not indigenous to northern Michigan; it had several Western-ranch-style buildings, including a bunkhouse and dining room, which were flanked by sixteen motel rooms. In addition, there were two trout ponds, all on two hundred and thirty acres.

Ted thought Ranch Rudolph would be a terrific satellite operation for the Park Place, and I guess he was right. In any event, I bought it for about $1,000 an acre, or $230,000. The only problem with the purchase, and this buttresses my point about the difficulty of running a business from a distance, is that we somehow neglected to be certain that the mineral rights were included in the contract. Consequently, when there was an oil and gas boom in the area a few years later and gas was discovered on the land, we did not benefit from it.

The hotel business is rich in everyday lessons about life. For one thing, it opened my eyes to the callousness people can display toward someone else's property. In particular it pained me to see the way our guests abused the furniture we had provided for their use and pleasure. And worse, we caught one guest going out the back door with one of our television sets under his arm.

Another thing the business taught me was what a fickle animal the public can be. No sooner did our hotel begin showing signs of health and vitality in what had been a rather depressed area than a Holiday Inn was built and some of our clientele immediately shifted allegiance to the lower rates offered by the chain operation.

Until the Holiday Inn came along, the Park Place was able to show a profit under Ted Okerstrom's direction, even with the cash drain of the rent it paid to me. The latter, at 6 percent of my investment, was substantial, since with what I had put into the various improvements and Ranch Rudolph, my investment came to almost $4 million . Competition from the Holiday Inn caused our occupancy rate to drop to about 68 percent, which is the ragged edge for any hotel operation. A few years later the competitive situation became even worse with the construction of a resort hotel in a development that generated a lot of controversy for a time because of its use of state and federal funds. That development is now called the Grand Traverse Resort Village.

Although the time I gave to developing Wolverine Broadcasting and the Park Place brought a certain measure of satisfaction, as had my service as regent, I missed the consuming involvement I had been accustomed to at UMI, which was becoming less and less the happy place I once knew.

M y position on the board of Xerox allowed me to protect UMI from some of the bureaucratic nonsense that was hatched in Rochester. But as the success of the 914 copier increased the administrative burden Joe Wilson was carrying, he was able to devote less time to me. Finally, he promoted Peter McColough to executive vice president and asked me to report to Peter.

Peter and I agreed that UMI needed more space, and that a campuslike environment in the countryside, which I favored, would be beneficial. Fortunately, I located a place that seemed exactly right, a twenty-five-acre plot on Zeeb Road. The property was on top of a deposit of gravel, so the drainage was excellent, and it contained an underground lake which would provide plenty of wash water (for film processing). I envisioned a swampy patch toward the front of the property being transformed into an attractive pond. After Xerox engineers looked it over and approved the site, the company financed the purchase, Alden Dow designed an attractive building for it, and we started construction in 1965.

This was when my conflict with the Xerox administrators began to fester. Joe Wilson moved up to chairman of the board of Xerox Corporation in 1966 when Sol Linowitz relinquished his post and put his thirty-five thousand shares of stock in trust to become ambassador to the Organization of American States. Peter McColough replaced Wilson as president. Peter asked me to report to Jack Rutledge, whose background was as a tough, hard-driving sales manager. My main disagreement with Rutledge was over his inconsiderate treatment of employees. For example, he made one sales representative move three times in one year; the individual was a married man who bought a new house and had to sell his previous one with each move.

Late in 1967, Peter McColough brought Archie R. McCardell in from Ford Motor Company and made him executive vice president of Xerox operations. I thought this was a major mistake. McCardell instituted an automobile-company approach that discarded the best parts of the Xerox philosophy that had been fostered by Wilson and Linowitz and replaced them with increased emphasis on short-term profits, and a Procrustean system of rules and reporting procedures.

About the time we were beginning to plan our move into the new building on Zeeb Road, Jack Rutledge told me he thought UMI's administrative staff needed to be bolstered and suggested that I bring in Jim Lundy as my second-in-command. I interviewed Lundy, who had been in Xerox headquarters in Rochester for several years and he seemed to be capable and likable. I asked him to take the job. Lundy had scarcely moved in when he began carrying out Rutledge's notion of "bolstering" by bringing in three more executives from Rochester: Bob Asleson as director of sales; Ernie Merlanti, director of personnel; and Joe Fitzsimmons, director of production.

I found this unsettling. I was not accustomed to delegating so much authority. My style was to immerse myself in our operations and keep in touch with everything that was going on. However, I knew we probably had grown too large for that approach now, and I was willing to go along with the Xerox directives.

Still, it came as a shock when Jack Rutledge told me he wanted Jim Lundy to take day-to-day responsibility for running UMI.

"Is that a suggestion or an order?" I asked.

"I am giving you a directive; I want Jim Lundy to be in charge," he said.

"OK, if that's what you want," I replied.

From then on, I developed projects that interested me and stood aside while Jim Lundy ran the day-to-day operations. When we moved into the new building, some of the ideas I had for beautifying the place were quietly shelved. There would be no flock of sheep to lend bucolic charm to the surrounding grounds and provide free fertilizer and mowing of the lawn; neither would there be trout stocked in our pond. The fact that some people in Rochester sniggered at such plans, referring to them as "Gene's folly," bothered me not in the slightest. What did rankle me, however, was the cancellation of plans to continue subsidizing operation of the cafeteria so employees would pay only the cost of the raw food. I considered our cafeteria a model of enlightened treatment of employees. As I mentioned earlier, I think it was the reason UMI had such strong loyalty among its workers, as evidenced by longevity records and by the fact that the employees emphatically rejected the only serious attempt a union ever made to organize our shop. Several employees even criticized the union representatives for asking them to vote on it. But our way of operating the cafeteria did not suit the style of the new management, and after several years it was abandoned. My fight against the union at The Park Place and my problems with the bureaucratic mentality of Xerox were nothing, however, compared with the ordeal I went through after being charged with conflict of interest in my role as regent of the University of Michigan.

O ne day in the fall of 1965, a U of M graduate student complained to the student newspaper, *The Michigan Daily,* that he was unable to obtain a book he had requested at the library because it was being photographed by UMI. This student worked part time at the library, and he supplied *The Daily* with photographs of cards indicating that books were loaned to UMI on a regular basis. He took pains to point out that University Regent Eugene Power was closely associated with UMI.

It happened that the editor of *The Daily* was a crusader for a residential college. He wrote editorials criticizing the university administration for not making a residential college a top priority in its planning. Somehow he got wind of the fact that I intended to make a gift of a million dollars to the university for a theater, and he wrote an editorial denouncing such a gift. He asserted that a theater would be a frivolous use of money, which would be better spent on a library for a residential college. In fact, I *had* considered donating a library to a residential college. But it seemed to me that the legislature might appropriate money for such a library, whereas it was unlikely to do so for a theater. It was unfortunate that the gift was attributed to me, because Sadye and I wanted to make it anonymously.

When the article appeared, Harlan thought it was a "tempest in a teapot" that would soon die down. But *The Daily* did not drop its attack. It simply shifted its focus directly onto me. My name had surfaced in the graduate student's complaint to the paper, and a reporter was assigned to interview Librarian Frederick Wagman for a possible conflict-of-interest story about me.

CONFLICT

Wagman, who had been with the Library of Congress before he came to Michigan and was a former president of the American Library Association, explained that libraries customarily allowed books to be photographed without charge, and that he would extend the courtesy to any of UMI's competitors. He also pointed out that he himself had invited UMI to install a camera on university premises for the convenience of the library.

On Saturday, October 23, 1965, *The Daily* printed a news story that presented innocent facts about UMI's dealings with the university as if they were high crimes. For example, the dissertations of University of Michigan Ph.D. candidates were filmed by the University, the negatives were stored by us, and included free of charge in *Dissertation Abstracts*. However, for some reason the agreement each doctoral candidate signed with the library—a document I had not known existed—stated: ". . . the negative [or microfilm] being kept on file at the University of Michigan Library where positive film copies [from the negative] will be made on request at the announced rates." Obviously, this was a mistake, but *The Daily* story presented it as if it were a deliberate misrepresentation.

The implication that we were somehow doing something underhanded made me boiling mad, because when I became a regent we had stopped charging the U of M for our services. Whatever the university wanted that we produced—English books, periodicals, dissertations—was given to them. This amounted to between $50,000 and $75,000 worth of free publication each year.

Doctoral candidates from other institutions paid UMI a

flat fee of $20 to have their dissertation published in *Dissertation Abstracts*. This was quite different from the arrangement with U of M doctoral candidates, who paid the university a publishing fee of $75. UMI received nothing from them or from the university. We stored the negatives and printed the abstracts. Our only income on the U of M dissertations came when someone not connected with the university selected a title from the abstract and ordered a copy of the dissertation, whereupon we made a copy from the negative and sold it.

What was downright mean, though, was an editorial that accompanied the article. It was titled, "Power— Regent, Businessman: A Conflict of Interest?" and fastened on the fact that we identified the U of M material in our catalog as the "University of Michigan Shelflist." It accused me of lying, stating "It is unbelievable that Power can be a regent for ten years and yet be unaware that university consent must be obtained to use the university's name. . . ." It quoted an unnamed "university official" as saying, "Power thinks that all his gifts make him lily-white and gives him the right to do anything he wants."

From then on *The Daily* ran a story almost every day about my alleged conflict of interest. One of the paper's reporters followed up on the rumor about the gift of $1 million in stock that Sadye and I had made for a theater at the university. He contacted the Securities and Exchange Commission and found out how many shares of Xerox stock I had received from the sale of UMI. Then he did some speculative calculations, concluding that I must have somehow made a lot of money off the university. A group of students from *The Daily* went so far as to invade my office, demanding to know how much money I had made from the sale of UMI. I was angry and told them it was none of their business. However, they could have obtained the information easily from *The Wall Street Journal.*

Despite my anger, I considered the situation to be so much fuss and feathers. Student newspapers stir up controversy— that is normal and to be expected. Earlier in my service as a regent I had defended the editorial autonomy of *The Michigan Daily* when it came under attack from conservative factions in the university administration. Some of my friends were more upset about the paper's charges than I was. I told them not to worry — opinions from two different state attorneys general had confirmed that there was no conflict of interest on my part, and my attitude was that the whole thing would blow over.

At the time *The Daily* launched its attacks, Sadye and I were preparing to leave for Japan to attend the inaugural meeting of the International Micrographic Congress, of which I was president. We deliberated about cancelling our trip but decided that to do so would dignify the paper's rantings and risk insulting our Japanese hosts.

We had an excellent trip. I was impressed with the vitality of the Japanese people and noted in my diary that "Perhaps more than any other country I have known outside our own, the expression which Emerson used to describe England in the 1850s could be applied to Japan: 'Their pulse is like a cannon.'" The meeting of the IMC went well. I stepped down as president and became a vice president for a two-year term, in part to provide continuity. Vernon Tate expressed his concern to me privately that the IMC would move in and take over the role of the National Microfilm Association and displace it. I did my best to persuade him that this would not happen, that the roles of the two organizations were different, and that he had no cause for concern. I think I was successful.

At the conclusion of the meetings, Sadye and I left Japan and went to Hong Kong, then to Bangkok, on to Tel Aviv by way of Bombay and Teheran, then to Vienna, and finally to England, where we took a flight back to the United States on December 5.

Back in Ann Arbor, I met with Harlan Hatcher, who showed me a report from a lawyer named Thomas Long, a senior partner in a prestigious firm in Detroit. At Harlan's request, Long had investigated the allegations made by *The Michigan Daily* and concluded there was no basis for any finding of a conflict of interest. Long stated that in his opinion I was "absolutely innocent." I was relieved.

However, *The Daily,* for reasons I have never been able to fathom, took the matter to a state representative from Detroit named Jack Faxon, chairman of the House subcommittee on higher education. Faxon was quoted as saying, "The dollar amounts are insignificant: the question is whether the law has been violated." He asked the new attorney general, a Democrat named Frank Kelly, to investigate and make a ruling.

As it happened, the legislature had just passed a new conflict-of-interest statute that had not been tested or interpreted by the courts. Kelly did not really investigate the

CONFLICT

situation. I was interviewed by his office for about twenty minutes, and it was clear that he would interpret the new law very strictly, which meant that any dealings I had with the university outside my duties as regent would automatically be considered a conflict. The fact that my use of the library was one that was available to any citizen as part of normal library operations was not considered. I was frustrated by the attorney general's complete lack of understanding of, and consideration for, the facts of how libraries work. Meanwhile, the press ran headlines about the situation every day, which was most unpleasant. One discovery they made was that UMI had mistakenly billed the university $43.10, and the university had inadvertently paid it. Normally, as I have indicated, we did not bill the university. But that fact and the amount of services we gave to the university each year cut no ice.

When Attorney General Kelly's opinion came out, it stated that a "completely unintentional but substantial conflict of interest existed" in regard to my role as a regent and UMI's business relationship with the university. I promptly resigned as a regent.

It was a regrettable conclusion to a sorry sequence of events (see Appendix E). Looking back on it now, however, I think that if I had stayed on as a regent, I probably would have been defeated in the Republican surge of 1972. (During my tenure on the board, its composition had changed from all Republican to six Democrats and two Republicans.) In any case, those who opposed me could never take away what I learned from my ten years of service. The experience increased my personal capacity as an adminis-

269

trator and public speaker and gave me firsthand knowledge about higher education that I shall never cease to consider invaluable.

Chapter Thirteen

Caxton

While I was in the midst of the tempest that led to my resignation as regent, a scholarly storm that was quite unrelated, but which soon would involve me, was developing in England. It stemmed from the discovery of part of the historic Caxton Manuscript and its subsequent sale at auction, on June 27, 1966, for 90,000 pounds ($252,000) to L. D. Feldman, representing the New York book dealer, El Dieff.

The discovery comprised the first nine volumes of Caxton's translation of Ovid's *Metamorphoses,* which had been missing for three hundred years. News of the find was, of course, tremendously exciting to English scholars. Ralph Bennett, a tutor at Magdalene College, Cambridge, was particularly interested, because the rest of Caxton's translation, the last six volumes of the work, was owned by his college, having been purchased by Samuel Pepys, probably at a sale in 1688, and left to Magdalene by Pepys with the rest of his library.

William Caxton was England's first printer and publisher (see Appendix F), and it is believed that his translation of *Metamorphoses*—from a French version, not direct from the Latin— was finished in 1480. Bennett and other scholars conjecture that Caxton never intended to publish the book commercially, that he planned instead to prepare a single, handsome, manuscript copy for presentation to a noble patron. However, what actually happened to it is murky. Two or three Tudor owners wrote their names on some of the manuscript pages. Then someone hacked the volume into two parts. The last 208 pages were what Pepys purchased. The first 272 pages disappeared without a trace. Nothing more was heard about the missing pages until 1964, when it became evident that they had been acquired sometime about 1870 by an eccentric London bibliophile named Sir Thomas Phillipps.

Sir Thomas was a busy if not particularly discriminating collector of all kinds of manuscripts. He was obsessive in his gathering: he would stop carters in the street and buy their entire wagonload of papers, most of which usually consisted of scraps and waste. Nonetheless, he would crate it all up and store it away. After he died, Sotheby's began sorting out his collection and auctioning the manuscripts, many of which were beautiful and valuable. These sales continued until the 1950s. The last three cases of Phillipps' papers were purchased as a lot, unopened, by Robinson Brothers, rare book dealers in London. When the cases were opened by Lionel and Philip Robinson, most of their contents were found to be worthless. In sorting through the stuff, sheet by sheet, however, a single page of Caxton was discovered, then another and another, until all 272 of the missing leaves were assembled.

Ralph Bennett was approached by several of his peers who suggested that Magdalene ought to buy the Phillipps part of the manuscript in order to reunite the two and forestall the rumored purchase by an American university.

A noble idea, but Magdalene had little money, and its administrators felt that the usual contributors were tapped out. They had been approached too often with requests for endowments and new buildings.

Instead, when the sale was announced, Magdalene enlisted the help of the British Museum and the Cambridge University Library in an attempt to keep the manuscript in England. In September 1966, their cause was advanced when T. C. Skeat, Keeper of the Department of Manuscripts at the British Museum, persuaded the government's Reviewing Committee on the Export of Works of Art to refuse an export license for the manuscript for three months. If the three institutions were able to match Mr. Feldman's bid within that time, they could claim priority as British subjects and the manuscript would stay in England.

But raising ninety thousand pounds was such an awesome task that the three institutions could not seem to agree on how to begin. Two months elapsed without action. Finally, with only three weeks left before the December 6 deadline and not a penny yet pledged, the Magdalene group[1] decided to launch their own last-ditch appeal. They enlisted the vice-chancellors of Oxford and Cambridge and several medieval scholars to sign a letter to the *Times* of London announcing an emergency fund drive. The letter was delivered to the paper on November 12.

"Unfortunately, public interest in the floods in Florence was just then at its height," Bennett recalled in an article he

---

[1] The Magdalene group consisted of Ralph Bennett, medieval historian; the late Jack Bennett (no relation), a Magdalene Professor of Medieval and Renaissance English; and the late Dr. Richard Ladborough, University Lecturer in French.

later wrote for the *Magdalene College Magazine and Record*. "The letter was not published in full, but only summarized in a corner of the sports page."

The disheartened scholars felt their cause was lost. But a glimmer of hope came in a call to Ralph Bennett from a Magdalene graduate named Henry Bailey-King, who owned a printing firm in London. Mr. Bailey-King had seen the truncated report and offered to print and distribute at his own expense a leaflet about the appeal. Several thousand of these leaflets went out, one of them to the editor of *The Times Literary Supplement,* who called Magdalene to ask for an article describing the Caxton Manuscript. This piece appeared in TLS on November 24 and gave what Bennett said was "the first authoritative—if still only preliminary— account of the importance of the discovery." The next issue of TLS, on December 1, carried a letter of comment on the article from the late Allan Stevenson, an American authority on Caxton's paper and watermarks, who was doing research at the British Museum.

At this point, coincidence stepped in to play a melodramatic role in this scholarly story. George Braziller, a New York publisher who had just brought out a successful facsimile edition of the *Hours of Catherine of Cleves,* was flying to England on business on December 4. He had brought along the *Times Literary Supplement* to read on the flight, and he saw Stevenson's letter. Visions of a facsimile edition of Caxton danced in Braziller's head. He thought of using part of the income from sale of the facsimile to pay the purchase price of the manuscript for Magdalene. Upon landing in London, Braziller contacted Stevenson, who was enthusiastic about the concept, and they then made a phone call to Magdalene. Bennett recalled that "the idea—it must be admitted—seemed to us thoroughly crazy in the light of the bare outline which we had been given on the telephone." But the two Americans went to Magdalene and "Before they left, our views had quite changed; Mr. Braziller had persuaded us that his plan was feasible in itself and that we ought to try it even though we had so little time."

In light of this new ray of hope, the scholars petitioned the reviewing committee for an extension of the deadline. Bennett says, "The committee took the unprecedented step of granting an extra month. We were grateful for this, but the Christmas holiday would reduce its practical value."

On December 13, Braziller held a press conference in London to announce his plan and painted a vivid picture of "a small Cambridge college fighting the battle of David against the American Goliath." Response was encouraging, but in the end raised only twenty thousand pounds. "In spite of all efforts," Bennett continues, ". . . there was still seventy thousand pounds to find in six days. Mr. Braziller had returned to America, promising to find someone to lend the balance until the edition could be put on sale."

A few days before Christmas 1966, the telephone rang in my office at UMI in Ann Arbor. "A Mr. George Braziller from New York for you," said my secretary, Mabel Peterson. I listened to Braziller's account of the Caxton situation and promised to contact him before the start of the New Year.

Obviously, Braziller was a terrific salesman. He had

touched my convictions concerning the sanctity of early manuscripts and my natural impulse to wish to see such a unique work reunited after three centuries; of course, the English context of the situation appealed to the Anglophile in me as well. There was also an element of drama in the need for immediate action and the fact that Braziller had approached other Americans, including Joe Wilson of Xerox, without success.

But, of course, I was not going to agree to anything without first checking on Braziller and investigating his story. I called my old friend Sir Frank Francis, director of the British Museum, who assured me that the facts were as Braziller represented them. He suggested I call Ralph Bennett, which I did, and he convinced me of the urgency of his college's need.

I decided to lend the seventy thousand pounds to Magdalene, and with Mike Hindert, my attorney and financial adviser from the Connable Office in Kalamazoo, I engaged in a marathon series of communications with London. It was a prickly situation since the value of the pound had been fluctuating rapidly and the manuscript, which was my collateral, was not in my possession. Mike Hindert solved the problem by taking out currency insurance; in other words, he insured the value of the pound sterling. When all the i's were dotted and all the t's crossed, Sir Frank and Ralph Bennett were named custodians of the Caxton Manuscript, which was to be kept in the British Museum—available only for the purpose of photographing it for the facsimile edition—until my loan was repaid.

Then, only twelve hours before the expiration of the reviewing committee's extended export embargo, I had the money cabled to London, and the Caxton Manuscript was saved for England.

S ince early 1965, Sadye and I had been traveling to Europe on the average of once every three months; I was keeping an eye on the progress of a monastic manuscript-filming contract that I will describe in the next chapter. There also was a need to visit Florence and investigate how UMI's microfilming capabilities might be used there to help salvage flood-damaged materials. We usually went to London first on these trips anyhow and, in view of my loan to Magdalene College, it behooved us to pay a visit there as soon as possible. Consequently, we departed for London on February 11, 1967.

The importance of my contribution to keeping the Caxton Manuscript apparently had not impressed itself on me as much as it had on British journalists. They awakened Sadye and me with telephone calls to our hotel room and hounded us with all kinds of questions. Their articles and cartoons left no room for doubt that I was a celebrity, at least for the moment.

At the British Museum, I gazed at last upon the Caxton Manuscript. Wrapped in paper, bound in tape, with a lead seal to ensure against tampering or substitution, it made a rather small and insignificant-looking package on the library table. I thought, "One would never guess that this item could have created such an uproar or be worth damn near a quarter of a million dollars." (In fact, it was the most expensive manuscript ever sold, with the exception of the

"In many ways I'd prefer them to take our manuscripts and leave us our scientists."

Codex Sinaiticus, for which the Russian government received one hundred thousand pounds.)[2] Then the keeper of manuscripts, Mr. Skeat, opened the wrapping and revealed a beautiful binding of recent vintage containing the manuscript, whose text was in bold, clear Gothic script on rag paper. It was lovely. There were fingerprints on the margins

[2] The 1968 *Guinness Book of World Records* (pp. 144-145) states: "The highest price ever paid for any manuscript is L-100,000 ($280,000), paid in December 1933, by the British Museum, London, to the U.S.S.R. Government for the manuscript bible *Codex Sinaiticus* originally from the Monastery of St. Catherine on Mt. Sinai, Egypt. . . . The highest auction price ever paid for any manuscript or book is L-90,000 ($252,000) for the illustrated incunabula of books 1 to 9 of the translation in 15 parts by William Caxton (c. 1422-1491) of the *Metamorphoses* ("Transfigurations") by Publius Ovidius Naso (43 BC-18 AD), the Roman poet known as Ovid. . . ."

of a few pages, one page was torn, and one illustration had been scratched by something sharp, but apart from these minor scars, it was in perfect condition. Caxton had planned to begin each of the fifteen books with an illustration and provided space for them, but only four of the illustrations had been drawn and colored. The text was complete, however, and the ink was very black and fresh-looking, although parts were more brownish than black, perhaps indicating places where the scribe changed ink bottles. A few lines of the manuscript are thought to be in Caxton's own hand. The rest probably was written by a scribe trained in the Netherlands. The similarity of the handwriting was one thing that proved the Phillipps part to be, indeed, identical to the Magdalene manuscript.

Ralph Bennett, whom Sir Frank Francis introduced to Sadye and me on our arrival at the museum, was an affable gentleman who made his gratitude obvious in an understated way.

Magdalene was having a dinner in my honor, which was for men only, since Magdalene was a men's college. I did not like the fact that Sadye could not attend, and I was surprised when Bennett told me it would be a black-tie affair. I had not thought to pack a tuxedo. I managed to rent one from Moss Brothers in London, but the only shirt they had in my neck size was far too small across the chest. This was a problem, since I do not wear an undershirt: every time I moved, the shirt would gap, giving others a quick flash of skin. An English friend of mine lent me a cummerbund, which helped some, but I think perhaps my hosts at High Table went away with the impression that my mannerisms were rather stiff. High Table, incidentally, is actually on a platform raised above the level of the rest of the dining hall. The students came in, had their dinner, and departed so quietly I was scarcely aware of their presence.

I was charmed by Cambridge, with its mellow old stone and brick buildings. After we returned to the States, following our visits to Florence and Vienna, I received word that Magdalene had elected me an Honorary Fellow of the college. The Master explained that the duties of an Honorary Fellow are none, and the privileges few. About the only privilege I have exercised, though strictly in a symbolic way, is the right to walk on the grass.

George Braziller proceeded according to plan on his facsimile edition of the Caxton Manuscript. He arranged to send the Phillipps part of the manuscript to Zurich to have color separations made by Schwitter, Ltd. That firm then traveled to Cambridge in July 1967 to do similar work on the Magdalene part in the Pepys Library. This trip was necessary because Pepys had been very explicit in his will, stating that the entire collection had to be kept under specific conditions and no item could be removed from Magdalene; if one was, the whole collection would go to Trinity College, Cambridge.

The facsimile was printed by Jarrolds of Norwich in a numbered edition of 1,200. I was supposed to receive Number 1, but what I received was Number 2, with the explanation that "Number 1 had to be given to the Queen." Braziller decided to print that many to enable him to sell them for $308 each. He was criticized for taking this

approach by John Carter, past president of the Bibliographi-
cal Society and a director of the influential periodical *The
Book Collector.* Carter and "some other hardened judges"
recommended half the number of copies, or less, at a
commensurately higher price.

As it turned out, Carter was correct in his estimate that
there was a worldwide market for only about six hundred
copies. Of course, whether those six hundred purchasers
would have paid $600 apiece is not known. We were left
with a considerable inventory of the facsimile, and
Magdalene was still $30,000 short of its goal. In the end, the
Power Foundation took the remaining copies as credit for
the balance of the loan and made charitable gifts of them to
libraries around the world that did not have a copy.

The important thing in my opinion was that this manuscript, recovered from limbo after three centuries, was made
whole and retained in an appropriate place in England.

Mr. L. D. Feldman, whose hopes of acquiring the Caxton
Manuscript were dashed by my intervention, was a perfect
gentleman about it, despite being cast as somewhat a villain
by the press in his "American Goliath" role. This picture of
him was one to which, John Carter wrote, "special color was
of course added by the many knowing persons who assume
(often quite inaccurately) that anything Mr. Feldman buys
is going to Texas, which is bibliophilically (if quite unrea-
sonably) the most unpopular State in the Union."[3] Anything
less than praise to Feldman for his actions would be unseemly. Not only did he recognize the appropriateness of

[3] *The Book Collector,* Spring 1971, p. 13.

reuniting the two parts of the manuscript, he even went to Cambridge and offered the authorities of Magdalene an extension of the official deadline for raising the necessary money. A Sotheby's official said Feldman "behaved throughout with commendable modesty, forbearance, and kindness." And as John Carter put it, "It must have been a bitter disappointment, and [Magdalene] did well to raise its hat to a good loser."

During my next visit to Cambridge I had an idea that has made my relationship there, especially to Magdalene, much more than symbolic. I thought it would be interesting if an exchange scholarship could be arranged with a graduate of Magdalene coming to study at the University of Michigan for two years and one of our graduates going over there at the same time. The idea arose, I am sure, as a result of Phil's Marshall Scholarship and his enthusiasm about his experience at Oxford. His development there made me realize the enormous value of studying under the tutorial system. Of course, although I did not study in England, I certainly had learned a great deal from my extended visits there. I suggested the idea at lunch at Magdalene one day in 1967, explaining that our newly established family foundation was willing to finance the scholarship. The response was extremely positive, and we immediately set about working out the details.

We decided to base selection of Power Scholars on ability alone, the characteristics judged being scholastic ability, leadership qualities, and physical vigor as exhibited by participation in athletics. The first pair of scholarships was awarded in 1968.

No limits are placed on the type of specialization to be pursued, as long as it is within the universities' curricula. It can be related to the scholar's major as an undergraduate or an entirely different field. Most American scholars in the program's twenty-two years of operation have chosen to take a second undergraduate degree, feeling that experience of the tutorial method of teaching at Cambridge would be most beneficial. American students at Cambridge usually take a B.A. degree. British students who come to the University of Michigan are expected to earn a master's degree.

Since Magdalene was a men's college, the Power Scholarships were at first open only to men. I came in for a lot of pressure on this point from Sadye; she knew, of course, that my own views were against discrimination on the basis of sex. Therefore, in 1978, we made an arrangement with New Hall, Cambridge, and female Power Scholars can go there. In 1988, Magdelene did away with its tradition of 500 years and opened its doors to women.

The only problem—apart from the difficulty the universities have in making final selections, which can be extremely agonizing— has been the rising cost of education. At present, the scholarship provides one round-trip fare between the United Kingdom and the United States, tuition and related fees, room and board, and an allowance for books and modest personal expenses. In addition, there is a limited allowance for vacation travel. I have been reluctant to cut back on the travel allowance, however, because I feel that travel consitutes a very important part of the individual's overall education abroad.

283

It has been extremely gratifying to see young men and women grow during their two-year scholarships. In 1988 we published our second report on all the Power Scholars over the years, in which they recount their experiences while in the program and tell about their current activities. They are pursuing a wide variety of careers, and all seem to be making their mark. Moreover, it is clear from the associations they have kept up that the scholarship is a lasting benefit.

I hope that the value of the Power Scholarships will be recognized by other Americans who can sponsor similar programs. Humanity's need for leaders of superior intellect and education continues to grow, and members of our business community can help insure that we develop such leaders by supporting arrangements for overseas study.

It has been suggested that, in the eyes of some corporate boards of directors, the high investment in educational resources required for effective educational philanthropy might act as a deterrent to such involvement. In that case, it might be possible to minimize those costs through a program of cooperative recruitment and screening of scholarship candidates.

Our colleges and universities are developing outstanding scholars. I believe it is up to individuals and corporations to provide the opportunity for educational enrichment that will help these young men and women achieve their full potential.

Chapter Fourteen

Travels

I have always agreed with the timeworn observation that the pleasure of travel is greater in retrospect than in the present, at the instant it is being experienced. I keep extensive journals and photographic records of my trips, and recollecting the experiences and emotions of a journey in tranquillity—even many years later— is wonderfully fulfilling. This probably owes something to the fact that my travels almost always had some business mission woven into them. As a writer once observed of me: "No purpose is ever solitary for Power. His interest in microfilm multiplies at the periphery of all activities, creating side projects. If he sees a library in an oasis, he parks his camel."

Travel is best with companions. Sadye and I often had someone else accompany us on our excursions abroad. Frank was a frequent and enjoyable companion, and he could always prescribe a cure for complaints, physical or otherwise. Phil traveled with us a great deal, of course, and he never failed to add zest to a trip.

On our trip around the world in 1955, when Phil was sixteen, for example, he remarked to us after a long flight on which he was seated next to Perle Mesta, the famous hostess to Washington, D.C. society, "I really enjoy traveling with you. I meet such interesting people; we discuss all kinds of fascinating things. But when they ask, 'And what do you

285

do?' I tell them I just finished my junior year in high school, and that ends our conversation."

Phil also gave us a few moments of parental anxiety. When we were visiting Moscow in August 1960 to attend an international convention of Orientalists, the Russians were suspicious of foreigners and there was a preoccupation with talk about the secret police and spying. Our family name created some apprehension because of the similarity to that of Francis Gary Powers, captured pilot of the U-2 reconnaissance plane the Russians had shot down two months earlier, ending President Eisenhower's hopes for a summit conference with Premier Khrushchev. Phil met a former U of M classmate, also American, who claimed that he and his Polish friend were being followed everywhere they went in Russia. That night Phil went off on a walk with them to see what was going on. I thought this was taking his newspaperman's tradition too seriously. In fact, we learned later, Phil was followed by Russian soldiers who stopped him and searched his bag.

Phil was frequently helpful to me on our trips because he spoke French and some German. After 1962, when he went to Oxford, Phil would often join us somewhere in the world to share part of a trip. We became an extremely cosmopolitan family.

I f we weren't able to arrange companionship, though, Sadye and I did not hesitate to go by ourselves. Our pattern of traveling to Europe about once every three months was one that developed, curiously enough, as a result of a visit I had from a Benedictine monk named Father

Oliver Kapsner, who belonged to the monastery at St. John's University in Collegeville, Minnesota. Father Oliver wanted UMI to film some manuscripts dated prior to 1600 that were held by monasteries in Austria. Why Austria? Because, he explained, many monasteries there had not been closed during the Reformation, as had those in Germany, France, and England. Therefore their libraries were intact, whereas those in France had seen most of their manuscripts sent to the Bibliothèque Nationale, those in Germany had given up most of their holdings to the state libraries, and those in England had seen their manuscripts packed off to the British Museum and dispersed among various private holders.

Such a project was a little outside UMI's general scope of operation. Most of our activities involved making multiple copies over time for a number of users. In this case, there would be little market for multiple copies. A manuscript is generally studied by only one person at a time, and a single copy is sufficient. On the other hand, the project was in line with our mission of using microfilm to bring to the United States materials that would otherwise be unavailable to scholars worldwide. It also would provide a means of preserving these valuable manuscripts, as we had done with manuscripts in England during World War II.

There was virtually no financial risk, because the project was to be funded by various organizations that supported St. John's. There was, however, a considerable potential obstacle in the fact that out of twenty-eight monasteries on Father Oliver's list, only one, Kremsmünster, had given him permission to photograph its manuscripts. The others had rejected many similar requests by other people in the past.

287

But Father Oliver was optimistic. He felt that as a fellow Benedictine monk, he would be able to persuade them.

Sadye and I arranged to depart from Washington, D.C., where I would join her, since I had to go to Rochester on business first. Sadye would drive down from Ann Arbor with Phil, who was living in the capital at this time, working as an administrative assistant to Congressman Paul H. Todd, Jr., from Kalamazoo. I had scheduled a meeting in Washington with Oliver Wendell Holmes, a relative of the famous Supreme Court justice and director of the Commission for the Publication of National Documents. I wanted to tell him about UMI's plan for publication of the Webster papers (which was later completed), but nothing much was accomplished. I found Holmes to be a dull sort of person who was extremely difficult to engage in conversation. The negative tone of that session was dispelled, however, by a marvelous cocktail party with people from the State Department and the Chinese and Thai embassies. Phil enjoyed it, too, and afterward we went out to a club with Mennen and Nancy Williams. The next day, Sadye and I got a royal sendoff in Pan American's Clipper Club at the Washington airport, courtesy of a public-affairs executive from Xerox.

Paris impressed me as being more civilized and hospitable this time than in the past. It also seemed busier and much more prosperous. I made a note that "The people are well clothed and well fed. They evidently have plenty of money judging by the price of merchandise in the stores. The prices are fully equal to those in New York."

Vienna was a distinct contrast to Paris. Everything about the city looked drab. However, my mission there was not to see the sights but to meet Father Oliver and make a preliminary survey of the local monasteries to determine what arrangements would be necessary to photograph their manuscripts. Our first call was on Klosterneuberg, just outside Vienna, which had approximately twelve hundred manuscripts. The director, Dr. Floridus Rohrig, was cordial and helpful. I explained that we would treat the manuscripts with great care and be certain they were not damaged. We also promised to present the monastery with a positive copy of its manuscripts, along with a microfilm reading machine. Dr. Rohrig brightened on hearing this. He agreed to let us do the filming and said he would provide us with work space. In looking over the manuscripts, however, I could foresee a number of difficulties that would have to be overcome, the principal one being that some of the books in which they were bound were large—eighteen inches high and as much as five inches thick—and very stiff. This would make them hard to position properly before the camera. I estimated that in this one monastery there were three hundred thousand pages to be filmed, which at a production rate of a thousand pages a day would take nearly a year. We next visited a monastery in the center of Vienna called Schottenstift, where we found conditions similar to those at Klosterneuberg.

Father Oliver wore an "I told you so" look. I was pleased, too, but I am afraid I did not display my enthusiasm as openly as he, because I was coming down with a touch of the flu. Sadye had it, too, and we stayed in bed for a day, dining only on milk toast and poached eggs. I took this opportunity to draft an outline of what it would take to do the manuscript

289

filming (see Appendix G) including the hiring and training of operators and purchase of equipment.

The next day, I called on the Vienna offices of Kodak, Ltd. and made arrangements for them to process our film of the manuscripts. I also paid a courtesy call on Rank-Xerox, which was under the direction of Dr. Kurt Rischka. Then Father Oliver and I went over my outline. He agreed to the procedure I proposed, including setting up a joint bank account and the purchase of a Volkswagen mini-van to be used by our operators. The following day we rented a car and drove to Stift Kremsmünster, about two hundred kilometers west of Vienna.

We were greeted by Dr. P. Wilibrod Neumüller, a big, burly monk who proved to be one of the most extroverted, engaging, and friendly men I ever met. He ushered us into his library, which was magnificent. In addition to its manuscript collection, it had a tremendous collection of early printed books, from about 1480 to 1800. I was impressed.

After visiting a few other monasteries, Sadye and I returned to the United States by way of London, where I met with Sir Frank Francis, who gave me a tour of reconstructed areas of the British Museum. I wanted to find out from him whether UMI could continue to get negatives from the British Museum if University Microfilms, Ltd. were to go out of business, which at that time seemed likely. Sir Frank assured me there would be no problem.

A couple of months later, we returned to Vienna and once again met Father Oliver. We had brought along two Kodak Microfile cameras, a model D and a model E, which we managed to get through customs without paying duty, because they were on loan and would be taken out again. We then met our two-man crew, Paul Steger and Hans Berger, whom we had hired with the help of the American embassy. Our Volkswagen van had been delivered, and we planned to drive out to Stift Kremsmünster and begin setting up shop. However, Father Oliver tried to discourage Sadye from going along.

"After all, this is a monastery," he told her. "You can't get inside, because women aren't allowed, and there isn't much to do in the village. So I suggest you stay here in Vienna." But Sadye wanted to come, so of course she did.

Father Wilibrod was not at the monastery when we arrived in a cold March rain. He was traveling to visit another library and was not expected back until the following morning. So after unloading the equipment and leaving Father Oliver, Paul, and Hans, who would be staying in the monastery, Sadye and I drove down to the village to find a Gasthaus for the night. In the village, I spotted Father Wilibrod walking up the street toward the monastery. I stopped the van and hailed him, and he came over and wrapped me in a mighty bear hug. He accompanied us to the Gasthaus, "to see that you get a good room." While we were getting settled, I asked, "Father Wilibrod, would you be interested in a little bourbon?" "Well," he answered, "I might have just a little for medicinal purposes." A little later he said, "I must be in worse shape than I thought; I need another treatment." The three of us were enjoying a lively conversation when Father Wilibrod pulled out his watch and eyed it. "Well, since I don't have to be back to the monastery officially until tomorrow morning, I think we

291

should have dinner together," he said.

He took us to a small restaurant tucked into the outer wall of the monastery. When we were seated, he announced that we must have some wine before dinner. We had a two-liter bottle of Austrian white wine, which I thought was OK since it is quite low in alcohol content. We had two liters more with our meal, and afterwards, two liters more. As we were drinking this third bottle, Father Wilibrod began relating some of the history of the monastery. "Only one woman has ever been allowed inside Kremsmünster," he said with an apologetic nod to Sadye. "She was the queen of the Belgians, and she was allowed to do so because she was a king!"

"Sadye is a king for me," I declared. After that Father Wilibrod addressed Sadye as "Mrs. King."

We had a little more wine as he continued his account of Kremsmunster's long history. Suddenly he paused and said, "Come, follow me!"

Jumping to his feet, Father Wilibrod led us into the night. His robes flapped in the damp wind as we marched through the medieval gates of the monastery and across the worn cobblestones of the inner court. Stopping at a low, heavy wooden door set into the wall, he stooped to open it with a large key. Inside, a narrow stone staircase led upward. We followed the wavering beacon of Father Wilibrod's flashlight up three musty, winding flights. Pausing at the top and putting a finger to his lips, he whispered, "They're all asleep in their cells." Then he proceeded to show us through the entire monastery. It was eerie but fascinating.

Back in our room in the Gasthaus at midnight, "Mrs. King" said she thought it had been one of the most unusual evenings of her life. I could not but agree.

The filming in Kremsmünster was successful; our crew did its work so quietly and so well that the other Austrian monasteries were easily persuaded to cooperate, and we moved to each in turn. I had to check the progress of the work periodically, so Sadye and I would travel to Vienna every three months, which was most enjoyable. We usually stayed at the Hotel Bristol, ate boiled beef and the famed Viennese Sachertorte, and listened to the city's endless succession of operatic and chamber-music peformances. We came to know Vienna pretty well and felt sorry about the ravages it suffered under the armies of occupation after World War II. The Russian soldiers were the worst. We were told they were so ignorant they thought faucets somehow made water. They pried all the faucets off the bathroom walls in the Hotel Imperial and sent them home, thinking they would have running water in their own houses when they returned.

UMI received five cents per exposure for the manuscript filming, and this enabled us to show a reasonable profit on the venture. Our efforts were given a marvelous, unexpected boost when a new administrator of the Staatsbibliothek in Vienna granted our request, which previously had been denied, to photograph manuscripts held by that library. We discovered more manuscripts there than in all the monasteries combined. The library photographer, Dr. Christl Pernold, was extremely competent. She helped facilitate our work, which took two full years. These films were incorporated into the St. John's project. At Father Oliver's suggestion, St. John's established a Monastic Manuscript

Microfilm Library, which was financed by the Hill Foundation, the Bush Foundation, and others. It is directed by Julian Plante, and it now has a collection of medieval manuscripts on microfilm that I believe is unequalled anywhere in the United States, if not the world. When we finished filming in Austria, the cameras went on to monasteries in Spain and Malta. We even did some work in Ethiopia, financed by a grant from the National Endowment for the Humanities, but the political upheavals in that country prevented any sustained effort.

While the enjoyment of foreign sights is ephemeral, part of the passing moment, the benefit of travel in the form of association with new and interesting people can last two lifetimes—yours and theirs.

I have many memories of people I have met in my travels with Sadye—enough to fill a separate book, I suppose. Here, in no particular order, are some vignettes of a few of these meetings over the years:

The Mysterious Russian. Once when Sadye and I were in London, after I had become rather well known there as a result of saving the Caxton Manuscript, we received a series of calls from a complete stranger who called himself Dr. Freibourg. He talked excitedly about books and his own exploits; he said he was a Russian expatriate, a concert violinist, an author, and all manner of things. Sadye was wary. She thought he was probably crazy. I was suspicious, too. Nevertheless, I agreed to meet him at the American Club, and found him to be charming. He was then eighty-two years old, though he certainly did not look or act it. He was a most amusing conversationalist. He showed me his book, an account in Russian of the atrocities of the Cheka, the security police or "Extraordinary Commission," which conducted the government's campaign of "Red Terror" during the early part of the Revolution, and I agreed to photograph it and make copies for him. We had lunch a few times after that, and his claim to be the best Russian cook in London was probably the only lie he told me.

The President. Our meeting with Lyndon Johnson in the Presidential retreat at Camp David, Maryland came about as the result of a broken dinner engagement.

Phil was pretty much tied down in Washington, D.C. by his work for Congressman Todd during 1965 and '66, so Sadye and I went there to visit him whenever an opportunity arose. One day I had arranged for the three of us to have dinner with my old friend Bob McNamara, who had been a member of our Economic Dinner Group in Ann Arbor.[1] He had just become president of Ford Motor Company in 1960, when President Kennedy appointed him Secretary of De-

---

[1] The University of Michigan faculty had two or three dinner clubs when I became a regent. I felt that I should belong to one, but they were academic, and I did not consider myself qualified. One day at lunch, Professors Paul McCracken and Russell Stevenson, the dean of the business school, and I discussed the value of a club in which leaders of business and industry would meet with members of the University of Michigan faculty and share views. I took the lead in organizing the Economic Dinner Group. At first we met at the homes of members, but that became a burden on the wives. When Bob Fleming became president of the U of M, he suggested we have our meetings at Inglis House, which had been given to the university for such uses. Robert S. McNamara is still a member and attends meetings whenever he is in Ann Arbor.

fense. On the day we were to have dinner, Sadye had an apologetic call from Bob saying that President Johnson had asked him on the spur of the moment to go up to Camp David for a meeting that evening. She told him that was understandable and I said I thought he should try to please his boss. A few minutes later, Bob called back to say the President had asked him to bring us along. So within a matter of hours, we all left by helicopter from the White House lawn with Bob and David Brinkley, the television commentator.

President Johnson was very cordial, very gracious. In no time at all, he had his arm around Sadye's waist as we walked through the woods, talking as if he had known us for years. I liked him. He was "old shoe." For example, a rabbit ran across the path, right in front of his beagles, Him and Her. They paid no attention and Mr. Johnson scolded them with mock severity for unbeaglelike behavior. Then he picked Him up by his ears and unceremoniously dropped him on top of the bush the rabbit was under. We all laughed as Him looked dumbfounded after the fleeing cottontail.

At dinner, Mr. Johnson was engaging, and he and Phil had a discussion about some piece of legislation that Phil clearly knew a great deal about. The President remarked to me as we were leaving the table, "That's a very bright young man you have there." A week later, he asked Phil to join his staff. Phil declined, saying he had a commitment to Congressman Todd, and I was glad he did, because Johnson was hard on his staff. They tended to burn out quickly.

One other thing sticks in my mind about that evening at Camp David: chairs were arranged before a screen and Mr.

Johnson announced, "We're gonna have a movie now. I'll
be asleep five minutes after it starts, and I hope you won't
be offended if I snore." Sure enough, shortly after the lights
dimmed and the film started, he was sound asleep.

The Press Lord. In 1949, while on a visit to London, I
had a call from Robert Maxwell, who asked me to come see
him in his office. At that time, Maxwell was viewed with
suspicion by many British businessmen and others. This
was due, in part, to his mysterious background during World
War II. After fleeing his native Czechoslovakia at age
fifteen, changing his name from Jan Ludwig Hoch, and
serving in the French Resistance, he joined the British
Army and changed his identity once again, to Ian Robert
Maxwell. After the war, he was put in charge of Berlin's
postwar democratic press by the British Army Control
Commission and, according to *The New York Times*, he took
a special interest in reviving Germany's academic-journal
business. He later acquired some of these journals as the
cornerstone of Pergamon Press, which became a leading
publisher of scientific and technical journals.

My British friends regarded Maxwell as a bumptious,
overly aggressive outsider. They nicknamed him "The
Bouncing Czech," and I soon found out why.

"So you own University Microfilms?" Maxwell asked
me.

"Yes, I do," I replied.

"I want to buy it from you."

"It's not for sale."

"What are your annual sales?"

"Adequate."

"What are your profits?"

"Sufficient."

That was the end of the conversation.

Maxwell went on to expand his communications empire, adding among many other publications, the British tabloids the *Daily Mirror* and the *Daily News*.

In 1987, after an abortive attempt to buy out Harcourt Brace Jovanovich for $2 billion, Maxwell finally seemed about to get his wish to acquire UMI, which by that time had become part of Bell & Howell. Fortunately, a group of Bell & Howell executives were able to band together and transact a leveraged buyout to keep the company out of the press lord's clutches.

The Foreign Correspondent. Bill Stoneman was a U of M graduate who gained quite a reputation for his coverage of combat during World War II for the *Chicago Daily News*. His wife, Ingrid, had been secretary to Trygve Lie, the first secretary-general of the United Nations, and they were an extremely interesting couple. They lived in London and were friends of Phil, who introduced them to Sadye and me. I shall never forget one evening we spent at the Stonemans' home with Sir Humphrey Trevelyan and his wife. Sir Humphrey had been ambassador to Egypt and Russia as well as chargé d'affaires in Peking for the British government, and our conversation was lively and informative. One point on which we agreed was that the United States and Russia would one day be forced to get together on a friendly and peaceful basis. In the light of events of 1989, that long-ago forecast seems rather perspicacious. We visited the Stonemans nearly every time we were in England, as we did Arthur and Phyllis Cain and, later, Ralph and Daphne Bennett.

The Sculptor. On one of our trips to London, we were joined by Phil, who had just come back from Istanbul, and we arranged to visit Henry Moore in the little village of Muchhaddan, where he lived in a sixteenth-century house. The home was decorated with models of sculptures he had done in the past, as well as African, Marian, and pre-Columbian figures.

Moore was older than I expected him to be from photographs I had seen, but he was energetic. Phil remarked later, "He uses words like chisels."

Moore took us to his workshop at the rear of his property and showed us two colossal iron rings which people would be able to walk through. He explained that he often made three versions of the same piece: a small one, a medium-size one (about one-third scale), and the large (final) one. I was intrigued by his figures and also by his method of working in plaster, which he said allowed him to add to something, cut away, and add again until he achieved just the shape he was seeking.

I raised the question of whether he might like to do a sculpture for the theater we were planning for the U of M. He looked at the renderings I had brought along and was interested in them. He said he would think about it, and I agreed to contact him again, but somehow that never happened.

EDITION OF ONE

Phil's recollections of our travels are interesting, and while I don't agree with his assessment of my personal motivations, I think his tape-recorded observations might give the reader a more rounded view:

My father loved to travel. It provided him with an opportunity for adventure, to express his personality in a hostile environment, and to overcome difficult situations.

I have one dominant recollection that brings to symbolic relief my father's approach to travel, which was that you pack into it as much as you possibly can—do it to the fullest. This made for a rather frenzied approach, as exemplified by this incident, which took place on our trip to Europe in 1952:

Father had bought a car and the idea was that he would put my mother and me on a boat in Le Havre and he would stay in Europe to conduct some further business. We got off to a late start that morning and my father figured he'd make up for that with his characteristic style of driving. We moved through the French countryside at a high rate of speed until we got to a river. The ferry had just left and there was no bridge. There was a lengthy pause while father phoned. Then the ferry came back and got us. Once across the river, we tore off at even greater speed and went through the streets of Le Havre with the horn blowing steadily and my father asking mystified Frenchmen rather crossly, in English, where the pier for the boat was. After three or four wrong turns, we finally screeched to a stop at the pier just as the gangway was being hoisted. Through sheer force of personality, waving and shouting, my father caused the gangway to be lowered and my mother and I got onto the boat and left.

You see, my father believes that when mischances occur on a trip, it is a function of the ineptitude of the environment and the foreign cultures, and in no way due to deficiencies in planning. My father hates to plan. The reason he hates to plan is because if you plan, you are then locked in by the plan. And because one purpose of the trip is to express your will on things, being locked

300

in by a plan is totally unacceptable.

On our trip around the world in 1955, we flew from California to Hawaii to Japan in stratocruisers, big planes that had berths. My father, of course, had booked berths. He always went first class. In Hawaii we had to go surfing. We surfed for an entire day, with the result that my father and I were badly sunburned. By the time we got to Tokyo, things were in a moderately alarming state. The bedspreads in the Imperial Hotel were of some artificial fabric that made severely sunburned skin feel as if thousands of fire ants were walking all over you. My father prescribed bourbon.

(Now you have to understand that mother carried a train case when she traveled, and in it were enough medical supplies to stock a serious pharmacy. Father would diagnose one's illness and prescribe. He did this during a later part of our trip for Perle Mesta, the Washington hostess; he was beginning to get exercised by her failure to follow his suggestions until mother said, "I think what Miss Mesta is trying to tell you, Gene, is that she is a Christian Scientist and doesn't like to take drugs." Father said, "Oh," and that was that.)

Anyhow, he prescribed bourbon—soaked into a washcloth and rubbed onto our skin. This produced a huge acceleration in the pain, but then anesthetized the skin for a while. Following the bourbon rub, we took some other medicines, antihistimines as I recall, from mother's pharmacy.

That night we were to have dinner with Mr. and Mrs. Otto LaPorte, who owned a beautiful Frank Lloyd Wright-style home with wide, natural redwood siding, next door to my parents' house in Ann Arbor. Mr. LaPorte was a scientific attaché to Japan. He was an extraordinary man, a theoretical physicist who was fluent in six languages, including Japanese and Chinese. It was a lovely dinner and we were enjoying it despite the jet lag, the sunburn, and all the medication we had taken. In the midst of the meal, Father said, "Otto, isn't it wonderful that the people who rented your house have painted it?" The LaPortes were aghast. Father paused, then added, "It's a lovely apple green." Then he shook his head dazedly and said, "What am I saying?"

He had fallen asleep sitting there, you see, and dreamed about the house being painted. Of course we all had a good laugh about that, and no one enjoyed the merriment at Father's expense more than he himself.

Late in October 1966, a prodigious storm struck Italy, causing widespread flooding and many deaths. Untold millions of dollars in damage was done to art treasures and books in Florence. American art scholars and technicians organized the Committee to Rescue Italian Art (CRIA), which raised money for that purpose throughout the United States. As was mentioned in the last chapter, news of the flooding eclipsed Magdalene College's fund-raising efforts to save the Caxton Manuscript. So there was a hint of irony in the fact that following my first visit to Magdalene in February 1967, I was heading for Florence to investigate how our equipment could be used most effectively there.

Sadye and I flew from Vienna to Milan on February 20 and went on by train to Florence, which had the atmosphere of a city devastated by war. There were no tourists, and the principal hotels were not yet reopened, although most of the mud had been cleared from the streets. We visited galleries and churches and libraries to see the way they were attempting to dry out walls by raising the temperature in the interiors of the buildings with large kerosene space heaters. In places such as the Pitti Palace and Santa Croce Cathedral we watched artists from CRIA working to preserve ancient frescoes that were in danger of crumbling because the plas-

302

ter on which they were painted was soaked.

I met Millard Meiss, a professor of fine arts and authority on frescoes from Princeton University, who was directing the CRIA operations in Florence. He arranged for one of his American associates, Eve Borsook, to serve as my interpreter. Eve and I hit it off immediately. She had lived in Florence for about fifteen years and had written two guidebooks to the city, which are still in use. Eve is also an authority on frescoes (she had been a disciple of Professor Meiss, but she broke with him after the flood over his project for removing Florentine frescoes in order to ship them to the U.S. for exhibition. She opposed the removal because it was so risky; the process involves covering the artwork with cheesecloth, which is then soaked with animal glue and, taking courage in hand, the workers grip the material at both ends and give a mighty yank. If they are lucky, the entire top layer of plaster containing the fresco comes away intact). I later arranged for Eve to give a series of lectures at the University of Michigan, and Sadye and I have stayed in touch with her. She comes back to the U.S. every year at Christmas to visit her invalid mother in California.

Professor Meiss introduced me to Dr. Emanuele Casamassima, director of the national library, the Biblioteca Nazionale. Dr. Casamassima showed me the marks on the walls of the library where the water had reached a depth of twelve feet, even though the building was four feet above road level. He was concerned about restoring the institution's collection of Italian newspapers, which had been inundated. The papers had been retrieved from the mud and oil in the basement (the flood had washed oil from residen-

303

tial heating-system storage tanks). The bindings had been hosed off and the papers they contained were removed and taken to a tobacco-drying facility in the area, where the single pages were hung to dry on racks like tobacco leaves. Then they were placed in plastic bags and stacked on the floor of the library, which completely immobilized the facility. I suggested that we place microfilm cameras in the library and send someone over from UMI to train operators to use them. Dr. Casamassima was delighted. Having the complete collection in microfilm form would preserve it and also open a large amount of storage space. I told him it would be foolish to restore and rebind newspapers printed since 1870 anyhow, since they would have extremely limited life expectancy at best.

Sadye and I visited Professor Meiss and his wife at the Villa I Tatti, a magnificent sixteenth-century structure that was willed to Harvard University with an endowment of about $1.7 million by Bernard Berenson.[2] The villa is administered by Harvard as a center for cultural studies. At that time it was under the direction of Professor Meiss, who later was succeeded by Myron Gilmore. On our subsequent trips to Florence, we stayed in this remarkable place, which was like living in an art gallery. The villa also has seventy-five acres of farmland on which nine families live.

When we returned to the United States, I persuaded Joe Wilson to have Xerox Corporation donate $50,000 to

[2] Bernard Berenson was an authority on Italian Renaissance art and author of several books, including *Aesthetics and History, Drawings of the Florentine Painters* and *The Italian Painters of the Renaissance*. Born in Vilna, Lithuania in 1865, he was raised in Boston and educated at Harvard. Though he remained an American citizen, he lived in Italy most of his life. He died in 1959.

purchase the equipment necessary to set up a complete microfilm laboratory in the Biblioteca Nazionale with five cameras, processors, a positive printer, and reading machines, which would be given to CRIA as a long-term loan to the library.

Dr. Casamassima assigned us several rooms to use for the photography, and Mary Lou Morrison went over from UMI in Ann Arbor to help get the newspaper-filming operation started. She did an outstanding job of training the staff. It was a massive project; there were 120 million pages to be put on microfilm, and I reckoned it would take the library six or seven years.

Unfortunately, Dr. Casamassima was transferred, and his replacement was less interested. The project seemed to lose momentum and, as far as I know, it was never completed.

Another project in Italy that *was* finished in good order was a complete set of government telegrams and various dispatches of Baron Sonnino, Secretary of the Italian Foreign Service during World War I, which Professor William Langer, the famous diplomatic historian from Harvard, said was "the most important discovery of manuscript material for historical research since World War II." The papers were found in four big wooden chests under a wine press in the home of the Sonnino family in Florence. There was some urgency about getting them photographed, because it was feared that the Italian government would confiscate them. I went to inspect them in April 1968. Sadye and I were accompanied on this trip by Mike Hindert. Mike is a loyal friend in addition to being an astute legal and financial adviser, but I think my driving on this trip brought him close to terminating our relationship.

In Paris I had rented a Mercedes 250 like the ones that had passed me so handily on the autobahn in Germany the previous year. The Mercedes handled beautifully and I enjoyed it. Mike did not.

E. M. "Mike" Hindert

He was disturbed by my French style of driving, which means taking advantage of every passing opportunity and accelerating sharply to get around.

I ignored his protestations at first, thinking he would get used to it. But when we reached Geneva he declared he was going the rest of the way to Florence by train. I was sorry. I really had not meant to alarm him. I promised to drive at a sedate pace thereafter and, much to my relief, he assented. We saw a lot more scenery I suppose, since we poked along behind big trucks for most of the rest of the trip, at a rate which Mike called *touring*.

Mary Lou Morrison came over again to set up our operation for filming the Sonnino papers, which presented some unusual challenges in that they were on four different colors of onionskin paper. For example, outgoing dispatches were typed in purple ink on peach-colored paper, and incoming telegrams were typed in purple ink on white

306

paper; some reports were on blue paper and others were handwritten on white paper. We had to experiment with various filters and exposures in order to get good images. Thanks to Mary Lou's efforts, we were able to film the papers without interference and make this unique collection available to scholars around the world.

This trip to Italy in 1968 occurred during a period of great turmoil back in the States. One feels isolated and somewhat insecure at such times.

On April 1, the day we left Paris for Florence, we learned that President Johnson had announced that he would not run for reelection that fall. His political career was brought down by intense criticism of his conduct of the Vietnam War. Students were demonstrating against him on campuses across the country, and there was an unsettling general atmosphere of rebellion. I was keenly interested in these events, not only as a result of my affinity for university life in general, but because I was active as a member of the board of Carleton College, a private school in Minnesota that had recruited me after my resignation as a regent of the University of Michigan. I felt sorry for Lyndon Johnson. He was in a no-win position between the doves and the hawks. I was proud of the fact that earlier that year he had appointed me to a six-year term on the Council of the National Endowment for the Humanities.

On April 5, my diary contains the following entry from Villa I Tatti : "We were greeted this morning with the news that Martin Luther King had been assassinated and all of us felt a great sense of foreboding as to the future and what the summer holds. . . ."

We certainly did not miss our share of the unrest. We returned home on April 19. On June 5, Senator Robert F. Kennedy was assassinated. The Democratic National Convention in Chicago that summer was accompanied by rioting in the streets.

In reflecting on our travels, I should add that not all of them were connected with UMI. Some of them also resulted from Sadye's interest in Planned Parenthood. She became involved with this movement back in the thirties as part of her interest as a counselor for students. Later, in the course of our travels abroad, we saw the price that some countries pay in human misery for allowing their populations to outgrow food supplies and economic opportunities. I echoed Sadye's interest in Planned Parenthood, of course, but I had strong opinions on the subject myself. I believed that unwanted pregnancies can lead to tragedy and that while no one likes the thought of abortion, it is a necessary last resort. In the early days, such topics were not considered suitable for discussion in public, and I admired Sadye and her associates for their courage in doing so.

In 1963 Sadye was named to the board of our local Planned Parenthood affiliate[3] and from 1969 to 1975 she served as a director of the national organization. During the latter period we helped organize Family Planning Medical Services. At the outset, FPMS was to be affiliated with the U of M. It would offer all kinds of clinical services specifi-

---

[3] The Washtenaw County League of Planned Parenthood, now Planned Parenthood of Mid-Michigan.

cally for women, including abortions. We raised $40,000 to buy a building; but before we could act on this, the local Planned Parenthood affiliate asked us to allow it to take over and administer the FPMS. After some deliberation, we gave them our blessing and the $40,000. Under Planned Parenthood's administration, this service has been extremely successful, even though it has been picketed regularly by "right-to-life" groups. I thought such protests would subside in time, but I was wrong. Moreover, following the election of George Bush in 1988, there was considerable speculation that the high court might reverse the Supreme Court's landmark *Roe vs. Wade* decision of 1973, which established a woman's right to have an abortion. Perhaps it will. Even if it does, however, I believe that in time reason will win out.

As a result of Sadye's position and our travels, we came in contact with leaders of Planned Parenthood like General William H. Draper, who was in charge of fund-raising for the national organization. General Draper invited us to attend the January 1969 International Conference of Planned Parenthood in Dacca, East Pakistan, now Bangladesh. It turned out to be a more exciting meeting than we had bargained for, because there was a lot of violence among religious factions in the country, and we were confined to the hotel where the meetings were held. The conflict was brutal; the combatants had the ugly habit of setting fire to the first floor of an apartment building to prevent occupants from escaping.

The conference itself was interesting. The Pakistanis had a fairly effective birth-control program. The Indians, on the other hand, had great plans but little in the way of results. Indira Gandhi's son, Sanjay, was in charge of India's program, and it was said that he gave his workers a quota for performing vasectomies. If not enough men came into their clinics (some of which we had visited on earlier trips and found to be rather primitive), the staff would simply go into the streets, collar some hapless passerby, and operate on him. It was not a very popular program.

From Dacca we flew north to Katmandu, Nepal, with Bill Draper, because Sadye and I intended to go on to Sikkim. I had been corresponding with the maharaja or chogyal, as he was called, of Sikkim at the request of Mrs. Chester Carlson.[4] The Institute of Tibetology in Gangtok possessed some important Buddhist manuscripts that had been smuggled out of Tibet by the Dalai Lama when he fled the country. Their safety was being threatened by a continuing border dispute with the Chinese communists, and Mrs. Carlson wanted to have the books preserved on microfilm.

Traveling with General Draper had some advantages: we were picked up at the airport in Katmandu, Nepal by U.S. State Department vehicles and taken on a highly informative tour. Bill stayed at the embassy and we attended a reception there, given by Ambassador and Mrs. Ellsworth Bunker, which was the usual dull diplomatic affair except for some interesting discussion of planned parenthood with a Kenyan man who was in charge of family planning for his country. We also had an opportunity to visit the hangouts of

[4] Mrs. Carlson, widow of Chester Carlson, the inventor of the process that formed the basis of xerography (see chapter Eleven, page 232). Both Mr. and Mrs. Carlson were Buddhists.

a large group of American expatriate "hippies" who had, in their own vernacular, dropped out (of American culture) and turned on (to drugs). They lounged around a restaurant in a slum-district alley smoking marijuana and hashish and listening to music from a record player. We were told this would be the end of the line for most of these young people; they would die here in a cheap, ecstatic trance. This seemed a pitiful waste; I felt sorry for their parents.

Sikkim was an absolutely stunning experience. We were met at the airport in Bagdogra by one of the royal vehicles, a jeep, and for seven hours we jounced and lurched and bounced up one of the worst roads I have ever seen, or rather felt, since most of the trip was in darkness. The driver was an expert; if he hadn't been, we probably would have gone off one of those sheer Himalayan precipices. We arrived with our clothes and luggage coated by a thick layer of gray dust. We were ready for bed, but the staff had stayed up to serve us, so we bathed as best as we could in the half-inch of warm water we managed to coax out of the spigot, and changed for dinner. It was two A.M. when we finally fell into bed.

Mr. Nirmal Sinha, director of the Institute of Tibetology in Gangtok, which was financed in part by the government of India, did an excellent job of introducing us to Buddhism and explaining the texts that were to be photographed. There were some twelve hundred of them, kept wrapped in cloth, each about twenty-two inches tall and twenty-four inches wide, a size that would pose some problems in photographing. But we were able to work out an acceptable approach.

Sadye and I were received for lunch the first day by our hostess, the Gyalmo, Hope Namgyal, the former Hope Cooke, a Sarah Lawrence graduate and New York and Washington debutante. She had become the envy of many teenaged American girls by marrying Crown Prince Palden Thondup Namgyal of Sikkim in 1961 and entering this exotic land as "Consort of the Deities" and "Queen of the Hidden Valley of Rice." She was charming, though I was a little put off by her heavy eye makeup and the fact that she spoke almost exclusively in a whisper. Her husband, the chogyal, was ill. But he recovered in time for dinner that night and we met several more times. I found him extremely intelligent, well educated (a graduate of Cambridge University), and interesting.

After our return home, I discussed the situation in Sikkim with Mrs. Carlson, and she said she wished to donate the equipment needed to do the photography and set up a permanent microfilm department in the Institute of Tibetology. This was carried out, after much correspondence with the chogyal, and Mary Lou Morrison went over and spent about four weeks in Gangtok, training Sikkimese camera operators.

I mentioned at the beginning of this chapter that I keep a "photographic diary" of my travels. Since the elements of photography were at the very heart of my life's work, it is natural that I would have a keen interest in it as a hobby. And what people see and learn in travel is greatly influenced by their individual interests. For example, Mike Hindert's interest is in figure skating, and his first concern on arrival in a foreign city is to locate an ice rink. On the trip he took with us in 1968, he did so much skating I told him, "Mike, I'm afraid your only impression of London will be of the inside of an ice rink." I suppose the same could be said of me and libraries. . . . But I digress. . . . My point is that my interest in photography has to some extent shaped my view of other countries. A favorite subject of mine is people in bazaars or marketplaces. One can capture a great deal about the temperament of people and get a basic feel for their culture by photographing them in markets. I don't pretend to be more than a dedicated amateur with a camera, but I have made enough photographs to have developed a distinctive style. I can always pick out a photograph I made from the style in which it is composed.

My most ambitious photography was done in Africa. I have at least three thousand slides and three and a half hours of videotape from our various trips to Africa. I was fascinated by the fact that lions will allow you to drive up beside them and stand there unconcerned, gazing off into the distance while you take their picture, giving the impression that they wished you would go away.

Our first trip to Africa was in 1963, not counting, of course, the time I was stranded in Portuguese West Guinea during World War II. Joe Wilson had said that when Xerox hit $100 million in sales, we would have a meeting in London. We did it in 1963, and Sadye and I went on to Africa —to Uganda, Kenya, and Tanzania—which had a joint university that was interested in getting periodicals on microfilm. We visited Kampala and Nairobi, and were so taken with the wildlife that we decided to go back on a safari, which we did in 1967, accompanied by my brother Frank and his son Tom. Phil had to cancel out because of an emergency that arose in his newspaper business. That was one of the few times we took a trip purely for pleasure, without some business connection. I was suffering some withdrawal pains; it was hard to adjust to the fact that Xerox was now in control at UMI. But things had changed, and I would have even more adjusting to do in the three years before my retirement.

Chapter Fifteen

New Beginnings

In January 1969, I told top management at Xerox that I was going on half salary at UMI, because I would be away from the office a lot in the future. For one thing, I wanted to devote more time to the affairs of the Park Place Motor Inn and Wolverine Broadcasting. For another, Sadye and I planned to do more traveling. Some of our trips would be related, in part, to my duties as chairman of UMI, representing the company at conferences and other functions. Others would be in connection with UMI special projects.

The way these special projects worked was that I would come up with an idea for one and set it up. Once I had it going, I would turn it over to someone else. It seemed like an ideal use of my abilities, because it was a continuation of the approach I had employed since I founded UMI. The filming of periodicals was developed in this way, as were dissertations and other successful ventures. Oftentimes such projects did not pay off immediately. It took time to nurture them, and the only rationale for them in their early stages was my own sense that they were needed and my certainty that they were right. This approach was foreign to Xerox, who wanted to show a lot of sales right off. It was possible to sell copiers that way, but not our products. I felt I owed it to Xerox to continue my efforts, even though they did not understand what I was doing.

I had begun concentrating more on my special-projects approach after Jim Lundy took over UMI's day-to-day operations. I enjoyed the freedom of operating this way, even though being out of the office so much caused me to gradually move to the periphery of things and lose touch with what was going on there. I didn't mind that; Xerox management was putting a lot of pressure on UMI, trying to make it fit into their corporate mold. I made it clear that I was available for consultation, and I assumed they would check with me in planning any major changes. My assumption was wrong. I was left out of the planning of some major programs, and this was unfortunate because what they came up with was based on a fundamental misconception of UMI's microfilm business. For example, they thought that UMI's rich store of negatives could be utilized to produce reprints of books, and that such reprints could be marketed profitably in the channels used by conventional book publishers. The move was wrongheaded, because the materials we had in negative microfilm were largely esoteric and specialized in nature. Consequently, the market for them was very limited, and bringing them out in reprint form was impractical. In fact, it ignored the very reason microfilm publishing was invented in the first place, to allow such low-demand works to be made one at a time as orders came in. Xerox was pushing for increased sales in a market that was not ready for rapid expansion. Another mistake was that in doing the reprints UMI did not use the company's own facilities. They went to outside suppliers for printing and binding, which sent production costs through the roof. As a result of this and similar problems, UMI lost money for the first time in its history.

I hope this does not sound like sour grapes, because it is not meant that way. In fact, I admired many of the improvements Xerox management made in UMI operations, such as creating a sales force and developing a sales-training program, which were instituted by Director of Marketing Bob Asleson, who later became General Manager, then President. My method of selling had involved only occasional personal contact; most of my sales were made by correspondence and telephone. Asleson set up a more broadly based marketing approach that called on libraries all over the country. This personal contact was vital in selling services like periodicals on microfilm.

Again, I did regret that I wasn't consulted on such major moves as getting into the reprint business. I think I might have saved them a lot of headaches.

My reaction when I learned about the reprint program was to consider it water over the dam. I would contribute everything I could through my expertise and special projects and make myself accept the fact that, under the management of Xerox, many things about UMI would be different.

How great that difference would be came through to me in dismaying fashion in the spring of 1969. I received a telephone call from Peter McColough, telling me that the Xerox board of directors had approved a new policy of mandatory retirement. Henceforth, he said, all executives in the main office in Rochester had to depart at age sixty; elsewhere in the corporation, including subsidiaries like UMI, the cutoff for all employees would be at sixty-five. I

317

was stunned. UMI's retirement age was seventy, and I had assumed that this policy would apply to me. But Peter made it clear that my retirement was mandated for the end of the month in which I turned sixty-five—June 1970.

Sadye's logical approach to problems was a great help to me in dealing with the shock of facing this unwelcome, and to my mind uncalled-for retirement. I should make clear in discussing my retirement that I was not unhappy with the terms Xerox gave me. In fact, I thought corporate management treated me very well. My quarrel was with the principal of the policy. I thought sixty-five was too young. I was still able and had much to contribute. Sadye understood my feelings and in her perceptive, persuasive way kept me from allowing my anger to color my judgment.

She encouraged me to focus on building up contacts that would bridge into new types of activity. I did so enthusiastically, because I did not want to fall into the trap of inactivity that has snared some men in retirement. Going from a full calendar to an empty one can be depressing. I think it can even bring on heart attacks and other physical ailments.

Fortunately, I had always been independent. Some corporate executives grow so accustomed to operating with the support of a large staff that they find it difficult to adjust to the kind of self-reliance it takes to be an entrepreneur. My friend Ed Cole, former president of General Motors, was a case in point.

It seemed obvious to me that I would need an office from which to work after June 1970, and Sadye was in complete agreement. The notion of my working out of our home never

318

occurred to either of us. I was not sure what sort of enterprise I would develop, though I had a feeling that whatever it was I would need my own office, and I was not inclined to rent space in someone else's building. This line of thought led me to acquire some land on Plymouth Road and hire Alden Dow, who had been the architect of the new UMI building on Zeeb Road, to design a building for me. I was glad I selected Alden, because my site presented a difficult design problem. The zoning regulations stated that floor space could not exceed 40 percent of the land area. There had to be one automobile parking space available for every 110 square feet of floor space, and the structure could be no more than three stories high. Dow met these requirements by raising the building on columns, with only a small entrance lobby and elevator area extending down to the ground-floor level. Most of the area on that level formed a parking lot beneath the rest of the building.

We started construction in the fall of 1969 and completion was scheduled for December 1970. This was inconvenient, since there would be a six-month gap between my retirement from UMI and the time I would be able to move into my new office. It worked out all right, though, because UMI still owned the buildings we had vacated on First Street; my old office there was available, and it made a perfect interim location.

The new building has worked out well. The second and third floors are in offices. My office occupies the entire southwest corner on the third floor, with a view across the U of M's North Campus area. I had a fireplace built into one wall and made certain there were adequate bookshelves and

319

space to display some of my Eskimo art. I engaged real-estate broker John E. Swisher, Jr. and his son, John E. Swisher III, to manage the property, and they have done an outstanding job. The design of the building, raised on stilts like some tidewater structures on the Gulf Coast, has proved to be an asset. Tenants appreciate having the covered parking area beneath the structure.

Xerox hosted an elegant retirement dinner at the Barton Hills Country Club, to which all the top executives from corporate headquarters came to pay their respects. If that sounds rather funereal, I suppose it reflects my mood at the time. I did my best to act casual and self-assured about my future prospects; I made small talk about the things I would be doing in my new office: Margaret Massialas (my assistant at UMI, an extremely capable Englishwoman) would be joining me; I told them I was taking a position on the boards of three companies; I said I was planning to put money into several start-up companies to help young entrepreneurs succeed. . . . In fact, however, I was a little fearful I would be at loose ends.

Those fears turned out to be groundless. Soon I was busier than ever, although I had no tangible product to sell. I found that people began coming to me for all sorts of advice. This was gratifying, and I did my best to help them.

The Environmental Research Institute of Michigan (ERIM) was one group that Margaret Massialas and I spent a great deal of time with in those first few months after my retirement. ERIM had been part of the University of Michigan, but was spun off as a result of student protests related to the war in Vietnam. ERIM was doing some classified research for the government and the students did not believe the university should be aiding a conflict they deplored.

Bill Brown, the president of ERIM and a very able guy, had to figure out how to raise capital for the company now that it was out from under the wing of the university. He approached me for advice, and after listening to his description of ERIM, which had tax-exempt status, it seemed to me that the State of Michigan would be the likeliest source of a loan. I turned to Margaret Massialas and said, "Would you please get Bill on the phone for me?"

Brown thought I was referring to Bill Pierpont, the business manager of the U of M, who was a good friend of mine. I'll never forget the expression of amazement on his face when he realized it was Bill Milliken, Governor of Michigan, on the other end of the line.

I explained the situation, and the governor (whom I had known since he was a boy in Traverse City and, as I mentioned in Chapter Six, had bought a sailboat from my brother and me) said, "Sure, Gene, we'll see if we can help out." The state loaned ERIM $2 million from its pension fund, and Brown was delighted. So was I, because the experience helped give direction to my still-somewhat-hazy notion of the type of service I would perform. It also validated my belief that new enterprises had needs I could help them fill.

Margaret Massialas adapted to our new setup quickly. She became my administrative adjutant. Her background with the British Embassy in Greece gave her a diplomatic polish that was invaluable in dealing with leaders in educational and political circles. She and I did a lot more consulting with

Brown and ERIM after we moved into our Plymouth Road office. Actually *consulting* is not quite the right word. Perhaps *facilitating* would be a better word to describe our role. I joined ERIM's board and our office provided a neutral environment where some of the more sensitive issues of its business could be worked out. An outgrowth of our work with

Brian Howard

Margaret Massialas

ERIM was involvement with Daedalus Corporation, which was started by Dana Parker, who had been a research engineer for ERIM. He developed a system of scanning terrain with a multi-spectral camera to produce maps that showed differences in surface temperatures. I made an investment in Daedalus and went on its board, and Margaret and I lived through all of the company's startup problems.

Because of Dana Parker's critical role in the company, Daedalus had taken out a $1 million insurance policy on his life. This turned out to be foresighted, because about a year after he founded the company, Dana died of a heart attack. His brother, Alan Parker, took over and Margaret and I went through many more days of meetings with him and others in the company, working out personnel problems.

One thing I learned from this experience is that many people have restricted vision. They can see an issue in only

322

one way. This almost always causes a breakdown of communication in a company, and the only way it can be bridged is to get the parties to see things from the other side. If they can't, then they often have to leave the organization.

Alan Parker came to believe that my position on ERIM's board created a conflict of interest with my role on his Daedalus board. I did not agree. I could see his point, though, and since I had an investment in Daedalus, I chose to resign from ERIM's board. In retrospect I think that probably was a mistake. After about ten years, I resigned from the board of Daedalus. Phil took my place, and I think he's doing a better job than I did. An odd-twist aside to the Daedalus episode is that a completely new group is running that company now and Alan Parker is working for ERIM.

In selecting companies to help with financial backing and advice, I preferred young, entrepreneurial organizations that had unique products. I felt that my experience would be most applicable to that kind of company and that type of product. However, I learned from my experience with GCO Corporation that a product can be too unique, too good for its own good.

Ralph Grant, who founded GCO, was a neighbor of mine in Barton Hills. He had invented a machine that through holographic imaging would reveal structural flaws in materials such as automobile tires and laminated sections of aircraft wings.

It was a terrific machine and I was impressed with Grant. His company had all the accoutrements of success: a beautiful office in an industrial park, a well-appointed manufacturing facility, even a corporate aircraft. I made a substantial investment in GCO and brought Sol Linowitz in as a member of the board.

GCO really had everything going for it—except sales.

Tire manufacturers, it seemed, were not really interested in paying $250,000 for a machine that would show up internal flaws in their product.

I arranged through Ed Cole for a demonstration of a GCO machine at General Motors. They bought one and were pleased with it. One of the major aircraft manufacturers bought one, too. But that was it. Without further sales, GCO was starved for cash. Finally, it was forced to disband, and once that process starts and the lawyers get involved, the money just seems to evaporate. I lost my entire investment, the largest loss I ever incurred.

After Ed Cole retired from GM, he formed International Husky Corporation. I invested in this venture and served on its board. Among the several interesting things we were working on was a flying-wing-type cargo plane that would be used to transport new automobiles from Detroit to the West Coast and bring back loads of fresh fruit and produce. It might have worked out if Ed had not been killed in a private-plane crash, which was a great tragedy.

Another of my directorships is with Domino's Pizza, Inc., whose headquarters are not far from my Plymouth Road office. It has an unusual and interesting board. Since Domino's is wholly owned by its founder, Tom Monaghan, there are no outside stockholders' interests to protect. The board is strictly advisory. Yet board members are kept fully informed about the company's operations and are charged with acting as a steadying influence in the event of Tom's death or disability.

When I was first introduced to Domino's I was surprised by the youth and vitality of its staff. It was brimming with energy and charging ahead in nine different directions at once. I found virtually everything about the company unorthodox, which may be the reason it appealed to me so much. Even the way I was introduced to it was unusual.

It had long been my habit at home in Barton Hills to go out early and pick up the morning paper from the drive. From time to time I would see my young neighbor out jogging. One day he loped up to me and introduced himself: "I'm Tom Monaghan, owner of Domino's Pizza," he said, standing there streaming sweat from his run. He told me about his home-delivery pizza business. A few days later, he called my office and made an appointment to see me at 11 A. M. June 30, 1978. He told me, "I've always admired you, Mr. Power, and I would like you to join my board." I was politely noncommittal. Frankly, I hardly knew or cared what a pizza was, and since my experience on other corporate boards had not been particularly successful or gratifying, I had decided I would not go onto boards lightly. But then Tom began sending a regular parade of his executives to my office to tell me about the company. After about four weeks of this, I decided I would agree to serve. I did not acquire any stock in Domino's, nor did Tom offer me any at that time.

At the very first Domino's board meeting I attended, on Wednesday, August 16, 1978, I was able to show them that some significant losses reported by their commissary in Ohio had to be caused by thefts. They corrected the situation immediately, and for a period of time thereafter, Tom thought I could walk on water. He says I taught him how to make money, and if that's true, I must have taught him pretty well, because Domino's annual sales are now more than $2 billion.

I also helped a succession of individual entrepreneurs on a less formal basis. I did not like to see a person who had a good idea be unable to try it simply for lack of money. For example, one young man came to me with an idea for starting a company that would reclaim welding flux for sale to manufacturers. He made an excellent presentation; it was obvious that he really knew the field, so I decided to help him with a loan. He bought the machinery he needed and started processing the flux. However, some of the customers he had been counting on to buy his product did not pan out. After about four months of searching for new customers, he came to me and said he was giving up. He couldn't seem to line up enough business. I figured that if he quit, my money would be lost anyhow, so I persuaded him to persist. I didn't exercise the option I held to buy stock in the firm, because I thought he should have his own company. After two weeks, he landed the Ford Motor Company as an account. That was all he needed; other accounts came in, and the business began doing very well. He paid me back and was able to build himself a fine house. His company has continued to flourish.

Not all my decisions about backing individuals have been sound. One man who seemed to have the qualifications necessary to make a go of the mattress company he wanted to start was a failure. I made him a loan, too, but as it turned out, no amount of money could have made up for his lack of entrepreneurial judgment.

M y transition into retirement did not reduce my physical activity, thanks to my water polo games three times a week with the Flounders. The only concession I had to make to advancing age on that front was wearing swim fins, which I learned were necessary one day when I jumped into the pool without them and damn near drowned. Water polo keeps one fit and alert, as the following commentaries by members of the Flounders will attest:

Andy Crawford
President, Ascott Corporation

I came to the University of Michigan to study industrial engineering, and I first met Gene Power in 1964 when I was a senior and business manager of *The Michigan Daily*; he, as a regent, was on the newspaper's board. I sat next to him at an awards dinner. We talked at great length and I was very impressed by him; I'm sure he doesn't remember that discussion at all, though. I went on to Harvard Business School and worked at a series of jobs, one of which brought me back to Ann Arbor in 1972. I then decided to return to school. I found myself back on campus with plenty of free time and felt I needed to get back in shape. I had played water polo in high school, so I joined the Flounders.

Gene was then about sixty-seven years old. He and Ken Pike were the senior citizens in the group, and my reaction, being much younger and stronger, was that I needed to be careful not to hurt them. I was disabused of that notion when Gene suddenly grabbed me around the neck in a grip I could not escape and held me under water. He'd let me breathe occasionally, so I just barely stayed alive. I learned pretty quickly to avoid that sort of thing. In the last few years, when Gene has not come onto the wall as he used to, he has still been able to stop me on a fast break.

EDITION OF ONE

Most people do not want to get between me and the wall, but Gene will. He'll attack me with every ounce of strength he has, and he usually holds me up long enough to get help.

There are no rules in this brand of water polo except the one Gene likes to quote: that you can't hold a married man under water for more than five minutes. It's a rough game and we have a lot of little injuries—broken fingers, busted eardrums (I was a little upset with myself in October 1988, when I hit Gene with my elbow and broke his eardrum), split eyebrows, scratched eyeballs—but no major traumas, because we play in deep water, not the shallow end, and the water cushions the blows. One day at lunch someone asked who in the group had not visited a hospital emergency room after a game. Only two hands went up: one, a new player who had not yet felt the effect of the law of averages; the other, a physician who admitted to treating himself.

In addition to being a great way to keep physically fit, the Flounders were a support group for me when I was launching my own business. Gene Power has been particularly helpful in this respect.

I use Gene as an example in the classes I currently teach in entrepreneurship at the U of M business school. He's a good role model for anyone who hopes to be a success in life as an entrepreneur. I wouldn't change places with him — he has faced enormous difficulties and he has hardened himself in some ways in order to overcome them—but I sure admire the life he has made for himself.

Ralph Loomis,
Professor of English,
University of Michigan

I joined the Flounders in 1959. For the first three months I wondered why I did it. I was weary, in pain, discouraged. Yet something kept me in, and I'm glad I stayed. I remember Gene as a wily, strong player. He's now the only player allowed to wear swim fins, and no one in the group would say him nay.

We have a tradition at lunch after our games that when someone is honored by getting his name in the paper, he has to buy coffee for the rest of the Flounders. Gene once got his name in the paper for getting a speeding ticket. He was urged to buy, but he denied that it was an honor. The group prevailed, but only after strenuous debate.

Being retired did not cause me to lose interest in what was going on at UMI either. The company suffered another drop in business after I left, and it was six years before it got back on track under a new president, Joe Fitzsimmons. Joe understands UMI's business mission and has led the company back to the kind of services it used to provide when I was run-

Joe Fitzsimmons

ning it. Joe agreed to tape record his recollections of our association for this autobiography, and here is a transcript of some of his remarks:

> I joined the company in 1966, coming in from Rochester as Jim Lundy and Bob Asleson had before me. I will never forget UMI's old building down on First Street. Just looking at all its rambling additions, you could see how it had grown with the fortunes of its entrepreneurial leader. I came from an engineering background, very structured, whereas Gene Power comes more from

the humanities side. His first question to me when we bumped into one another in the corridor was, "What do you do here?" I told him, "Sir, my title is Chief Industrial Engineer." He said, "I didn't know we needed one of those."

I didn't know what to make of that, but I liked him immediately. He was dominant, prominent, and knowledgeable about the business to the point where he wanted to run everything himself. I'm not sure what he thought of my work at that time, but I know he saw me as an Irish Catholic from the East Coast. When my wife became pregnant with our fifth child, Gene called me up to his office and asked, "What are your views on birth control?" I thought for a minute and said, "None of your goddam business!" After that we were fine.

He would challenge you every which way. That was one reason we did well. I admired his deep understanding of the business. But back in 1967 I thought sure he was going to fire me.

We were then doing about two-thirds of the filming for *The New York Times*, a contract Gene had set up years earlier, and I thought, "Baloney, we can do the whole thing better than anyone else." So I grabbed our marketing manager and said, "Come on, let's make a sales call on *The New York Times*." We got nowhere. The day after I returned, Gene called me up to his office and said, "Fitz, you know what happened? We lost *The New York Times* contract!" I thought I was history!

The fact of the matter was that *The Times* had decided to buy a company in the business and do all their own microfilming. We didn't get that contract back for eighteen years—in 1985—and that was a big milestone in my life . . . but this is supposed to be about Gene, so I'll skip that epsiode. . . .

He established the company's culture, and it was unusual and admirable. I say *unusual* because it reflected his own varied interests. I learned something about the extent of those interests when I was put in charge of our move to the new building on Zeeb Road. Gene's old office was spacious by anyone's standards; he

330

had cases of wine stacked in there, because he was running a wine-import club. Down in the shipping room he had a canoe hanging from the ceiling. A building across the street was full of Eskimo sculptures and prints for another nonprofit business he was running. I wondered, "What in blazes am I gonna do with all this stuff?"

When he left the company, we lost a lot of credibility. The strategic direction we were taken in was wrong. It led to a four-year hiatus in UMI's business of providing access to information, because we had gotten into the reprint business. We bought a company in California, PLS (Professional Library Services), that was doing cataloging, and we became a library-services company, producing a lot of different products. Those were wrong moves. Now we've gone back to the basics of preserving periodicals and newspapers, doing doctoral dissertations and other scholarly materials. I keep an "Edsel shelf" in my office of reprints like the *March of America* series to remind me to stick to the basics.

This doesn't mean we have stopped innovating. We've developed a whole line of electronic services—putting our materials on optical disks that can be searched and accessed rapidly by computer and displayed on a CRT screen. But this technology won't supplant microfilm; it simply augments it. And the approach is merely another extension of Gene Power's original concept.

I visit Joe from time to time and stroll through the plant to say hello to the older employees, many of whom have been there most of their working lives. I never fail to get a sense of excitement from these visits and wish I could be back there in the thick of things again. The feeling is akin to homesickness. After all, there's a lot of me in that company, and I'm not talking about the oil portrait of me that hangs in the lobby. The feeling passes quickly, though, because I have so many new things I am involved in. For example, administration of the Power Foundation requires constant attention; scarcely a day goes by without several new and interesting requests for grants arriving in the office.

Sadye and I established the foundation in 1967 as a means to share with others the good fortune which life has brought us. The foundation represents only part of our giving activities, however, and in many respects it is a smaller part. We also make personal gifts. In fact, we give away most of our income each year.

My thinking on giving was shaped to a large extent by what I learned from my service as a member of the Council of the National Endowment for the Humanities. I had accepted appointment to the council from President Johnson in 1968, because I felt it was an opportunity to make use of what I had learned about educational needs from my years as a regent. And, indeed, that was the case. In the process I also found out how foundations work and came to appreciate the great need for financing individuals and programs that can benefit society.

Sadye and I agreed that one use of our gifts, whether personal or from the foundation, would be as seed money to help an organization get started. There is now a long list of such recipients. An example is the Ann Arbor group called Soundings, which was formed to provide programs and counseling for women who are displaced homemakers or are undergoing mid-life crises such as widowhood or divorce. We also helped many established groups such as Planned Parenthood, the Council on Foreign Relations, and various cultural organizations.

One of the nice things about our approach, using both private and foundation funds, is that we can operate flexibly. For example, we heard about an unsuccessful effort to raise funds for the purchase of Marion Island, a 156-acre island in Grand Traverse Bay, eight miles north of Traverse City, for the purpose of preserving the island in its natural state. A developer wanted to acquire the island and subdivide it into building sites. With the help of the Nature Conservancy, we bought the island and donated it to Grand Traverse County with the stipulation that it was to be used strictly for daytime public recreation and left in its natural state in perpetuity; it could not be improved with buildings or settled or sold. I think our action was a good thing, and apparently so did the people in the area, for they renamed the preserve Power Island. The name cannot be changed on navigational charts, though, until after I die.

One reason I found so much satisfaction in helping others, I think, is that it was an extension of my business philosophy. My whole approach to business—making need rather than projections of financial return the test of whether a new project should be undertaken—was reflected in the way I approached helping others.

Another thing that influenced me was the help I received years ago from the Carnegie Corporation and the Rockefeller Foundation. Without their grants, UMI might never have developed and prospered as it did. Nor would I have grown personally as I did, thanks in part to the travel in Europe that their grants made possible.

I suppose the real roots of my concern for others, though, can be traced to my mother. Her interest in social welfare, typified by her work among the Indians of Shobbytown, made an enduring impression on me. In any case, the desire to help others has always been part of my makeup. And I have always felt it most markedly when it seemed I could help a young person get started. I think, for example, of a young woman named Barbara Nissman, who wanted to become a concert pianist.

Barbara was completing her work on a Ph.D. in piano performance at the U of M when, at the request of the dean of the School of Music, Alan Britton, I went to hear her doctoral recital on April 25, 1969. She was a star in the music school. Britton had high hopes for her future, and he told me that any help I could give her would be appreciated. Her teacher, Gyorgy Sandor, also approached me in her behalf. I was impressed by her playing and went backstage afterward to congratulate her. She told me about her dream of concertizing.

Coincidentally, I was having lunch the following day with my friend Eugene Ormandy, conductor of the Philadelphia Orchestra, who was in town to conduct performances for the University Musical Society's May Festival. I first met Ormandy at a function for regents and had invited him and his wife Gretel to our home for dinner. Oddly enough, Ormandy and I did not discuss the interests we had in common, such as fast cars and photography. We talked about music, which he was as driven and demanding about, I'm sure, as I was about microfilm. He had been a child prodigy on the violin in his native Budapest, and he delighted us with stories of his career. His favorite violin concerto was the Beethoven, which he recorded with Isaac Stern as soloist, and this piece

334

became perhaps the most frequently played by Sadye and me in our nightly concerts on the hi-fi set in our bedroom.

Anyhow, I was having lunch with Ormandy and I told him about Barbara Nissman. He said he would like to hear her play, so off we went. Barbara was rather shaken when we arrived unannounced at her practice session that afternoon —there she was in bluejeans, without makeup, in the presence of the great Ormandy—but she collected herself and played. When she finished, he said he would like to dictate a letter. I took him to my office, where he dictated a letter to his manager in Holland, Johanna Beek, asking her to be Barbara's manager in Europe. She accepted.

With some financial assistance, Barbara went to Europe, and Beek arranged for her to play some concerts there. Later she was hired through the Affiliate Artists program by the John Deere Tractor Company of Moline, Illinois, to entertain employees with classical music in the lunchrooms of its plants across the country. This provided her with an income for two years. After that, she returned to England, and we were able to help her in making contacts there, providing her with letters of introduction. Among other things, she signed to do her own TV program, *Barbara and Her Friends*, on the BBC. She later moved to New York City and married Daniel Haberman, a poet. (When Ormandy first met her, somewhat to my discomfort, he had counseled her to "fall in love . . . have an affair," because he thought her playing needed more passion.) It is especially difficult, I think, for women to make it as concert pianists. Barbara is coming along, though, and in addition to a series of engagements in Europe, New York, and St. Louis, she obtained a contract to record the nine Prokofiev piano sonatas, which were brought out in 1989 to honor the centennial of the composer's birth. She has several other recording contracts as well.

I have mentioned the long-standing interest Sadye and I have had in the performing arts, and in recent years we have enjoyed being able to support the Ann Arbor Summer Festival.

The idea for this series of musical and theatrical presentations originated with Jim Packard, who was in the engineering school at the U of M. He regretted the absence of high-quality theater in the community. I decided he was right and that I would do something about it. I incorporated the Ann Arbor Summer Festival as a nonprofit organization in 1978, but for a variety of reasons, not the least of which were economic—high inflation followed by a recession— we were not able to present our first festival until 1984. Remembering my experience with the Dramatic Arts Center, I had made certain that both the City of Ann Arbor and the U of M would be involved in the Summer Festival. The bylaws called for half the trustees of the organization to be appointed by the Board of Regents of the University, the other half by the City Council. We felt our way through the first two seasons, because we did not know what kind of programs the public wanted. Each subsequent season has been a learning experience. We now know with certainty that lighter fare sells better than classical works in the summer. In 1987, as we began working on the fifth season, I attempted to reduce my own role in the planning and day-to-day activities. It was consuming far too much of my time as well as that of Margaret Massialas. After the 1988 season was ended, I resigned as chairman. I felt we had put the festival on solid footing, and it was now up to its fulltime staff and volunteers to keep it going. Of course, I am still on the board and will continue to help by contributing ideas and advice as needed. The 1989 season was a success; it had seven sellout performances; only the theatrical perform- ances did not sell well, but we know from experience that professional theater in Ann Arbor often must be subsidized.

I would not want to pick one of our projects as being more worthwhile than another, for the results of some of the smaller, individual grants have been as gratifying as larger ones to major groups. If I were to choose a favorite, however, it would be our exchange-scholarship program between the U of M and Cambridge University, England (Magdalene College and New Hall).

My long-term goal for the Power Scholarship Program is to foster a closer, more harmonious and understanding rela- tionship between the United States and the United King- dom. An American student who lives in England for two years and travels there should develop an appreciation for that country which sees beyond cultural stereotypes. There- fore, he or she should become a champion for England after returning to the United States. The same follows, of course, for English students who come here.

My reason for establishing this goal transcends mere An- glophilia. I believe it is absolutely essential, given the present world situation, that our two countries understand one another and work together.

Our scholarship grants are administered by the institutions, which receive and process all applications and make the selections,[1] narrowing the field down to six or seven candidates apiece. This has its advantages; certainly we do not have sufficient staff to handle that much work. In fact, the correspondence and record-keeping we provide, which includes following up on all of our scholars, takes up a considerable portion of Margaret Massialas's time. We have been pleased so far with both the quality of candidates and the variety of fields of study they represent. We have all kinds: music majors, nuclear biologists, mathematicians, poets . . . which is what we want.

We interview all the candidates on the short list before the final selections are made, which as I mentioned earlier is an extremely difficult process. Once a decision has been reached, though, there has seldom been occasion for doubts or regrets. I attribute much of the success of the program to the work of Margaret Massialas. It happened that she had outstanding qualifications for helping set up the scholarship program, because she had a good knowledge of the English education system and its regulations, which are quite different than those of American schools. And as the years have gone by she has taken on most of the responsibility for seeing that the program is carried out.

To give you an idea of what the experience of Power Scholars is like, I would like to share just a few of the comments, taken at random from the letters we have re-

---

[1] The selection of the scholar is based on academic record, breadth of intellectual achievement, qualities of character, physical vigor as shown by participation and success in sports, and capacity for leadership and public service.

ceived over the years:

Andrew Sprague Becker
University of North Carolina
B.A. Michigan, 1982; B.A. Cambridge, 1984

Before I went to Cambridge, one of the Power Scholars told me that this old and respected university does not court its students; if I wanted to win it over, I would have to do the courting myself. This exhortation proved to be a valuable stimulus in both my academic and nonacademic life at Cambridge.

The tradition and reputation of Cambridge can be daunting, but behind it are dons and students who are willing and often eager to discuss, debate, or otherwise share the fruits of their study. It is an intellectual community in which one must actively take part. Magdalene College's interdisciplinary academic society gave me a good introduction to the combined pleasures of learning and socializing at Cambridge.

It is deceptively easy for an American to believe that he need not adjust to England. After all, aren't they just like us? Nonacademic activities provided the opportunity for understanding, and consequently forgetting that I was a foreigner. Through several societies I tried to avoid the trap of associating only with other foreigners and to find some shared activities with a large number of students. Once I discovered that positions of responsibility are very open to Power Scholars, I became co-chair of the Magdalene-Newnham College Classical Society (the Dipsophilists), president of the Magdalene graduate students (the Middle Combination Room), and captain of lower boats for the college crew team. Eight people trying to blend together as a unit early in the morning on the Cam have a way of diminishing their differences; it carries beyond appearing clad in tuxedos at a graduate dinner or the satisfaction of being a part of two boats which won oars in the May Bumps.

My studies continue as a Pogue Fellow here at the University of North Carolina at Chapel Hill; I am working on my disserta-

339

tion on the analogy between rhetoric, poetry, and art, as seen by the ancient Greeks and Romans. The people I met as a Power Scholar—academically, socially, and athletically—remain a large part of my life here. Their thoughts, now through letters and visits, still stimulate my own (and I hope the reverse is true). Several friends and Power Scholars continue to provide good excuses for visiting Australia, Spain, Greece, Canada, and England itself.

The Power Scholarship allowed me to receive a kind of training in my field which supplemented very well my education at the University of Michigan; professional contacts made there are a great help in my present studies. More important, however, was the social side of Cambridge, which introduced me to several of my closest friends, including a number of previous and subsequent Power Scholars. —June 1986

Howard E. Flight,
London, England
B.A. Cambridge, 1969; MBA Michigan, 1971

While I was at Ann Arbor, I ran the Finance Club at the Business School and was also resident adviser at Bates Housing. I travelled extensively through the States. My most valuable experience was getting to know and becoming life friends with both Americans and graduates of other nationalities at Michigan, and also having the chance to meet with a number of particularly interesting and influential Americans.

My ongoing contact with Ann Arbor has remained essentially through the Power Foundation. I have unfortunately not had the occasion to revisit Ann Arbor, but hope to do so in the near future with my wife. I continue to remain in contact with Magdalene and Cambridge and have now acted for some years as Secretary of the College Association.

I have intermittent contact with other Power Scholars, some of whom have met with me before going off to Michigan.

NEW BEGINNINGS

My main career to date has been as a merchant/investment banker working in London, the Far East, and then returning to London.

I presently run the investment department of one of the London Accepting Houses with particular strength in retail funds and overseas management but also with a growing involvement in venture capital. . . .

For future Power Scholars, my main points of advice are, first of all, don't expect it to be like Cambridge! Secondly, the most valuable experience is getting to know a wide circle of American contemporaries, many of whom will remain friends for life. I believe it is important to be able to travel widely in the U.S.A. and, in essence to become "bicultural" of both the U.S.A. and Britain. — September 1985

Clare R. Snook
Ann Arbor, Michigan
A.B. Cambridge, 1986; B.A. Michigan, 1988

I have only been in Ann Arbor for one complete term at the time of writing and for this reason what I have to say about my activities and experiences relates mostly to my process of acclimatisation, such as learning the rules of American football, remembering which way to look when crossing the road, and sorting out what credit hours really are. I spent Christmas in Boston with friends who subjected me to a ruthless Americanisation programme that included taking elevators (not lifts) up 50 floors, burning popcorn in the fire and becoming less ignorant about Dr. Martin Luther King, Jr. We drove up to Montreal; earlier in the fall I visited a friend in North Carolina.

At the moment I have just become involved with a student environmental group with which I go canvassing in small midwestern motortown suburbs and meet vast hordes of Real Americans. This is a welcome relief as I was beginning to think the States were entirely populated by poets and business students. . . .

—February 1986

341

It is apparent by now, I'm sure, that although my resignation as a regent in 1966 was traumatic for me, it did not sever or even strain my other close ties to the University of Michigan. The initial $1 million gift Sadye and I made for a theater at the university, which *The Michigan Daily* deplored so indignantly, was to have kicked off a fund-raising campaign to celebrate the U of M's sesquicentennial in 1967. I had proposed this campaign at a regents' dinner in 1963; Harlan Hatcher asked what I thought we could raise, and I said the amount I had in mind was $35 million, which was a big goal at that time. The most the university had raised in the past was $7 million for the Phoenix Project.[2] Harlan thought the campaign was a good idea. He took it up with his administrators and, after considerable discussion, the goal was set at $55 million, hence the designation *The 55 Campaign.* Many people thought even my original figure was too ambitious, but the campaign actually raised nearly $74 million, more than any publicly supported insitution had ever raised to that point, and it became the model followed by other universities in the future.

Plans had been drawn up for the theater (the renderings I showed to Henry Moore) and a model was made. However, public donations to *The 55 Campaign* were mostly restricted, earmarked by donors for certain uses, and there were not sufficient funds to cover the balance of the theater's cost. A further problem, I think, was that some members of the faculty were opposed to allocating funds for a

---

[2] The Phoenix Project was a nuclear-physics laboratory and classroom facility with the first nuclear reactor at any university in the country. It was built on the university's north campus.

theater of *any* kind. In any case, the plans and model were filed away, and the donation we had made remained in the endowment fund. Our gift was in the form of 3,000 shares of Xerox stock, which at the time it was transferred in 1963 was worth about $1 million.

In 1968, Robben Fleming, who succeeded Harlan as president of the university, approached Sadye and me and said he was very interested in the theater project; he asked us to expand our gift in order to get construction started. We agreed to add significantly to the amount over a period of ten years. This, plus the accumulated interest[3] and an amount added by the university would provide enough for a truly great building. Ground was broken early in 1969 for what is now the Power Center for the Performing Arts. Robert Schnitzer and his wife, Marcella Cisney, directed the theater program at the U of M, and they steered the design toward dramatic uses.

I deliberately stayed out of the planning process—for political reasons—and I now think this was a mistake, because several unfortunate things transpired, such as the orchestra pit being too small and the acoustics being designed strictly for speech, not both speech and music. The latter problem was later corrected with the installation of an acoustical shell for music programs, which we also financed.

The building was dedicated in 1971. Schnitzer and Cisney were very pleased with it, but they left not long afterward. Unfortunately, at the outset, the Power Center was not used

---

[3] Our total donation to the project was approximately $4 million.

343

as much or as broadly as I hoped it would be. That situation has been corrected, apparently, and use of the building has increased significantly in recent years. One use has been for performances of the Ann Arbor Summer Festival. The Power Center lends itself to this very well, because the large pavillion that forms the roof of its adjacent parking structure —called the "Top of the Park"—provides an excellent outdoor area for entertainment, refreshments, and movies on warm summer evenings.

R eflecting on these various projects now, I can say without reservation that helping others is extremely satisfying. I recommend it to anyone who is fortunate, as I have been, as an entrepreneur. I think it is important to recognize that gaining wealth carries with it an obligation to help others. Furthermore, being able to help others can be a great source of satisfaction when age and illness begin to deprive one of the ability to help oneself.

I have always been a robust, active person, and thoughts of infirmity never entered my mind. But there was no escaping it in 1972, when both Sadye and I were told we had Parkinson's disease.

Chapter Sixteen

Reflections

A frica had been beckoning to Sadye and me since we returned from our 1967 trip with Frank and his son, Tom. We decided to make another safari in 1969, even though Sadye was having some problems with her back. Frank and his wife, Margot, agreed to accompany us, and this mix of personalities would be almost as interesting as Africa itself.

Sadye had always had a close relationship with Frank, much the same kind of rapport she'd had with my mother. Sadye had a knack for sparking Frank's ready wit, and he had a way of setting her at ease in virtually any situation. The two of them would develop and sustain hilarious verbal rallies. I took part in the fun, of course, but I was less articulate. For the most part, my contributions merely added ballast to their rollicking conversations.

The Sadye, Gene, and Frank trio was already well established by 1936, when Frank and Margot were married, and the trio never became a quartet. I'm not sure why. Part of the reason, I suppose, was chemistry. Margot was more an individualist. She seemed more comfortable outside our circle. Part of the reason, too, was the physical separation; Ann Arbor is more than 200 miles from Traverse City. Margot and Frank had four children: Jocelyn, Roberta,

Thomas, and Jeffrey. Like many physicians, Frank had to spend more time looking after his medical practice than he did at home, so Margot was more actively involved in raising the children. Both boys became lawyers. Tom is now in the state legislature in Lansing and Jeff is with the firm of Warner Norcross & Judd in Grand Rapids. Jocelyn is a housewife and mother, and Roberta is a statistical analyst at the University of Washington.

Our safari would be the first time that Margot had been in a close proximity with Sadye and me for such an extended period, and I think we all were a little anxious about how we would get along. As it turned out, we had a splendid time. Margot is a strong-minded person. She grew up a tomboy in Windsor, Ontario, where her father was an engineer for Canadian Bridge Company. She was a good athlete; in fact, she and Frank met on the badminton court at the U of M on Thanksgiving Day, 1935. One night on our safari, she gave us her account of that day. She had been a gym assistant in charge of a round-robin badminton match, and Frank and I came in so late that we forced her to stay and miss her Thanksgiving dinner.

"I was extremely irritated," she said. "I played on Gene's side with Frank opposing me, and I amused myself by seeing how often I could smash the bird into the shiny silver buckle Frank wore on his belt. I did it several times, and by the end of the session I rather liked the guy, because most men under those circumstances wash out. They don't like it when a woman does that kind of thing to them. This guy kept fighting."

Margot was then in her first year of graduate school in

business administration
and Frank was already a
qualified M.D., doing his
five-year residency in surgery. After their marriage
the following year, they
moved to Traverse City,
where Frank started his
practice and Margot be-
came active in community
affairs. She was on the
board of the Michigan
League of Women Voters

Frank and Margot Power, 1971.

during the period when the League was reassessing its
position on foreign trade and foreign aid, and she led the
Michigan organization through its evaluation of those issues. She is still on the Leelanau County Planning Commission as well as the township commission and is busy
drafting amendments to the county zoning ordinance.

In planning our 1969 safari, I hired a guide named Bob
Lowis, an Englishman whom I had read about two years
earlier in *Glimpse of Eden*, a book on African wildlife by
Evelyn Ames. I was impressed by the conservationist outlook Bob expressed in the book. I was even more impressed
by his professionalism on safari; every aspect of his organization and execution seemed perfect. He had new trucks that
were smaller than those most white hunters operate, which
enabled him to obtain permission to drive into the valleys
and along streams that were off limits to heavier vehicles.
This put us right down among the animals, which was

347

exciting. We were among the privileged few allowed to camp inside the famed Ngorongoro Crater, which harbors its own ecological system.

Bob's Japanese wife, Yasuyo, supervised the staff who cooked our meals over open fires. These were multi-course repasts that would have been outstanding in any fine restaurant. Out there in the bush, with Kilimanjaro as a scenic backdrop, they were truly extraordinary.

Frank and Margot were excellent companions, and Bob Lowis was able to sense the psychological currents among our group and harmonize with us beautifully. Bob had been in Africa for twenty-five years. He was an avid amateur ornithologist, and he took pleasure in pointing out fascinating aspects of the seemingly innumerable varieties of brightly colored birds we saw. For example, while driving across a bare stretch of plain at Amboseli, a plover suddenly appeared in front of our windshield and hung there fluttering madly; Bob swerved sharply to avoid it. Then he stopped the truck and showed us a single egg on the ground, camouflaged almost perfectly by the earth tones of its shell. Bob told us that a plover would pull the same fluttering act in front of a running herd of wildebeest, and the animals would swerve round her, leaving her egg intact.

Bob also had an uncanny ability to locate and approach animals. We were able to watch elephants pass by us at close range. The majestic animals walked silently in single file, and though they seemed to be moving slowly, a man would have had to trot hard to keep up with them. We also watched the birth of a giraffe calf, a process which, carried out on the open plain with predators all around, filled me with awe at

348

the paradox of life—its strength and abundance contrasted with its constantly threatened fragility.

Sadye and I began talking about going back on another safari before we returned home from that one. However, events of the next two years kept us from going. These included Phil's marriage in 1971 to Sarah Goddard, daughter of Wendell and Katherine (Kitty) Goddard of Grosse Pointe, Michigan.

Phil was doing extremely well in his career by then. He had bought the Livonia, Plymouth, and Farmington community newspapers in 1966, and he was well established as a publisher, with a chain of twenty-two papers, when he and Sarah were married. Sadye and I were delighted with the match. Sarah was a Vassar graduate, extremely bright, and she and Phil seemed ideally suited to each other.

By 1972, Sadye's back was worse. She had severe pains that seemed to start in her back and run down her legs. She also complained of a peculiar sensation in her knees. She said they felt "as if they were being pulled." We decided that if we were ever going to make another safari in Africa, we should do it that year. Phil and Sarah came along, as did Jack and Emma Dawson and Sarah's mother, Kitty Goddard (Sarah's father had died two months earlier).

I was fortunate to be able to engage Bob Lowis to be our guide, and once again Bob's detailed planning and intelligent, informative observations, combined with the splendid camp cooking and congenial companionship, made every day of the trip a pleasure. And once again I was impressed by the constant juxtapositioning of life cycles as hunters, prey, and scavengers fulfilled their roles in nature. One day we came upon fifty or sixty hippos snorting and cavorting in a pool like so many exuberant eighth-grade boys. It seemed they had nothing to do but bellow and blow and push one another around. We also found a pride of lions we had observed on the '69 trip—they had changed greatly in three years: the pride was smaller, some older animals were missing, and some of the young ones showed the scars of life in the wild—and we visited the log cabin Jane Goodall had lived in[2] when she was doing her study of hyenas.

I had taken many still photographs on the '69 trip. This time I was equipped to take movies. I wanted to capture the natural actions of the animals. Most filmmakers tend to focus on key movements, shifting to other things when the animal is standing still or resting, but I dwelt on individual specimens for extended periods of time. I was quite pleased with the results.

The most pleasurable parts of the trip for Sadye and me, though, were the evenings filled with sparkling conversation. The stars shone as if blazing through holes cut in a vast tent of black velvet. There was always a great deal of amusing repartee and laughter around the dinner table. This would be followed by long discussions by the campfire. Phil and Jack Dawson often sat up talking politics long after the rest of us had retired.

On July 8, 1972, our last evening in camp, Sadye and I held an "awards" ceremony, at which everyone appeared in costume. Jack Dawson was a Masai chieftain, carrying a tent pole for a spear, with Emma as his *bebe*, draped in a

---

[2]Goodall describes this cabin in her book about hyenas, *Innocent Killers*, Houghton Mifflin, 1971, pp. 31, 32.

350

piece of cloth she had purchased in Nairobi. Sarah was a young Masai girl, bedecked in beads and other jewelry and wearing a feather in her hair. There were extravagant speeches and Sadye and I presented some citations we had prepared, such as the Guide of the Year award to Bob and Best-Dressed Guide of the Year to his assistant,

Jack and Emma Dawson on safari.

Fred. Jack Dawson received the Hippopotamus Award . . . and I can't remember all the others. Phil and Sarah were the "Harambee Singers." They presented a skit, a takeoff on songs, mostly Gilbert and Sullivan, which "roasted" each of us in the group in turn. The hunting beasts of the night must have been amazed at the clamor of our merriment.

Sadye was brave during the trip, but she felt ill much of the time, and I had a feeling it would be our last safari.

From Africa, we went to London and had a good visit with Ralph and Daphne Bennett. Work on the facsimile edition of the Caxton Manuscript was completed and we were wrestling with the problem of distributing copies, so we had plenty to talk about.

Sadye and I had made our usual pilgrimages to our favorite London art galleries. Back when we were visiting Europe four or five times a year, Sadye would spend a great deal of time in museums and galleries while I was working.

If she made some unusual find, we would arrange to see it together. My favorite painters are 15th and early 16th century Italians, especially Florentine, but I also like Pieter Brueghel the Younger. There is an uncompromising zest for life in his work, and I enjoy the richness and honesty of detail he captures. The fact that so many of his works are miniatures also appeals to me, perhaps because I feel in them a similarity to microfilm.

All things considered, it was a wonderful trip. But the news we received after our return in mid-July was dismal. Sadye went to see Dr. Russell de Jongh, chairman of the department of neurology at the U of M, and his grim diagnosis was Parkinson's disease.

The cause of Parkinsonism is not known. Nor is there any cure. It attacks the central nervous system, reducing control over all voluntary muscular movements and producing a stooped posture, slowness of movement, loss of control over the tongue and lips, making speech and chewing difficult, and an uncontrollable tremor of the arms and legs. These symptoms worsen slowly but inexorably.

Researchers believe that the motor symptoms of Parkinsonism are linked to depletion of the chemical neurotransmitter dopamine in the brain, and the drug L-dopa often eases the symptoms. Unfortunately, Sadye could not take L-dopa; the nausea it produced as a side effect was intolerable. I discovered a drug called Sinemet, an improvement on L-dopa developed in Europe. It had not been approved by the FDA for sale in the United States, but it was available in England, and I obtained some from there. Sadye responded fairly well to Sinemet, with only a few side effects, so I continued to obtain it from England until it was approved by the FDA in May 1975.

By that time I was taking Sinemet myself.

Two months after Sadye's diagnosis, I was told that I, too, had Parkinson's. I understand it is very rare for both a husband and wife to have this disease, but it is a distinction without honor and one that Sadye and I would gladly give up.

I found soon after my diagnosis that my skill in sports was gradually deteriorating. My golf game fell off, and there seemed to be nothing I could do to correct it. My balance and coordination were affected, too, though I continued to play water polo regularly with the Flounders. For despite my medical sentence to a progressive decline and the apparently inevitable conclusion that claims most victims of Parkinson's—death from choking—I was not ready to submit. Neither was Sadye.

For the next seven years we continued to travel, though with increasing difficulty, and I continued to push ahead with my activities. Coping with the same ailment helps us understand each other's problems, and the handicaps we have had to deal with have made the enjoyable moments— and there have been many of them—all the sweeter.

One of those enjoyable moments was my election to membership in the American Philosophical Society (APS) in the fall of 1974. The APS was founded in 1743 by Benjamin Franklin, who had a strong belief, as I do, in the value of associations for useful ends. In establishing the society, he called for a "constant correspondence of virtuosos (men of scientific interests) throughout the colonies."

There was a requirement that members must have contributed to public knowledge. The society grew and, at some point in its more than two hundred and thirty years of existence, passed the rule that membership would be limited to five hundred Americans and fifty individuals from other countries. Being elected to such a distinguished group was, of course, very gratifying.

In March 1976, I received a telephone call from Julian Boyd, librarian of Princeton, editor of the Jefferson Papers, and president of the APS, who asked if I had read the report on the front page of *The New York Times* about the proposed sale of the site of the Battle of Hastings. I had not, and Julian proceeded to read it to me:

London, March 13—The hundred-acre field where William, Duke of Normandy, defeated Harold, King of England, in the Battle of Hastings in 1066 is going to be sold to the highest bidder next June.

The battle, which gave the Norman duke control of England and the title William the Conquerer, has been termed "one of the battles which at rare intervals have decided the fate of nations." It was the last time a foreign invader vanquished the English. Norman rule and civilization left their marks on Britain, and the French language enriched Anglo-Saxon speech.

Yet the battlefield, part of a 573-acre estate that is on the market, will be auctioned as ordinary property at the Mayfair Hotel in London on June 24 unless it is sold privately before then. The present owners cannot afford its upkeep, and the inheritance taxes would force its sale eventually, they say.

England is so rich in historical buildings "littered all over the place," as a spokesman for the Department of the Environment said today, that a battlefield is not automatically protected as an "ancient monument" as it would be in the United States.

354

Wouldn't it be a shame, Julian said, if the battle site were thrown into a commercial deal—just so many more clods of earth? I agreed. But I wondered what was actually on the property. Well, according to *The New York Times* story, Julian replied, William gave thanks for his victory by founding a Benedictine abbey on the battlefield, and although the original building was a ruin, a gatehouse was still standing and an abbot's house nearby was tenanted by Battle Abbey School for girls. Julian's idea, he explained, was that Americans might raise enough money to buy the battle site and abbey. We could then present the deed to Queen Elizabeth when she came to Philadelphia for the celebration of the United States Bicentennial on the Fourth of July. Did I agree? Indeed I did. Would I work on the project with him? Absolutely!

We ended our conversation with Julian promising to keep me posted on the results of further research he was conducting. What he found made Battle Abbey seem all the more important. Its altar had been built on the spot where King Harold had raised his standard at dawn on October 14, 1066, as he arrayed his troops along the top of a ridge to do battle. He'd learned that the sections of land containing the battle site and abbey comprised 156 acres, and informed opinion was that they might be had for about $400,000.

The next meeting of the American Philosophical Society, the following month in Philadelphia, was the last at which Julian Boyd would preside. We elected Dr. Jonathan Rhoades as the new president, and he and the executive council listened attentively as Julian proposed our plan. They approved it immediately and asked me to head the fund-raising effort, which I gladly agreed to do. Louis Wright, a Society member and Director of the Folger Library in Washington, D.C., was asked to contact the British ambassador to initiate correspondence with the proper authorities.

To Wright's dismay, the ambassador did not seem very interested in our plan. He finally agreed to write to London, but the letter went astray in rather Dickensian fashion. When we had no response after a month, the ambassador was approached once more. He traced the letter to Buckingham Palace, where for some reason it had been sitting for nearly four weeks on someone's desk in the protocol department. Nothing had been done about it. After that, though, we received a series of telephone calls and cables of steadily increasing urgency from various officials. It was apparent that they had finally become extremely interested in our proposal.

Our fund-raising campaign also encountered some situations that seemed like they, too, must have been plotted by Dickens. There were three principal beneficiaries of the trust that was selling the 573-acre estate, which Henry VIII had given to his Master of Horse, Sir Anthony Browne, during the dissolution of the monasteries in the sixteenth century. The estate had passed through a number of hands, and the beneficiaries now disagreed about the battle site. One of them wished to withdraw that 156-acre section from the main estate and sell it privately; one did not want to separate the battle site under any circumstances; and the other one was unable to act, being under the care of a guardian. Therefore, the trustees felt obliged to sell only through a public auction. I contacted Sir Frank Francis for advice, and he put me in touch with a solicitor in London who agreed to represent the APS in the transaction. After a few days, the solicitor called to tell me that the British Department of the Environment would bid for the entire 753 acres, and if they were successful, they would sell the battle site to us.

By this time we had raised $390,000, in large part through Julian's efforts. Unfortunately, the American Philosophical Society realized that due to IRS regulations, it could not participate in the purchase, because the specific object of the gift was being directed through the APS to a foreign country. Under these circumstances, I decided to proceed directly in behalf of the seven individuals whose contributions had been made to support the project, rather than the APS.

Happily, the bid by the Department of the Environment won, and our solicitor worked out a purchase arrangement for the 156 acres we wanted. Our problem now was how to get the money to England on a basis that would allow the donors to obtain a charitable deduction for their contributions. After considerable searching, Julian found the Royal Oak Foundation, a branch of England's National Trust, which had been established in New York to accept grants for specific purposes in England from sources in the United States. After receiving a multipage opinion from the IRS, the Royal Oak Foundation agreed to handle the transfer of funds, which was to take place on September 29, 1976.

Sadye and I decided to go to England for the ceremony at Battle Abbey that was to follow my signing of the transfer documents in London. We had not been abroad for four years, because Sadye's physical condition had been so delicate. The acute pains in her legs and back, we discovered, had nothing to do with Parkinson's. She had three discs that were pressing on spinal nerves and two vertebrae that had calcified inside, further compressing nerves. She became unable to travel at all. During the summer of 1975, she was virtually bedridden, but she underwent back surgery that September, and her condition slowly but steadily improved.

We left September 28, 1976, on a Pan American 747. We had considered taking the *Concorde,* which makes the trip much shorter, but decided that the seating space on the *Concorde* would be too cramped for Sadye. I managed to have her stretched out on a row of four seats, and she endured the flight well.

I knew we would not be going to our old London haunts this time. In fact, I felt we would be lucky if Sadye were able to get around much at all. She was hampered more than usual because she had fallen on some stairs the night before we left and bruised her elbow and both knees. A Pan Am service representative in London arranged for us to be taken through customs in an electric cart, which expedited matters. The morning after our arrival, I left Sadye at the hotel and went to the law office on Cheapside where I was to meet our solicitor and Roland Ditchfield, who was in charge of Ancient Monuments for the Department of the Environment. The funds I had brought were transferred in a series of document exchanges between lawyers for the Royal Oak Foundation, the British government, the trust representing the owners of the property, and me.

358

REFLECTIONS

That night, Sadye and I went to dinner at Peggy Crowther's house near the London Zoo. Peggy was the widow of Lord (Geoffrey) Crowther who had been involved in University Microfilms, Ltd. Geoffrey was editor of *The Economist* when I first met him in 1956 in Ann Arbor, where he was visiting Dean Clare Griffin of the U of M Business School. He had asked Clare to arrange a meeting with me. After some discussion, he asked if he could be an investor in our London company. I had not thought about that sort of thing, but it seemed reasonable, and he took a minority interest, about 15 percent as I recall. I had given Arthur and Phyllis Cain some stock when the company was first organized. The operation was always a source of frustration for me; it just couldn't seem to do very well. When I sold UMI, I did not feel I could put a very high value on the London company, since it had been a losing proposition from the beginning. I think Geoffrey made about a 25 percent return on his investment and, in retrospect, I think I made a mistake. I should have put a higher value on the company. I think the Cains felt rather disappointed with what they received, when UML was sold in 1962, and justifiably so.

As a result of two or three misadventures after going to the theater, when we could not find a taxi and were forced to walk, Sadye began having real difficulty with her legs. This kept us pretty much confined to the hotel.

Nevertheless, we made it to the ceremony at Battle Abbey on October 13, 1976, and a grand occasion it was. The organizers had kindly arranged to have a wheelchair for Sadye, so she was able to tour the grounds, too. That evening at the reception, which was very formal, with a herald in a bright red jacket announcing the names of all guests as they entered, my heart flew into my throat in a lump to see Sadye standing up, looking so lovely in a long white dress with colorful flowers, a gold necklace, and a cerise scarf on her hair.

I was sorrier to leave London that mid-October of 1976 than on any previous occasion. Perhaps it was because of the difficulty we had faced and overcome in making the stay enjoyable; or perhaps it was the "last visit" syndrome manifesting itself for a country and people I had known and loved so well and might not see again.

Yet in the months following our return to Ann Arbor, the spirits of the Power household improved greatly. Sadye was gaining more strength and experiencing less pain in her back and legs. This process was aided by spending the coldest months that winter in the sunshine of Indian Wells, California. Our friends Eugene and Gretel Ormandy graciously rented their home in the Eldorado Club to us (we continue to spend time there each winter). We were buoyed up, too, by the happy progress our son and daughter-in-law were making in their respective fields. Phil's merger of his Observer papers with the Eccentric papers was successful. His loss in the U.S. Senate primary race in 1978 appeared to solidify his orientation to the newspaper business, though his interest in politics certainly continues.[3] Sarah was

---

[3] Phil was an adviser to Jim Blanchard, both during his first campaign for governor and through his first two administrations. Phil also was chairman of Michigan's State Job Training Coordinating Council and served on the Governor's Commission on the Future of Higher Education.

elected a Regent of the University of Michigan in 1974.

Things were going so well, in fact, that Sadye and I decided to return to England in September 1977. So almost a year to the day since we had last been in Ralph and Daphne Bennett's home in Cambridge for lunch, we were seated around the table there once again. The telephone rang and Ralph answered, cocking his head quizzically. Then he cupped a hand over the receiver and shouted, "Stop talking! Everybody, stop talking, please!" When he had our attention, he said, "I have an important announcement for you, Gene. It's Margaret Massialas calling from the States to tell you that the Queen has made you a knight!"

Ralph and Daphne Bennett.

A stunned silence fell over the room, and as I rose to go over to the phone and talk to Margaret, Sadye exclaimed, "I think I'm going to cry."

The ceremony bestowing the honor on me was held that November, appropriately I thought, in the rare-books room of the Clements Library at the University. Harlan Hatcher presided, since the current U of M President, Robben Fleming, was out of town, and the gold and blue enamel Cross of King George, suspended from a red ribbon with white center stripe, was draped over my shoulders by Peter Jay, Britain's ambassador to the United States.

361

In his remarks[4] Ambassador Jay said, "In a world which increasingly, alas, is becoming short of space, Mr. Power was one of the first to develop the all-important science of

U of M photo by Paul Jaronski

After my knighting ceremony, I share a toast with Peter Jay, Sarah, and Phil.

miniaturization—in his case, microfilm. We in Britain will long remember, with a deep sense of gratitude, at a time when our shores were under a severe threat of attack, his gift of *lebensraum* for so many of our precious archives and libraries. He helped, literally, to transfer the inheritance of English language and culture to the United States, with whom we share these precious things . . . and last year there

[4] For complete text, see Appendix H.

362

was widespread and grateful recognition of his typical generosity in association with Professor Boyd of Princeton and others who have remained anonymous, in donating the famous Battle Abbey Estate in Hastings, England, to the British Crown. . . ."

Frank came down from Traverse City and took pictures of the ceremony and the champagne reception that followed. In all, it was an important and moving occasion. I appreciate the recognition, although both the British code on orders of chivalry and the U.S. Constitution ban the titular prefix in addressing holders of such honorary titles, so I'll never be known as Sir Eugene Power.

The dozen years following that ceremony have passed with incredible swiftness. Time seems to accelerate as one grows older; events fold into one another, collapsing the present into the past in a rapid glissando of joys and sorrows, triumphs and disasters.

I have kept busy on the affairs of the Power Foundation, Eskimo Art, and other interests, such as the Ann Arbor Summer Festival, and my work on the board of Domino's Pizza, Inc. A project I recently helped develop for Domino's is a center for senior citizens called Domino's House. The idea came from Lois Jelneck who, with her associate, Ingrid Deininger, operates Individualized Home Nursing Care (I.H.N.C.) in Ann Arbor. Lois is one of Sadye's nurses, and I thought she and Ingrid were correct in their assessment that many families have elderly members who need a place that can look after them during the day while the younger folk work. It took a great deal of time and effort to get the pilot project started in space leased by Domino's in a local schoolhouse, and I hope that one day the company will be able to replicate it across the country.

My activities have been slowed down by Parkinson's. The disease affects my balance, which is inconvenient; it has caused me to fall and break my glasses, and my nose. The insidious thing about Parkinson's, though, is the frustration

Karsh, Ottawa

Sadye in a rare formal portrait.

and anger it produces, because one feels imprisoned in one's own body. There is nothing wrong with our minds—Sadye's thoughts are as stimulating and insightful as ever—but due to loss of control of her speech and diction as a result of Parkinson's, she cannot express them to most people. I can understand her, so can Phil, and so can the nurses who are on duty around the clock in our house now. Some of her friends like Mary Bromage can understand her better than others. Mary and her husband, Arthur, were members of our RAMS and LAMS social set. After Mary retired as a professor of written communications at the U of M Business School, she wrote a book titled *Writing for Business* and became a consultant on that subject for major companies and the military. Mary tape-recorded some thoughts about Sadye, from which the following was excerpted:

> I met Sadye Power for the first time when we were both young women. Someone pointed her out to me at a style show. She wasn't given to style shows, but she was a very stunning figure. I asked, "Well, who is Sadye Power?" The woman I was with said, "Oh, she's a psychological counselor at the university. She's not a doctor, but she is one of the strongest counselors they have."
>
> I visited Sadye at her home recently and the subject of choosing a new president for the U of M came up. She struggled very hard to make a point—it is so difficult for her to speak, you see—but I could see from the intensity in her eyes that it was important to her. Finally, she got it out: "Have they considered a woman?"
>
> Sadye, as you may know, was responsible for having women as well as men made eligible for Power Scholarships. Sadye still participates in the interviews with Power Scholarship candidates, and I believe her judgment is in large part responsible for

the high academic success record of the students who were selected.

Sadye's difficulty in talking is complicated by her loss of hearing, which I do not think is caused by Parkinson's. I have devised a hearing aid, with two sets of earphones, using parts from a radio-supply store, and this gadget makes it possible for the two of us to carry on a reasonably normal conversation.

We were sitting in our living room holding hands one evening in 1975, and I noticed that Sadye's pulse seemed very slow. I counted it at 35 beats per minute, which is less than half the normal rate, so next day I took her to the doctor. The upshot was that she had a pacemaker implanted, and in the last fourteen years, she has gone through six of them. The technology of pacemakers has improved greatly during that time, and the device she currently has is tiny by comparison with the first one. It also is designed so that its functioning and battery strength can be tested by the specialist over the telephone and it will last for seven years.

Sadye and I were shaken by my brother Frank's death on January 27, 1978. It was a great blow for both of us. Yet the way he died was fitting, I suppose, considering his dedication to the medical profession and his love for the outdoors.

Frank and Margot lived back in the woods on Lee Point on the shore of Grand Traverse Bay.[5] They were snowbound that day, but Frank said he had to get to the hospital; he had an operation scheduled. So he called the sheriff and ex-

---

[5] Frank had used part of the money from my 1964 gift to build this place; one of the conditions I had placed on the gift was that he *had* to use it—he couldn't squirrel it away.

plained the situation, saying he would snowshoe out to the main road if the sheriff would meet him there and drive him to the hospital. He made it to the main road all right, but the strain of that long hike on snowshoes in the bitter cold was too much for his heart. He died in the sheriff's car. Margot gave me the following tape-recorded recollections of what happened thereafter:

Frank died on a Friday and the snow was so deep that no one could get in here, which in a sense was great. Gene called on the Saturday, very worried because I was alone up here. I was touched. Then two snowmobiles came in: one the sheriff, who brought my daughter and grandson, the other was Ted Okerstrom, who ran the Park Place Motor Inn for Gene. The next morning the county snowplow came in before it had cleared the rest of Lee Road and made a swath down the half-mile that dead-ends in my turn-around.

But it was close on a week before you could really get around. I had Frank cremated in Grand Rapids. When Gene and Sadye came up, they picked up Frank's ashes on the way and brought them home. We talked about a memorial service. Frank and I always felt that unless you were a very prominent person, funerals should be private. Weddings are different. We felt weddings should be public, and acknowledged by all, but not funerals.

Frank and I had discussed our burial wishes, and we agreed that his ashes should fertilize his birch trees—he had a hangup about those birches; he had been trying for years to get the damn things to grow—so my son Jeff cleared a path out to the birches. After everybody arrived, Gene and Sadye, Phil and Sarah, and my children and grandchildren, we all trooped out and made a circle around the birch clump. The snow made a sort of altar next to the trees, where Jeff had dug a hole for the casket of ashes. We sprinkled some of the ashes on that altar, and Gene took a handful to sprinkle into the bay, where he and Frank had sailed for so many years. There was still a bit of open water near the point, and as we slogged through the snow to get there, two swans that Frank and I always fed came swimming up to meet our party. Phil ran back to the house to get some bread for them, and we tossed bread to them and Gene sprinkled the ashes. It was beautiful. Then we went back to the house and had brunch. We reminisced about Frank, and I think Gene felt very good about the whole thing.

When one reaches the age of eighty-four, death has become an old acquaintance, but there is no way of inuring oneself to its increasingly frequent visits. This is especially true when those it takes are young and seem to have the most promise, as was the case with our daughter-in-law Sarah, whose suicide in March 1987 was a great shock to all who knew her.

Children are the best antidote to death's loss and grief, and our grandson, Nathan, whom Phil and Sarah adopted in 1982, has been a constant joy to Sadye and me. He is a bright, energetic youngster, and at age seven he's already an enthusiastic fisherman.

I missed Frank, not only for his companionship, but for the sound medical advice he always gave me. I recall the last big trip we took together, just Frank and me, a fishing expedition to Panama in 1974. It was one of those rare occasions when I grew absolutely weary of pulling in fish and longed to go home—the Caribbean sun was too hot, the very atmosphere oppressive—and had it not been for Frank's agreeable companionship, I probably *would* have gone home early. Somehow I managed to cut a nasty gash in one of my fingers, and though Frank had no suturing material, he used silk thread and sewed it up so expertly I scarcely felt pain.

I felt his absence very acutely in the spring of 1988, when I had a serious problem with my stomach. I went to the hospital with some bleeding from an ulcer. Later the ulcer spread and ruptured a nearby artery, which began hemorrhaging and did not seem to want to stay cauterized. Three days later, as I was getting ready to be released, the real hemorrhage let loose. The physicians poured seventeen pints of blood into me in an attempt to make up for what I was losing. I now realize what a near miss I had. My recovery was speeded by the expert care of Dottie Normand, one of Sadye's nurses, who spent the greater part of each twenty-four hours at my bedside.

Fortunately, I was able to get out of the hospital in time to join Sadye, Phil, Nathan, and an amazingly large group of UMI employees, both past and present, to celebrate the company's Golden Anniversary. Sixteen hundred invitations were sent out and fourteen hundred people showed up. It was held June 1, 1988 in the Power Center for the Performing Arts, and it was a gala evening. The doctors thought it would be OK if I went on stage in my wheelchair. I would have anyhow—I could not have sat by in silence after seeing all those people who had contributed so much to the company over the years and hearing Joe Fitzsimmons's stirring tribute. Phil wheeled me onto the stage, and I managed to walk toward the podium, leaning on my "Father Time" staff. I was beginning to think I had made a big mistake, that I wasn't going to make it, when the orchestra in the pit below began playing "Hail to the Chief." Well, of course, that lifted me over those last few steps, and I was able to say some words of my own, apologizing for whispering because the tubes that had been pushed down my throat in the hospital had rubbed my vocal cords raw.

A month later, I went to England with Margaret Massialas and Joe Fitzsimmons for another celebration of UMI's anniversary at Magdalene College. I was sorry that Sadye could not go this time. I had hoped that Vernon Tate would be able to, but his health was too poor also. Vernon had contributed a great deal to the field of microfilm, and his presence would have added luster to the occasion. But I must say it was a memorable event anyhow. I had the feeling my speech went well, and Ralph and Daphne Bennett and Margaret later assured me that it did. And Joe Fitzsimmons was positively eloquent. He spoke about the "Genesis" of UMI, saying:

> About 1454, Johann Gutenberg invented the art of printing from movable type cast in lead. Through the generations thereafter, technology kept improving on Gutenberg's idea, finding better and faster ways to transfer an image onto paper. Offset, or photolithography, developed in the early 1900s, was one of these methods.
>
> In 1934, Eugene B. Power, a 29-year-old offset-printing-company executive, conceived the idea of microfilm publishing. Power saw that photographic film, used in the process of making offset plates, could itself become a form of publication when produced as a positive and illuminated in a projector. Subsequent users of his product would read an image that was only light and shadow.

REFLECTIONS

University Microfilms, Inc. was formed by Power in 1938 to pursue the commercial potential of his idea. As with print publishing, technology has brought a continuous series of improvements on the basic idea.

Now, as it celebrates its fiftieth anniversary, UMI, a subsidiary of Bell & Howell Company since 1985, has expanded Power's idea to new markets. This growth includes adaptation of his idea to the electronic age, disseminating materials on video disks.

The prism of history separates forces in the spectrum of human events, and even the relatively short span of fifty years makes clear that Power was the right man at the right time for the invention of the idea of microfilm publishing.

He then gave a rather moving summary of my career, describing events that have already been discussed here. So suffice it to say that he gave five reasons for his assertion that I was the "right man at the right time": (1) my background at Edwards Brothers and my understanding of academics and their needs, plus the wide contacts I had with them, thanks in large measure to Sadye; (2) the influence of Randolph Adams, William Warner Bishop, and Warner Rice; (3) my technical ability and the influence of Robert Binkley and Vernon Tate; (4) the growth of photography as a library tool, with the consequent interest of my contacts in the American Library Association; and (5) the influence of George McCarthy's check-copying "flow" camera for banks and other developments, such as Draeger's copy camera. Joe went on to say:

> [he] assimilated the varied elements of these interests and associations and considered them creatively rather than logically. His intuition, informed by technical understanding, seemed to dispense with logical steps, going from problem to solution

371

in a single bound. . . .

Hindsight tends to make seminal ideas seem obvious: of course a light bulb must eliminate oxygen by forming a vacuum in order to prevent the filament from igniting. Of course a needle with an eye at its point can make a chain stitch in cloth without removing the needle. But it took the genius of Edison to come up with the incandescent bulb and the insight of Elias Hunt to patent a sewing machine. And so it was with Power's idea, which was the first ever to allow economical and practical publication of a single copy. It *is* obvious now, but at the time of its conception it ran counter to all the prevailing wisdom about printing.

I appreciated Joe's remarks, which he concluded by mentioning my "humanitarian contributions and work in preserving social and cultural institutions."

Certainly I intend to keep up those latter activities as long as possible. However, I don't go into the office as early or stay as late these days as I once did. I want to spend more time with Sadye. For whatever else I have done in my life that may seem important to others, all dims by comparison to the importance of my marriage to her.

Married life is not an easy undertaking. Even the closest of couples are bound to have stormy moments and periods of stress. This is especially true, I think, when both partners are strong individuals, like Sadye and me. She was a force in the community long before I was; in fact, when we were first married, I was known around Ann Arbor as "Mr. Sadye Power," an appellation I did not resent. Indeed, I was rather proud of it.

Our love has helped us to overcome the differences that from time to time came between us, though, and there has never been a moment when either of us questioned the support and affection of the other.

An interviewer named Enid Galler, who spent consider-able time compiling an oral history for me, asked toward the end of our work together what ideas I would like to pass on to my grandchild. And my response makes a fitting conclusion to this autobiography, I think, because the thoughts contain much of what I have learned over the years from Sadye and, of course, from my own experience.

I hope my grandson will live his life for what each day holds—that he will not make himself unhappy for what has happened in the past or what may happen in the future. Today is here and today is to be used, to be lived to the fullest. I don't mean that he should adopt a kind of fool-hardy, devil-may-care point of view about the future—or anything else. I mean simply to use what the day brings and be satisfied with it.

I hope that he will use the talents with which he was endowed for the benefit of those around him. It is difficult to know how to do that. It is a thing one must learn for oneself.

I hope he will learn that each individual represents a unique set of experiences that condition his or her attitude toward life. Therefore, he should be very careful in assess-ing any blame on any individuals for their actions.

I hope he will learn that no person can ever truly view a situation through the eyes of another. For that reason we must be tolerant and be helpful. People are basically good. We must have affection for people, even if we do not understand them.

I hope he will learn to be honest with himself, because if he can do that, he will always be honest and truthful to others and follow the Golden Rule. And I hope he will draw from each experience that which is good and beneficial to him and not be discouraged. Fear and discouragement are such deadening, self-defeating emotions. They must be overcome.

Finally, I urge him to realize that he came onto this globe and into this life as mere potential—unformed and undifferentiated—but what tremendous potential! Each individual has that potential to live life according to his or her convictions and ideals. I could not wish for more for any youngster on earth than that he recognize his own potential and do his best to make the most of it.

Appendices

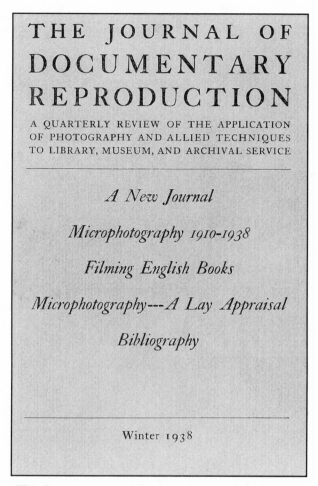

THE JOURNAL OF
DOCUMENTARY
REPRODUCTION

A QUARTERLY REVIEW OF THE APPLICATION
OF PHOTOGRAPHY AND ALLIED TECHNIQUES
TO LIBRARY, MUSEUM, AND ARCHIVAL SERVICE

A New Journal

Microphotography 1910-1938

Filming English Books

Microphotography---A Lay Appraisal

Bibliography

Winter 1938

First issue cover reproduction, about half actual size.

The frontispiece states: "The need for an independent, critical, impartial journal in this field, published on a coöperative non-profit basis, has been felt by scholars, scientists, archivists, librarians, editors, authors, and other concerned groups. This JOURNAL, in attempting to meet this need, urges other periodicals to continue disseminating helpful news concerning scientific aids to learning, and seeks their coöperation, as its editors and publishers are motivated only by the spirit of scientific inquiry and service to scholarship."

377

A PLAN FOR

Publication of Scholarly Material by Microfilm

Low Cost Publication of Material Intended for Limited Distribution

by Eugene B. Power

The invention of printing provided the means for the tremendous expansion of scholarly research through the duplication of man's ideas, and the years that followed demonstrated the value of this new technique. For centuries printing methods fulfilled the requirements of scholars as a means of reproducing the results of research. With the turn of the century it has been increasingly apparent that the greater specialization of scholarship has resulted in a decrease in the potential market for books and monographs in any one field. This same printing press which at one time provided the release from the restricting influence of book production by scribes is now exerting a similarly restricting influence through a reverse process.

Our printing facilities today are all geared to the production of a large number of copies on an extremely economical basis. However, they are not able to produce a small number of copies economically, and with this decrease in the size of the market, publication of scholarly material becomes an increasingly difficult problem unless accompanied by subsidy.

Present-day publishing involves an estimate of the number of copies of a given book which can be sold, producing a sufficient number to make them available at a saleable price, with the hope that enough will be sold to recover the initial investment made in type, paper, press work, and binding. Too often it develops that but a portion of the edition is sold, the balance remaining on the shelves to collect dust. This represents an expenditure of the available funds of scholarship which are tied up in stock which cannot be recovered.

What scholarly publishing needs is a method of distribution which gives sufficient and adequate publicity to a title or list of titles so that the information regarding what is offered is readily available to prospective users, combined with a means of production which can produce as demand materializes at an economical and uniform rate.

The newly developed microfilm technique offers an ideal solution and this booklet sets forth a proposal which, it is believed, meets these requirements in a singularly satisfactory manner.

Briefly, this is a plan to provide a means of production and distribution for the products of scholarly research which, because of their nature, command too small a market to warrant publication through the ordinary and established channels. This is conceived to include two general types of material, one being the monograph, and the other the dissertation.

The service of University Microfilms which is offered here, would operate in the following manner:

1. This service is available to scholars possessing a doctorate degree or those having a doctorate dissertation for publication.

This restriction is made in order to maintain a certain amount of control of the material submitted, for it is not proposed that University Microfilms will assume any responsibility for the content or the scholastic standard of the material submitted; the sole purpose being to aid and facilitate distribution.

2. Each author will be required to submit a carefully typed manuscript accompanied by an abstract of 300 or 400 words with the deposit of the usual fee for this service.

The original typewritten manuscript will be returned to the author as soon as it is photographed, and the negative placed on file.

3. In the case of doctorate dissertations, the abstract must have the approval of the candidate's committee before it will be accepted.

4. The abstracts thus collected from several sources or authors, will be published in a booklet of abstracts issued at periodic intervals, each abstract occupying one page. At the bottom of each abstract will appear a statement to the effect that a film copy of the complete manuscript can be had at 1 1/4 cent per page, and a total figure for the entire book.

5. For each title in the booklet of abstracts, two library cards will

be prepared, a subject and an author card.

6. One copy of the booklet of abstracts and one complete set of cards will be distributed without charge to 200 of the leading libraries in the United States and abroad.

7. The same titles contained in the booklet of abstracts will be incorporated into certain of the standard widely distributed and current bibliographies.

8. Copies of the booklet will be sent to the leading scholarly journals for listing of the subjects within their field for comment or review.

9. The author is in no way restricted from publishing by any other means than film. If he wishes to publish a condensation of his manuscript in a journal or revise it and print it in book form, that is his privilege.

10. If sufficient demand materializes to indicate that there is interest enough in the title to warrant printing the book by some one of the conventional methods, this will be suggested and help given in arranging such publication.

11. The Bureau of Copyrights has stated that they will consider as publication this method of production and distribution, and therefore will accept two film copies of the manuscript as fulfilling the requirements for copyright should the author wish this protection.

12. The only charge to the author or his institution will be $15.00 which will cover the cost of printing and distributing the abstract, and photographing the manuscript.

In actual use the plan will operate in the following manner: Anyone working in a given field will find the titles listed under this service in either the current bibliographies, the card catalog files in his library, or in the current literature, all of which will refer him to the abstract printed in the booklet of abstracts.

From examination of this abstract he can then determine whether or not the complete manuscript covers the material in which he is interested, which is not possible from the mere title or very brief descriptions which are offered at present. If this proves to be the case, he can then order a film copy of the complete manuscript at a very reasonable rate.

While the usefulness of this method of publication depends somewhat upon the availability of reading machines, most scholars who would use a service of this type, and who are working with this type of material, are located in institutions already possessing such equipment. Further, the development of low cost reading machines which is going rapidly ahead, indicates that the distribution of these machines will be widespread and, therefore, easily accessible.

Under such a plan as this, the only cost to scholarship involved in the publication of a manuscript is $15.00—less than the cost of typing it. If there is no demand for such material the loss is slight. If the demand is there and the material is needed, it is available at a reasonable cost. The microfilm technique makes possible the production of copies upon demand, and for the first time we are released from the restrictions of the printing press which specifies that a comparatively large number of copies be produced so as to bring the cost per copy to a low level.

A sample abstract and catalog card covering a typical dissertation, which will show how the information will be distributed are shown below.

Specimen Abstract

THE HIGH PLAINS OF MICHIGAN

Charles M. Davis Thesis (Ph.D.)
University of Michigan, 1935

The purpose of this study is to describe and explain the landscapes which make up the High Plains, an area in the northern part of the southern peninsula of Michigan. Parts of this area had been mapped in detail by state agencies, in others it was necessary to construct the general outlines from reconnaissance mapping based upon this previous work by the state. The conclusion of this study points out that:

The position of the High Plains upon the patterns of the world distributions of climate, vegetation, and population undoubtedly underlies the broader facts of its geography, but these larger distributions neither mark the regionality of the area nor orient its internal differentiation. As the study presented here has attempted to show: *The distribution of the landscape-forming elements and the resulting landscapes follow in general a fundamental pattern based upon a distribution of the surface features and soil materials which were laid down by the retreating ice of the last glaciation.* Upon this original fundament the weathering of the glacial material into soils and the development of the cover types proceeded in a direction consistent with the existing climate. Until the time of the occupance of the lumbermen this process of landscape development had gone ahead almost

382

APPENDIX B

to the harmonious codistribution of cover associations and soil types. Thus far the activities of man had not altered the nature of things in the High Plains to any significant degree, but a new occupance took over the area, changed the cover, introduced new elements into the course of development, and initiated the modern landscape.

Into the slow and orderly process of the evolution of the natural landscapes were thrust new cultural factors: clearing, fire, and agriculture. The result was an almost complete change in the cover associations and the introduction of new types in one way or another suited to survive in the new regime. The basic framework of the soil and the surface remained practically unaltered.

From the debris of this overturn the modern landscapes are taking form. Slowly they can be seen to emerge as an image develops upon a photographic plate. Although their outlines are not yet sharp and their details are obscured by the "fireweed" associations and by the ebb and flow of human adjustment, nevertheless their distribution is apparent and it is seen to follow the same fundamental pattern of the surface and the soil.

Microfilm copy of complete manuscript
245 pages plus 5 maps at 1 1/4 cents, total cost, $3.20
Available from University Microfilms

Specimen Catalog Card

AS   Davis, Charles Moler, 1900-
36   The high plains of Michigan by Charles M.
.m6 Davis . . . [Ann Arbor, Mich., 1936]

     See Abstracts, University Microfilms
        Vol. I, No. 1, p. 16, 1938

          cover title, 303-341, [1] p. illus. (maps) pl. XLIII-
     XLV. 23 1/3cm

     Thesis (PH. D.) --- University of Michigan, 1935

     1. Physical Geography -- Michigan. 2. Michigan
     I . Title

383

British Manuscripts Project

A checklist of the microfilms made in England and Wales by
University Microfilms, Inc. under a grant from the Rockefeller
Foundation to the American Council of Learned Societies
1941 — 1945
Note: The collections listed are not complete.
Only those portions of particular interest to
American scholars were microfilmed. The
microfilms are in the possession of The
Library of Congress, Washington, D.C.

BATH
Marquises of. Library, Longleat
Coventry Papers
Devereux Papers
Dudley Papers

BEDFORD
Dukes of. Library
Manuscripts

BRITISH MUSEUM
Department of Manuscripts
Additional Mss.
Additional Charters
Arundel
Class Catalog of Mss.
Cotton Appendix
Cotton Augustus
Cotton Caligula
Cotton Claudius

Cotton Cleopatra
Cotton Domitian
Cotton Faustina
Cotton Fragments
Cotton Galba
Cotton Julius
Cotton Nero
Cotton Otho
Cotton Tiberius

EDITION OF ONE

Cotton Titus
Cotton Vespasian
Cotton Vitellius
Egerton
Hargrave
Harley

Lansdowne
Royal
Sloane
Stowe
Department of Printed Books
Thomason Collection

CAMBRIDGE
University and College Libraries
Lettered Manuscripts, A through Z
Supernumerary Mss.
Christ's College
Manuscripts

Emmanuel College
Manuscripts

Fitzwilliam Museum
Manuscripts
McClean
Marlay

Gonville and Caius College
Manuscripts

Jesus College
Manuscripts

Newnham College
Manuscripts

Pembroke College
Manuscripts

Later Manuscripts

APPENDIX C

Peterhouse
Manuscripts

Queen's College
Manuscripts

St. Catherine's College
Manuscripts

St. John's College
Manuscripts

Sidney Sussex College
Manuscripts

Trinity College
Manuscripts

Trinity Hall
Manuscripts

DOWNSHIRE
Marquesses of. Library
Trumbull Manuscripts

ETON
College Library
Manuscripts

PUBLIC RECORD OFFICE
Great Britain
Admiralty
Colonial Offices: Carolina, North Carolina, South Carolina, Georgia, Maryland, Massachusetts, New Hampshire, New Jersey, New York, Pennsylvania.
Foreign Office
Home Office: Disturbances, Domestic
Special Collections
Star Chamber
Treasury: American Loyalist Claims
War Office: Amherst Papers

HOLKHAM HALL
Leicester, Earls of. Library
Deeds
Manuscripts

HOLKHAM HALL Cont.
Miscellaneous
Billingford Court Rolls
Burnham Court Rolls
Castleacre Court Rolls
Creake Court Rolls
Dunton Court Rolls
Elmham Court Rolls
Fulmodestone Court Rolls

Holkham Court Rolls
Longham Court Rolls
Massingham Court Rolls
Tittleshall Court Rolls
Warham Court Rolls
Wellingham Court Rolls
Wells Court Rolls
West Lexham Court Rolls
Wighton Court Rolls

LINCOLN CATHEDRAL
Cathedral Library
Manuscripts

MIDDLETON
Barons of. Library (Birdsall House)
Manuscripts

MISCELLANEOUS COLLECTIONS
London, Royal College of Music
Manuscripts
Singer, Dorothea (Waley) Bibliography
Manuscripts
Imprints
Smith, Vernon
Manuscripts
Victoria and Albert Museum Library
Catalogs

NORTHUMBERLAND
Dukes of. Library (Alnwick Castle)
Manuscripts
Dukes of. Library (Syon House)
Ten Lettered Collections

APPENDIX C

OXFORD
Bodleian Library

Additional Mss.
Archivum Seldenianum
Ashmole
Auctarium
Ballard
Bodley
Bodley Rolls
Canonici
Carte
Clarendon
Digby
D'Orville
Douce
English Bibles
English History
English Miscellaneous
English Poetry
English Theology
Fairfax

Gough Ecclesiastical Topography
Greaves
Hatton
James
Junius
Latin Liturgies
Latin Miscellaneous
Laud Greek
Laud Miscellaneous
Liturgical Mss.
E. Musaeo
Music
Rawlinson
Rawlinson Liturgical
Rawlinson Poetry
Selden Supra
Tanner
Topography
Unidentified

PENSHURST
De l'Isle and Dudley, Barons of. Library
Penshurst Deeds
Penshurst Muniments
Robertsbridge Deeds
Sidney Deeds
Tattershall Deeds

SACKVILLE
Barons of. Library (Knole Park)
Papers

WALES
National Library

Aberdar Mss.
Additional Mss.
Carreglwyd Papers, Series I
Cwrt Mawr
Evans Ms.
Llanstephan Mss.
Merthyr Tydvil Mss.

Mostyn
Panton
Peniarth
Puleston Documents
Puleston Mss.
Wrexham

Part I: Supplement
Oxford University, Bodleian Library
Carte Mss.
Northumberland, Dukes of. Library (Syon House)
Two Documents

COLOR FILM
Oxford University, Balliol College
Manuscripts
Oxford University, Bodleian Library

Additional Mss.
Ashmole
Barocci
Bodley
Buchanan
Canonici Greek
Canonici Liturgical
Canonici Miscellaneous

Douce
E.D. Clarke
Latin Theology
Laud Latin
Laud Miscellaneous
E. Musaeo
Roe
Selden Supra

New College
Manuscripts

Part II: Index

Microfilm as a Substitute
for Binding

by Eugene B. Power

Of increasing urgency for libraries in the United States, and other countries as well, is a satisfactory solution for the storage problem. The number of books, of periodicals and newspapers which must be saved for future use is rapidly exceeding the physical capacity of the buildings now available or likely to be constructed. Even if one discounts the estimates of reputable authorities that a research library such as Yale University will tend to double its size every sixteen years,[1] the growth of collections and rise of building costs present formidable difficulties.

Two classes of material especially, periodicals and newspapers, crowd library shelves. Both have many issues each year, and both are bulky. Journals and newspapers have another characteristic in common—a high reader interest immediately following publication which diminishes more or less rapidly, depending on the subject. Recent studies by Fussler[2] and others reveal that in the fields of chemistry and physics interest rapidly declines after three years. This same pattern of use in a more intensive form surely holds for newspapers as well. Yet any good research library must have available back files of periodicals and newspapers, often covering 100 years and more, if it is to be worthy of the name. This situation presents an odd dilemma. The material is used but rarely and is filling stack space to overflowing, but still is essential when needed.

A possible expedient for the reduction of storage costs is the use of microfilm.[3] Under this plan the library circulates periodicals either un-bound, or in inexpensive pressboard covers, for the 2-5 year period after

---

[1] Rider, Fremont. *The Scholar and the Future of the Research Library,* New York, Hadham Press, 1944.

[2] Fussler, Herman, "Characteristics of the Research Literature Used by Chemists and Physicists in the United States," *Library Quarterly,* XIX, 19-35,1949.

[3] For a full description and list of titles included in this service see "The Problem of Periodical Storage in Libraries," University Microfilms, Ann Arbor, Michigan, 1950.

publication during which the use is the heaviest, and at the same time a microfilm copy of the same material is purchased. The cost of the microfilm is no greater and is usually less than the cost of binding, and there is consequently no increase in over-all expense. When the demand for the original paper copies tapers off, they are discarded and the microfilm substituted for general use.

Nearly 800 leading periodicals are already available to subscribers to this service. Through the use of high-reduction microfilm it is possible to produce microfilm copies of journals to sell at the rate of 1/4 cent per page, which is just about the cost of binding the equivalent material. The film varies in reduction ratio from 14-1 to 20-1 as a maximum, reproducing forty pages to each foot. On a reading machine with an enlargement ratio of 17 to 25 times, the resulting image is clear, sharp and satisfactory. Low enlargement readers are not satisfactory, since the type is too small for comfortable reading.

The virtue of the program just described is that the library is able to acquire the microfilm at no additional expense since the cost is no more than the charges for binding. When the paper copies are discarded, most of the shelf space that would be required by the bound volumes represents a net saving and all without restriction of library service, though with a change in the nature of the material offered the reader.

A few detailed examples will make clear how great the saving really is. In terms of storage costs, a periodical fifty years old used once in five years is just as expensive as a periodical used fifty times in one year. When an estimate of what the cumulative storage charges for a periodical purchased on subscription, bound and stored for a period of fifty years or more is made, the result is astonishing. A realistic method for making such an estimate is outlined below.

Assume t = time in years during which a periodical file is stored, and that
v = The number of volumes per year
a = cost of storing one volume for one year
k = cost of binding one volume
n = number of volumes stored
b = cost of storing one volume in microfilm for one year
m = cost of microfilming one volume of newspaper
e = cost per page of microfilm copy of periodical
p = cost of making one positive microfilm from negative
y = number of pages in one volume
c = cost

APPENDIX D

The cost of storing a completed file of a journal which is no longer published can be expressed by the formula

$$c = a\, n\, t, \text{ if bound, and } b\, v\, t, \text{ if on microfilm}$$

Further:

$$c = 1/2 \ a\, v\, t^2$$

represents the cost of storing a continuing bound publication, and k v t the binding costs.

$$c = m\, v\, t$$

represents the cost of microfilming a continuing publication, and

$$c = 1/2 \ b\, v\, t^2$$

the cost of storing a continuing periodical on microfilm.

$(m + p)$ vt the cost of one positive microfilm, while $\frac{(m + 2p)\, vt}{2}$ the cost of one copy when two copies are made from the same negative.

y e v t would represent the cost of a positive microfilm of a continuing periodical where "e" is the cost per page.

When actual cost figures are substituted in these formulae, the results are revealing. While it is true that some of the necessary figures are not readily available, the estimates and formulae here provided are ample to enable any librarian to draw useful conclusions.

In a typical American library stack one square foot of floor space will accommodate on the average fifteen books, eight periodical volumes, or one volume of newspapers. Space of this type is worth from $1.50 to $2.50 per square foot on an annual rental basis, including heat but not light or upkeep. This means then that "a" is at least $1.50 for each newspaper volume, 20 cents for a periodical, and 10 cents for each book. Binding a newspaper volume of approximately 700 pages costs $7, while for periodicals the average is $3.50 for a volume of 800 pages. The usual microfilm storage cabinet requires nine square feet of space for 612 volumes of books, newspapers, or periodicals, including the aisle space in front for use. Thus the figure for "b" is 2.2 cents.

If the cost figures for various methods of storage discussed above are

393

computed and plotted on a curve, some interesting comparisons and relationships are revealed. Let us assume a newspaper of approximately thirty pages daily, stored over a period of fifty years.

Newspapers bound:

$$c = 1/2 \, a \, v \, t^2 + k \, v \, t$$
$$c = 1/2 \, (\$1.50 \times 12 \times 50^2) + (\$7.00 \times 12 \times 50)$$
$$\$22,500 + \$4,200$$
$$c = \$26,700$$

Newspapers—microfilm: [4]

$$c = 1/2 \, b \, v \, t^2 + (m + p) \, v \, t$$
$$c = 1/2 \, (.022 \times 12 \times 50) + (15 + 6) \times 12 \times 50$$
$$c = 330 + 12,600$$
$$c = \$12,930$$

It will be seen that even when only one copy of the microfilm is made, film cost is substantially less than the storage of the original. If, however, two copies of the film are made, and the cost of photography divided between two libraries, it will be found,

using the formula $c = 1/2 \, b \, v \, t^2 + \frac{m + 2p}{2} \, (vt)$,

that the cost of bound volume storage equals film cost in ten years. After ten years the spread between cost lines which represents the saving becomes increasingly great. (Fig. 1) The same reasoning applied to periodicals using the formula $c = 1/2 \, a \, v \, t^2 + k \, v \, t$ for bound files, and $c = 1/2 \, b \, v \, t^2 + y \, e \, v \, t$ for microfilm, yields more impressive results, since a large number are already being offered on microfilm at a cost approximating that of binding the original paper edition. (Fig. 2)[5]

Frequently a library keeps a file of a journal no longer published. A comparison of the cost of storing a single volume in its original form or of purchasing a microfilm and storing the film is shown in Figure 3[6] using the

---

[4] Microfilm negative of 100 feel per volume at $15, and positive at $6.

[5] Based on an average of 800 pages per title per year, a binding cost of $3.50 per volume and a microfilm cost of 1/4 cent per page.

[6] A cost of 1/4 cent per page can be realized only if ten or more copies are made over which the cost of the negative can be spread, combined with the use of a high reduction ratio.

formula $c = a\,n\,t$ and $c = b\,v\,t + y\,e$. From the graph it will be seen that the storage cost for ten years of a defunct periodical is just about equal to the cost of purchasing and storing a microfilm copy; thereafter a saving results. Where space is at a premium it may be more than merely a matter of dollars

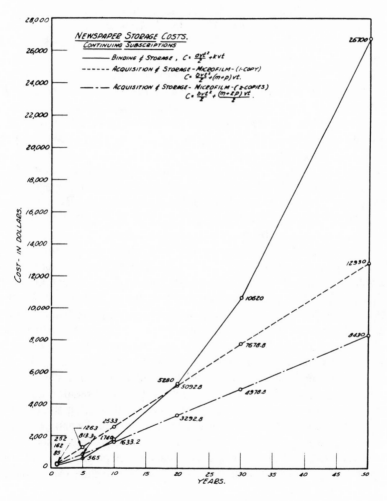

Figure 1

395

and cents. It may be a question of giving adequate library service or none at all.

Just as books require shelving, microfilm requires storage cabinets. A cabinet in popular use, costing $180, accommodates 612 100-foot rolls of 35mm film, or the equivalent of 612 volumes of newspapers, or the same number of volumes of periodicals. Double faced shelving will accommodate fifty volumes of periodicals and less than seven volumes of newspapers per running foot at a cost of $18. Thus, for periodicals, shelving costs 36 cents and film cabinets 30 cents per volume. For newspapers the shelving cost is much greater than the cabinet cost for microfilm, or $2.57 per volume.

It should be noted here that this comparison of costs does not take into consideration other factors which have a bearing on the extensive use of microfilm. Among these certainly would be the cost of the reading machines necessary to service a large film collection, or the additional space or facilities which the use of reading machines might require. Whether the cost of servicing the collection is more or less for film than for books is dependent upon a number of factors. For example, heavy newspaper volumes in a distant part of the stack are difficult to service, whereas the microfilm can be conveniently located and quickly serviced. Because of the small amount of space required, a substantial collection on microfilm can be kept readily accessible near the reading machines.

If the materials kept on film are only those items for which there is a substantially lessened demand, a few reading machines will serve for a sizable collection of periodicals or newspapers. Dr. Warner G. Rice, Director of Libraries at the University of Michigan, has estimated that a research library of the sort he heads would need one reading machine for each 100 graduate and faculty readers, even if a substantial part of the collection were on microfilm. Present day reading machines well engineered and built will, with reasonable care, last twenty years. Thus the annual replacement charges would not be more than 5 percent.

A table model reading machine together with its user requires not more than 50 percent more space for comfort than a reader sitting at a conventional study table. Since at any given time not more than a small fraction of places will be devoted to microfilm reading, space requirements should not be excessive. The recent appearance of satisfactory portable reading machines on the market means that like books film and machine can be loaned for use in office or home.

There is no doubt in view of the comparative inexperience in the use of microfilm by scholars that some additional servicing is required. Inexperienced hands can thread film incorrectly and tear it, and many users require some assistance or instruction. It is equally true that a little practice greatly increases proficiency.

From the foregoing it can be seen that we now have techniques at our disposal to forestall to a considerable degree the mushrooming growth of

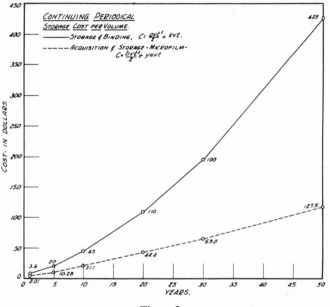

Figure 2

library buildings and costs, at the same time preserving material in a medium considerably more permanent than many paper copies current today.

If the possibilities outlined above are to be fully realized, certain decisions must be made. The initial success of the high-reduction film may point the way to a solution for some of the perplexing problems surrounding standardization. If the two basic types of microfilm currently supplied in the United States, notably low-reduction 1-10 to 1-15 microfilm for copies of books, manuscripts and other originals made for individual users, and high-reduction microfilm 1-161/2 to 1-25 for newspaper reproductions and for periodicals of the type mentioned above can be widely accepted and

397

standardized, much existing confusion would be eliminated. Future models of reading equipment could be designed to provide dual magnification in low and high ranges and more attention could be devoted to considerations of legibility and use. Incidentally, on the basis of experience with high reduction microfilm, the opaque screen seems to yield a sharper and more adequate image than the conventional translucent screen, though either may be used with good results.

Librarians, therefore, can meet the requirements and needs of users with two types of equipment. One type is the large permanent reading machine of finest quality and greatest flexibility. These may now be obtained on the market at a cost of from $300 to $725. The second type of reading machine is the smaller less universal portable unit which should ultimately be available for from $75-$150. The larger universal machines could be used within the library, and the smaller could be loaned to the user with the film for use outside the library. Instrument manufacturers have repeatedly pointed out that the problem of the small low-cost instrument is insoluble until definite use specifications are evolved. Once the requirements are known, the production of a suitable model is not a matter of great difficulty.

From the foregoing it would appear that a number of conclusions can be drawn from the data presented having a direct bearing on future library policy. Among these are the following:

1. The purchase of older back files of periodicals, often at premium prices, is not a wise investment. Age almost automatically means infrequent use. The same needs can be adequately served by a microfilm copy. In bound form space costs continue at a high rate year after year, whether the materials are used or not; in microfilm the fixed charges are greatly diminished.

2. Storage of newspapers in bound form is not warranted. The space required is excessive, the binding expensive, and the use after a short period of time is infrequent. Moreover the cheap wood pulp paper will disintegrate after 25-40 years and the total investment is lost. A microfilm copy is small, compact, satisfactory to use and permanent.

3. Through the proper use of microfilm pressing problems of space can be substantially eliminated. Files necessary for adequate library service can be kept and maintained without frequent expansion of stack capacity and new construction at the present high building costs.

4. Present library service can be maintained or expanded through the use of microfilm, as publications can be kept on microfilm that otherwise would have to be discarded because of space considerations.

APPENDIX D

5. As the number of desirable publications is itself increasing in a parabolic curve, storage of many titles on microfilm may become inevitable if costs are to be kept within manageable limits. With many libraries it may become a question of using microfilm to give adequate service, or severely curtailing the resources made available to their users.

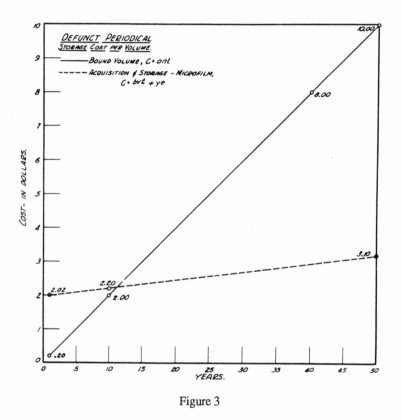

Figure 3

Ed. Note: The numbering of footnotes and figures in this adaptation is different from that of the original article as published in *American Documentation*.

Regent Power's Resignation

Following is an extract from the Minutes of the
Proceedings of the University of Michigan
Board of Regents, March 1966

The President said, "It is with reluctance and regret that I announce to you the resignation of one of the members of this Board, Mr. Eugene B. Power.

"Last Friday, March 11, the Attorney General of the State of Michigan made public his opinion on the relationship of Mr. Power, University Microfilms, Inc., which he heads, and The University of Michigan. That opinion said that 'a substantial conflict of interest' existed in regard to the business relationships between Mr. Power's corporation and the University.

"Immediately following the release of this opinion to the public, Mr. Power announced his resignation 'In the best interests,' as his statement phrased it, 'of the University and the corporations which I represent.'

"When word of Mr. Power's resignation reached me, I immediately released to the press the following statement:

" 'I am shocked at the sequence of events. I regret them deeply. Regent Power is a devoted public servant and has served the University and the state faithfully and generously.

" 'When he became a Regent a decade ago, he asked and received from the State Attorney General at that time approval of guidelines for the conduct of his unique service to libraries and scholars while a Regent of the University.

" 'He is respected by scholars and librarians all over the world for his contributions and has received their grateful thanks. His work was noted in the recent U.S.-Japan Cultural Exchange Conference in Tokyo. Over 2,000 colleges and universities benefit from his enterprise.

EDITION OF ONE

" 'It is indeed a harsh choice that deprives the state of Mr. Power's direct service to the University and to higher education. It is mitigated only by his continued contributions to the scholarly world.'

"On Tuesday of this week, March 15, Governor Romney announced that he had received and accepted Mr. Power's resignation from the University of Michigan Regents, which had been submitted to him in accordance with the provisions of the Michigan Election Code."

Regent Power's letter of resignation and his public statement follow:

March 11, 1966

The Honorable Board of Regents
The University of Michigan
Ann Arbor, Michigan

Gentlemen:

It is with deep regret that I write this letter submitting my resignation as a member of the Board of Regents. My reasons are contained in a public statement which I have released; a copy is attached.

The ten years I have served on the Board have been interesting, exciting and satisfying. They have provided an opportunity to participate in the development of one of the great universities of the world. It now appears that this era of my life must draw to a close. I take this step with great regret but take with me many fine and happy memories of the association with the Regents and the members of the University family.

Sincerely yours,

s/EUGENE B. POWER

402

APPENDIX E

Statement of Regent Eugene B. Power, President, University Microfilms, Inc., following release in Lansing, March 11, 1966, of the Michigan Attorney General's Statement

Working in the interests of extending the boundaries of knowledge is a rewarding experience, and for a long time my relationships with the University of Michigan have been satisfying ones. These satisfactions deepened when 10 years ago the people of Michigan first bestowed their honor and trust by electing me a Regent of the University.

When I started working with microfilm more than 30 years ago, it was a curiosity. It has now become one of the significant ways for students, scholars, and institutions of learning to exchange knowledge and for new libraries to build their collections. University Microfilms, Inc., presently serves more than 1,000 colleges and universities throughout the world. The work consists of supplying microfilm and xerographic copies of books, periodicals, and manuscripts as well as doctoral dissertations to libraries and scholars.

When I took office in 1956, I was aware that there might be some question regarding my being a Regent and at the same time continuing to supply services to the University as I had for many years. Accordingly, I asked the Attorney General's office for an opinion. The advice I received has served to guide University Microfilms, Inc., in its relationships with the University from that time on. Since the Attorney General indicated I could no longer sell to the University under state law, I made arrangements to donate to the university the full range of services offered by University Microfilms, Inc.

Last fall questions were raised publicly about the relationships between University Microfilms, Inc., and the University of Michigan. I immediately asked for a full-scale review of these relationships. As a result of the thorough study that followed, neither the independent counsel retained by the University to examine our relationships nor the Regents found any impropriety.

Now I have learned that the Attorney General has given his

403

opinion that my holding office as a Regent of the University of Michigan is in technical conflict with my business affiliation with University Microfilms, Inc.

Despite my distress at this view of a relationship that I in good faith believed was consistent with the law, I wish to acknowledge the Attorney General's recognition of my service to education and his clear statement that there is no question about my motives or integrity.

It is difficult for a layman like myself to understand fully how different lawyers can arrive at such divergent opinions on the same facts. But this is beside the point. That the Attorney General, in pursuit of his duties as guardian of the public interest, now deems the relationships under consideration inappropriate, must be regarded seriously.

I have always held the view that a man in public office must conduct his affairs, and those of any business or institution with which he is connected, with careful attention to the law — and in my case this applies to the law as it is now interpreted by the Attorney General.

Under the present situation it becomes impossible for me to continue to serve both as Regent of the University and as an officer of University Microfilms, Inc., especially in view of the plans for increased participation in the field of education by both University Microfilms, Inc., and Xerox Corporation of which I am a director.

Therefore I have decided that it is in the best interests of the University and the corporations with which I am connected if I resign at once from the office of Regent, and I shall submit my notice to the Board of Regents later today.

The close association which I have had with the University for more than three decades has brought an exciting experience of being an active part of one of the world's great universities. It also has brought the satisfaction of contributing a little to its progress. Therefore, my decision to resign is not an easy or a happy one for me or my family. I take this step because I would not willingly or knowingly let the slightest question of conduct cloud a relationship I hold precious.

APPENDIX E

Regent Murphy offered the following resolution on behalf of the Regents:

Eugene B. Power, Regent of the University of Michigan from 1956 to 1966, has been proud of its stature and impatient for its continued growth. From the first motion he seconded in February,1956, to the many motions he initiated throughout the decade of his service, his intent has always been to strengthen his Alma Mater in its place among the world's leading universities.

Expert in microphotography and the field of documentation, he has generously shared his knowledge and his abilities not only with this University but with universities and libraries throughout the world. His invention of Projected Books has brought to thousands of physically incapacitated people the ability and comfort of reading. Particularly sensitive to his University's cultural needs, he has worked unceasingly for the expansion of its libraries and of its program in the theater arts. His generous gifts to these aspects of the University's life are the tangible proof of the profound concern he has for its welfare.

The Regents of the University of Michigan recognize his highly significant and meaningful service to the University. They are pleased to appoint him Regent Emeritus and extend to him best wishes for his good health and happiness.

On William Caxton

The following biographical notes on Caxton appeared on the First Day Cover of British stamps issued on September 29, 1979:
"Five hundred years ago, in the autumn of 1476, William Caxton set up his workshop in the Almonry of Westminster Abbey, and became the first printer to work in Britain.

"Born some 55 years earlier in Kent, he was apprenticed to a wealthy London mercer. His activities in the cloth trade took him early in his career to Bruges, now in Belgium but at that time the chief city of the duchy of Burgundy. After many years of residence he became the leader of the British mercantile community there, with the title of 'Governor of the English Nation,' a post not unlike that of a modern consul-general.

"Caxton left the cloth business and his diplomatic post in 1469 to enter the service of Margaret, Duchess of Burgundy, the sister of King Edward IV of England. For some time he had been spending his leisure in translating French books into English and the duchess encouraged him (somewhat imperiously, to judge from his own account) to pursue his literary hobbies. In 1471 he completed a translation of a long book of stories about the Trojan War, which proved very popular among his court acquaintances, who began asking for copies.

"At that time printing was little known, and was practised at less than a dozen scattered places in Europe...Caxton...resolved to travel to Cologne and learn how to print himself. The following year he was back in Bruges ready to practice the new craft, and in 1474 his translation was in print. By the time he returned to England in 1476 he had issued five more books from his press in Burgundy....

"The first book Caxton printed in England was *The Dictes or Sayings of the Philosophers*, published in Westminster in 1477... Caxton died in 1491 and was buried in the churchyard of St. Margaret, Westminster...."

Appendix G

From Eugene B. Power's Notebook, 1965

Benedictine Monastery Manuscripts - St. Johns Univ. - Father Oliver Kapsner in charge.

1. Scope - All mss in 16 Austrian Monasteries = 10,000 of average of 300 pages each = 3,000,000, or 1,500,000 or p. Maybe more later.
   a. All in black & white -- 35 mm.
   b. Selected ones or pages in 35 mm color
   c. Will send one operator from US.
   d. Three to seven years
      1. If use one locally
2. Procedure - Equipment needed.
   a. One model O + one model E microfilm camera.
   b. One ... reader for inspection.
      1. Each to be equipped with book holder.
      2. 220 volts, 50 cycle. —
         a. Voltage regulators?
      3. Set of spare parts most needed.
      4. Extra magazine or head for model O.
      5. Film - either a HU or regular p an negative.
   b. Processing
      1. Can be done in Vienna perhaps - (best) — check —
      2. London -
      3. Should have small developing tank for tests
   c. Inspection
      1. An MPE reading machine for inspection.
      2. splicer.
      3. lens. (loupe)
   d. Titles to be typed - no board needed.
      1. Print face typewriter.
      2. a supply of ## 5x8 cards.

409

2

    e. Volkswagon or other vehicle for transportation of staff + equip.
      1. Buy in Austria. - probably.
      2. Truck type - rear loading -
    f. Voltage regulator — (2)
    g. 150 ft of cable — one end blank - other - 2 outlets .
                  two with ground .

2. Bibliographic procedure.
    a. Fr. Clever will do. He will prepare a card describing and dating
    each. MS., number of leaves, size, scribe, etc
      1. This will be filmed first + at end.
      2. Cards will constitute a complete file of work.
      3. Can be used to prepare published catalog.

3. Finances.

   a. Must open bank account from which expenses can be paid.

     1. Joint signatures - Fr. Oliver + Am. operator.

     2. Will need references ∞ from A.A. bank.

4. Miscellaneous ..

   a. Better visit Rank Xerox office + pay respects.

     1. What capacities do they have?

   b. Set time schedule to begin with Fr. Oliver.

     1. Will partly depend on availability and training of operator

   c. We will need a statement regarding unauthorized use, to go at the beginning and end of film.

5. Personnel

   a. One American - trained in A.A.

     1. What kind of person -

       a. Technician.

       b. Scholar with language.

   b. One Austrian - as camera operator.

     1. Recruited from Vienna

carried over   1886.00

~~Profit on Camera~~
Travel expences - from US.   100.00
Overhead _ um 2 — + profit   250.00
                                              $ 2231.00

4460.2 ÷ 2231 :   2231 ÷ 44000 = 5¢ per exposure
2uote 6¢ = 2640 ᵐ per mo.

If can be done faster - say 1000 a day per camera the cost would
reduce to 4¢ per exposure.

Send Fr. Kapsner copy of S.J. article on project.   ✓

To do   8/17/65   also reads
1. ~~Order camera from Kodak.~~ Vienna _ Peter Schmidt   ✓
2. Order Volkswagon. Gerhard Maresch _ c/o Auto haus _ Vienna
3. Send check to Harold Folgar. Verubardstein. 10,000 sh. ✓
4 Write Kapsner _ to tie ~~down~~ the operator. ✓
5. Follow up on items to be shipped from here
     a. Model E camera.
     b. Rack for holding ms.
     c. Bookholder for E +O
     d. Voltage regulators for model E.
     e Cable
     f splicer, winders. lenses etc.
     g. Developing tank and change bag.

6. Costs.
   a. Might consider cost plus 10% -
      1. Include all costs except this one trip.
   b. X per exposure -
      1. Difficult to estimate —

7. Estimate of costs. -
1000 exp. per date - per camera. × 2 = 2000 exp
2000 × 22 days = 44,000 per mo.

Labor. (2 operators)
     Am.   900   7 00
     Asst.   100 + 250 min. = 400
                              1100.00   1100.

Film - 8 exp per foot.
   44000 ÷ 8 = 5500
   5500 × 7¢ =   385.00   385.—

Developing 55 rolls @ 1.75   96.—

Equipment depreciation @ 100= per mo.   100.0
     Car 2000
     Cameras 3500
     Misc. 1000
                7500

Miscellaneous expenses.   100.0
     Legal.
     Gasoline
     Insurance   100..
Contingency   1881.

6. To be acquired in Vienna —
   a. Model III V.-2 camera - EK.!
   b. Bus. ',
   c. Film
   d. Reading machine. !
   e. Typewriter
   f Processing of film. !
   g Operator. !'

7. One camera operator to come from U. M. Lts.
   a For six months only.

Procedures

1. A record kept of all checks written, ~~why~~ and sent to me
   a. Fr. Oliver sign.
   b. Check for Paul — twice a month. ~~4845~~ shipping each time
2. A weekly report on exposures completed & hours worked.
   a. ~~Hitt~~ Paul.
3. Monthly report on use of car: - personal and otherwise
   - a. Paul.
   b. One trip to Vienna - personal - allowed.
   c. Business as needed.
   d. Expenses - gasoline, repairs, millage
   e. shipping
4. Separate report of film shipped
   a. Weekly.
5. Heim
   a. maintain an inventory
   b. Test films
   c. Matching camera sheets & film.

6. To be acquired in Vienna —
   a. Model III V. - a camera. EK.
   b. Bus.
   c. Film
   d. Reading machine.
   e. Typewriter
   f. Processing of film.
   g. Operator.

7. One camera operator to come from U. M. Lts.
   a. For six months only.

Filming Procedure   4/0/65

1. Film title card containing (28 frame)
   a. Discription + name of ms.
   b. Catalog number of MS.
   c. Scale in inches + cam.
   d. Consecutive number of ms filmed.

4. Fill out camera wo
   sheet.

2. 2 blank frames

3. First page and ocessive openings until finished. -12-1 to 18-1

4. Tilt card and scale at end.

5. When roll finishes - send to Kodak. GmbH.
                        Jacquingasse 29,
                        Wein. III

   for processing
      a. Film to be returned to Monastary
      b. Inspect immediately on reader.
         1. check for filming defects.
              corret titles
              density.
              missing pages.
              gutter.

6. Post film to Ann Arbor; in packages of 3 roll each.
   a. Each package numbered consecutively.
   b. Mail copy of title cards separately using same number.
   c. Enclose camera work sheet!

Things to acquire + Do

1. Title cards,
   a With imprint at bottom.
      6. Carbon paper.
2. Raw film. - Kodak.
3. Camera and reader- Kodak.
4 minibus.
5. See lawyer.
6. Customs broker.
7. Have monastery sign letter.
8. Arrange for insurance - liability -
9.

Checks drawn to date.

1. Harold Fogler -   10,000
2 Custom house
3 Kodak   5000
4. Auto haus
                      10,000
5. Roland Binnet   38,700 - balance on tax.
6. Paul Sager.   51 copy boards.
7 Heinz Richter   813. misc exp.
8. Paul Sager.   240   "   "
Deposits   500 - Petty Cash.

Feb. 25,638. - EBP letter of credit
2/26 127,520
3/14   14,000
4/14   25,600 -   "   "   "

Account 50-03892.
Creditanstalt Bankverein
Karntner Ring 1.
Wein. I.

417

Remarks by Ambassador Peter Jay in Knighting Eugene B. Power

It is a very great pleasure to be with you this afternoon for this rare and special occasion. I am delighted that my visit to this great and famous university, with which Eugene Power has had such a long and distinguished association, should have included this particularly happy element.

In a world which increasingly, alas, is becoming short of space, Mr. Power was one of the first to develop the all-important science of miniaturization, in his case in photography. We in Britain will long remember, with a deep sense of gratitude, at a time when our shores were under a severe threat of attack, his gift of *Lebensraum* for so many of our precious archives and libraries. He helped literally to transfer the inheritance of English language and culture to the United States, with whom we share these precious things. Mr. Power's great interest in Britain has continued to be expressed through the Power Foundation, from which my own university, Oxford, and some others that exist in Britain, has benefitted so much. And, last year, there was widespread and grateful recognition of his typical generosity, in association with Professor Boyd of Princeton and others who have remained anonymous, in donating the famous Battle Abbey Estate in Hastings, England to the British Crown.

This is a simple ceremony, and reflects the simple nature of this award, which expresses our affection, respect, and gratitude for a life of honorable service and unusual distinction.

Britain has two assets which give our honors system a significant character: The Monarchy itself, and the venerable age of our traditions. Sometimes we like to believe that in the great American Republic we can offer a compliment of unique value. Whether or not that is true, in making this presentation today, I am acting in a very personal sense as her Majesty's representative in the United States;

and this award marks the bestowal of the Queen's own approval and appreciation.

It is a pleasure and an honor for me to greet you at this ceremony to receive your award. I offer you my very warmest congratulations on this most appropriate recognition of your distinguished career.

I will now read out the formal authority for me to make this presentation on behalf of Her Majesty The Queen:

"By command of Her Majesty Queen Elizabeth II, by virtue of the authority vested in me as her Britannic Majesty's Ambassador and Plenipotentiary at Washington in the United States of America, it is my honor and privilege to present you with the Insignia of the High Honor which the Queen has been graciously pleased to bestow."

Index

Adams, Paul, 208, 210, 216-17, 232
Adams, Randolph, 11-13, 29, 89, 118, 371
Affiliate Artists program, 335
AFL-CIO, 206, 207, 208
Albareda, Reverend A. M., 105, 150
Alien Property Custodian (U. S. State Department), 143
Ambrosiana Library (Milan), 104
American Archivist, The, 148
American Council of Learned Societies, 100, 127, 147; advisory committee for microfilming European materials, 122, 126; Joint Committee on Materials for Research, 15; Medieval Academy of, 16
American Culture Series, The, 118, 119
American Documentation, 160
American Documentation Institute (ADI), 188, 189, 190
American Hospital (Neuilly, France), 86
American Library Association (ALA), 33, 112, 157, 159, 371
American Periodical Series, The, 118, 119
American Philosophical Society (APS), 100, 353-54, 355, 356
Ames, Evelyn: *Glimpse of Eden*, 347
Amherst College Library, 94n

Amherst, England, 134
Ancestry, 37-43
Ann Arbor, Michigan, 1, 6, 21, 197, 198, 200, 201, 202, 345
Ann Arbor Dairy, 205
Ann Arbor News, The, 113, 227
Ann Arbor Railroad, 204
Ann Arbor Summer Festival, 201, 336-37, 344, 363
Antrim Ironworks, 40
A Plan for Publication of Scholarly Material by Microfilm, 89-93
Archives of the Indies (Seville, Spain), 162-63
Argus, Inc., 32, 145
Armstrong, Stanley, 69
Art Institute (Chicago), 173
Arts Theater, 199-200, 201
Asleson, Bob, 262, 317, 329
Association of Deans of Graduate Schools, 91
Association of Governing Boards of Universities and Colleges (AGB), 220-21
Association of Information and Image Management (AIIM), 192-93. *See also* National Microfilm Association (NMA); National Micrographics Association
Association of Research Libraries (ARL), 165-68
Athenia, 110

421

INDEX

INDEX

423

INDEX

Churchill, Sir Winston, 108, 117, 221

Cisney, Marcella, 343

Citizens Military Training Camp, 51

Civil Defense Women's Auxiliary, 152

Clapp, Verner, 129

Clements Library, The, 11-12, 118, 361

Coco, Jimmy, 199

Codex Sinaiticus, 278

Cole, Ed, 318-24

College and Research Libraries Journal, 95

College Art Journal, 95

Colonial Williamsburg Foundation, 194

Colorado Springs, Colorado, 251, 252, 253

Commission for the Publication of National Documents, 288

Committee to Rescue Italian Art (CRIA), 302, 303, 305

Comstock, William Alfred (Michigan governor), 22

Connable, Al, 163, 215, 216, 220, 237

Connable, Dorothy (Mrs. Al), 163

Connable Office (Kalamazoo, Michigan), 276

continuous developing machine, 141

Coolidge, Blanche (Mrs. John), 43

Coolidge, John (uncle), 43, 68, 73

Coordinator of Information (COI), 128, 134, 135, 136, 137. *See also* Office of Strategic Services (OSS)

Copenhagen, Denmark, 138

Copyflo II machine (Haloid Xerox), 229-30, 242

Council of the National Endowment for the Humanities, 307, 332

Council on Foreign Relations, 332

Council on Library Resources, 238

County Mental Health Department (Milwaukee, Wisconsin), 63

Cragie, Sir William, 14

Cranbrook Science Museum (Bloomfield Hills, Michigan), 174, 175

Crawford, Andy, 327-28

Cross of King George, 361

Crowther, Lord (Geoffrey), 359

Crowther, Lady (Peggy, Mrs. Geoffrey), 359

Cudlip, Bill, 210

Cushing, Bert, 11

Dacca, East Pakistan. *See* Bangladesh

Daedalus Corporation, 322, 323

Dagron, René, 139

Daily Mirror, 298

Daily News, 298

Dalai Lama, 310

Davis, Watson, 26, 28, 122, 127, 188

Dawson, Emma (Mrs. Jack), 163, 188, 199, 349, 350

Dawson, Jack, 163, 188, 199, 205, 206, 207, 212, 213, 349, 350, 351

Dawson, Peter, 223

Day Street house, 76, 77-78, 97

Deininger, Ingrid, 363

de Jongh, Dr. Russell, 352

Democratic Party, 107, 187, 206, 208, 217, 220, 250, 251, 269

INDEX

425

INDEX

Ellsworth, Ralph, 165-68
encephalitis, 51-52
Environmental Research Institute of Michigan (ERIM), 320-21, 322, 323
Esdaille, Arundel, 29-30, 84, 108, 124-26, 127, 139
Eskimo Art, Inc., 174, 176, 182, 183, 184, 185, 363
Eskimos, 174, 176, 177-78, 179-80, 182-83, 185
Estoril, Portugal, 133
Ethiopia, Africa, 294
Evans, Luther, 129

Fairbanks, Alaska, 223, 224, 245
Fairchild, Nancy (Mrs. Red), 245
Fairchild, Red, 245, 246
Family Planning Medical Services (FPMS), 308-9
Farmington, Michigan, 37, 39
Faxon, Jack, 268
Feldman, L. D. , 271, 273, 281, 282
Fellow of the Association (National Microfilm Association), 191, 193
FID Review, 95
Fidelity Mutual Life Insurance, 42
55 Campaign, The. *See* University of Michigan, sesquicentennial fund-raising campaign
First National Bank (Traverse City), 96, 204
fishing, 44-49, 57, 67-68, 76, 153, 172, 368; fly-fishing, 45-47
Fitzsimmons, Joe, 262, 329-331, 369; UMI Golden Anniversary speech, 370-72
Fleming, Robben W. "Bob" (President, U of M), 221, 343, 361

Flight, Howard E. (Power Scholar), 340-41
Florence, Italy, 104, 273, 274, 277, 302, 303, 304, 305, 306
Florer (U of M professor), 71
Flounders, The, 227, 327-29, 353
Folger Library.
  See Folger Shakespeare Library
Folger Shakespeare Library (Washington, D. C.), 18
Ford Motor Company, 262, 295, 326
Forsdyke, Sir John, 123, 136, 137, 147, 154
Francis, Sir Frank, 231, 276, 279, 290, 357
Frankfurt, Germany, 82, 149, 150
Freedman, Sam, 235, 236, 239
freedom of the press, 108, 267
Freibourg, Dr., 294
French Underground, 135
Fries, Charles (U of M professor), 13, 14, 15, 18, 79
Frost, Wallace, 114-15
Furlong, Tom, 69
Furstenburg, Albert C. (Dean, U of M Medical School), 212

Gach, Bob, 30
Galler, Enid, 373
Gandhi, Sanjay, 310
Gangtok, Sikkim, 310, 311, 312
GCO Corporation, 323-24
General Motors, 324
General Precision Corporation, 236, 237
Geneva, Switzerland, 103, 306
German Property Branch (U.S. State Department), 143
Gilbert, Benjamin, 32, 245

INDEX

INDEX

Holmes, Oliver Wendell, 288
honey business, 8, 76, 77, 79
Hoover, President Herbert, 21
horseback riding, 97-98, 158
hotel business, 250, 253, 254, 255, 256, 257-58, 259, 260
Hotel Bristol (Vienna), 293
Hotel Imperial (Vienna), 293
Houghton, Arthur A., Jr., 181, 183
Houghton Library, 181
Hours of Catherine of Cleves, 274
Houston, Jim, 171, 172-73, 174, 176, 177, 181-82, 183, 184, 185
Howse, Bob, 145
Hudson's Bay (trading post), 177, 182
Huntington Library (San Marino, California), 18
Hydrick & Struggles, 258

Illinois State Mental Hygiene Clinic (Chicago), 63
Indian Wells, California, 360
Individualized Home Nursing Care (I.H.N.C.) , 363
Innocent Killers (Lawick, Hugo, Baron van and Lawick-Goodall, Jane, Baroness van), 350n
Institute of Tibetology (Gangtok, Sikkim), 310, 311, 312
International Federation of Documentation, 103
International Husky Corporation, 324
International Labor Office (Geneva, Switzerland), 103
International Micrographic Congress (IMC), 267, 268
International Peace Conference, 103

intuitive thinking, 46
Inuits. *See* Eskimos
Itek Corporation, 234-35, 237, 239

Jackson, Mrs. Laura, 77-78
Jarrolds of Norwich, 280
Jay, Ambassador Peter, 361, 362-63
Jelneck, Lois, 363
Jewett, Dick, 202
John Deere Tractor Company, 335
Johnson, Albin, 52, 53
Johnson, President Lyndon B., 295, 296-97, 307, 332
Journal of Documentary Reproduction, The 33, 93-95, 117, 118, 160
Journal of Higher Education, The, 95

Kaiser-Frazer Corporation, 172
Kampala, Uganda, 313
Kappa Kappa Gamma, 62, 99
Kapsner, Father Oliver, 286-87, 288, 289, 290
Katmandu, Nepal, 310-11
Katzen, Maxwell, 71
Keller, Herbert, 126, 127
Kelly, Frank (Attorney General), 268-69
Kenya, Africa, 313
Keogh, Andrew, 18
Keppel, Frederick, 100-101, 119
Kibre, Adele, 105, 138-39, 150
Kiel, Germany, 81, 82
Kingston, Bob, 199
Kingswood School, 114, 153
Klosterneuberg (Austrian monastery), 289

428

INDEX

INDEX

Madrid, Spain, 85
Magdalene College (Cambridge,
England), 271, 272, 273, 274,
275, 276, 277, 279, 281, 282,
283, 302, 337, 370
*Magdalene College Magazine and
Record*, 274
Malta, 294
Mann, Matt, 60, 61, 62
Marantette, Ken, 75
Margaret, Princess, 247
Marion Island (Power Island), 333
Marshall, Bill, 207, 208
Marshall, John, 16
Marshall Scholarship, 224, 247, 282
Martinez, Don, 47-48
Massialas, Margaret, 320, 321, 322,
337, 338, 361, 370
Maxwell, Robert, 297, 298
May Festival (U of M Musical Soci-
ety), 334
Meisel, James (U of M professor),
223
Meiss, Millard (Princeton Univer-
sity professor), 303, 304
Melcher, Fred, 156, 231
Merlanti, Ernie, 262
Mesta, Perle, 285, 301
Metamorphoses (Ovid), 271
Metcalf, Keyes, 100
*Methods for Reproducing Research
Material* (Binkley), 15, 25
Metropolitan Museum of Art (New
York), 181
*Michigan Alumnus Quarterly
Review*, 95, 130-31, 133
Michigan Daily, The, 56, 222, 264-
67, 268, 327, 342
Michigan Hotel Association, 255

Michigan State University, 56, 206,
213, 218-19
Michigan Union, 56
Microfile camera (Kodak, various
models), 112, 128, 134, 138, 290
Microfilm developments during
WWII: aircraft blueprints, 142;
combat intelligence, 134-36,
138-39; preservation of British
manuscripts, 127-28, 134,
142; scientific and various other
publications and documents,
128; Shostakovich's 7th Sym-
phony smuggled out of
U.S.S.R., 139-40; V-Mail, 140
Microfilm Research Foundation
(MRF), 238
Microfilms, Incorporated, 143, 144,
228
Microphoto, Inc., 235-36
Milan, Italy, 104, 151, 302
Miller, Mina, 58-59
Miller, Dr. Norman, 98
Milliken, Bill (Michigan governor),
121, 321
Milwaukee, Wisconsin, 63, 66, 73
Mimeograph, 240
Ministry of Information (London),
134
MIT, 168, 189
Modern Language Association, 119
Moholy, Lucia, 135
Moller, Dr. Joseph, 103
Monaghan, Tom, 324, 325-26
Monastic Manuscript Microfilm
Library (St. John's University,
Minnesota), 293-94
Moore, Henry, 299, 342
Morrison, Mary Lou, 305, 306, 307,
312

430

INDEX

431

INDEX

Park Place Motor Inn, 253, 254, 255, 256, 257-58, 259, 260, 263, 315
Park Place Motor Inn Corporation, 255
Pennland, S. S., 79, 83
Pepys, Samuel, 271, 272, 280
Pergamon Press, 297
Pernold, Dr. Christl, 293
Peterson, Mabel, 275
Philippines, 138, 158
Phillipps, Sir Thomas, 272
Phoenix Project, 342
photographic travel diary, 312-13
Pierpont, Bill, 321
Pike, Ken, 327
Planned Parenthood, 308-9, 332
Plante, Julian, 294
Plough, Alice, 11, 22, 29
Plymouth Road office, 319, 322, 324
Pooh-Bear Honey, 77, 79
Pope, Anna Marie, 175
Port of Spain, Trinidad, 245
postal money orders, 22-23
Povungnituk, Quebec, 180
Power, Annette (mother, Mrs. Glenn Warren), 29, 43, 46, 64-65, 84-86, 95, 120, 123-24, 333-34
Power, Antoinette (grandmother, nee Cloise), 40-42
Power, Arthur, 37-38
Power, Bob, 39
Power Center for the Performing Arts, 343, 344, 369
Power, Eugene (grandfather), 39
Power, Eugene B.
    American Philosophical Society (APS), elected to, 353-54
    Award of Merit (NMA), 193
Battle Abbey saved for England by, 357, 358
    birth, 1
    Caxton manuscript saved for England by, 276-77
    college attendance, 52-53; graduation, 67
    Eskimo Art founded by, 174
    honorary degree, St. John's University (Minnesota), 181
    Honorary Fellow of Magdalene College, 280
    knighted by Queen Elizabeth II, 361
    merges UMI with Xerox, 247
    President, International Micrographic Congress, 267
    Regent, U of M, 201; campaign and election, 205-10; conflict of interest. *See* University Microfilms, Inc.; performance as, 211-21, 224-25; resignation, 269;
    retirement, 4, 318
    University Microfilms, Inc. founded by, 2-3, 34-35
    Xerox board of directors appointment, 4, 247
Power Foundation, 281, 332, 363
Power, Frank (brother), 44, 49, 65, 68, 86, 124, 204, 224, 313, 346, 347, 348, 363, 366-68, 369; European travels, 14, 79-83, 285; honey business, 76-77; Panama fishing trip, 368; sailing, 120-21, 122
Power, Glenn Warren "Gov" (father), 42, 45-47, 65, 96, 97, 113, 203-4

INDEX

INDEX

INDEX

soapstone carvings, 171, 173, 174, 175, 176, 178
Social Science Research Council: Joint Committee on Materials for Research, 15
Sonnino, Baron, 305
Sonnino papers, 305, 306-7
Sotheby's, 272
Soundings, 332
Spain: monastic filming in, 294
Spooner, Vera (Mrs. Willett), 113
Spooner, Willett "Will," 113, 122, 124
Staatsbibliothek (Berlin), 106, 135
Staatsbibliothek (Vienna), 293
Staebler, Burnette (Mrs. Neil), 99, 102, 105, 108, 163, 199, 201
Staebler, Neil, 34, 51, 99, 145, 163; college experiences, 58-59, 60-61, 67, 73; European trip (1939), 102, 105, 106-7, 108; Democratic party and, 187, 188, 250; regency campaign and, 209; theater and, 199, 202
STC (Short Title Catalogue of English Books from 1475 to 1640), 14; extension of (1641-1700), 231
STC books: as trial for editions of one idea, 28-29; microfilm book camera built to film, 29; 1935 European filming project, 84, 127, 134
STC books *Early Modern English Dictionary* project, 14, 15, 18, 79
STC book-subscription service, 31-32, 34, 95, 96; announced at ALA meeting (1936), 30; base for UMI business, 34, 96, 111;

filming at Edwards Brothers, 29
Steer, Edith, 12
Steger, Paul, 291
Steinman, Father, 180-81
Stern, Isaac, 334-35
Steuben Glass Company, 181, 182
Stevens, David, 16, 33
Stevens, Roger L., 198
Stevenson, Allan, 274, 275
Stewart, Jimmy, 164
Stift Kremsmunster (Austrian monastery), 290, 291, 292, 293
Stillwagon, Alan, 247
Stineman reels, 31, 113
Stock, Frederick, 69
Stockholm, Sweden, 138, 139, 150
Stoneman, Bill, 298, 299
Stoneman, Ingrid (Mrs. Bill), 298, 299
Straub, Bob, 63, 68, 69
Sunbelt Broadcasting, 253
Swain, Florence, 56
Swain, Jessie, 56
swimming, 49, 55-56
Swisher, John E., Jr., 320
Swisher, John E. III, 320
Swiss National Library (Bibliothèque Nationale, Bern), 151

Tanzania, Africa, 313
Tate, Vernon, 100,133,140; Draeger camera and, 28; editor, *American Documentation*, 160; editor, *Journal of Documentary Reproduction*, 93, 117, 160; National Archives microfilm labs and, 33; National Microfilm Association, and, 189, 190, 191, 192, 193, 268, 370, 371

435

INDEX

teaching machines (film), 236, 237, 239, 247

Thermofax, 240

Theta Chi Fraternity, 57, 67, 71, 72

Thompson, Walt, 49, 52, 53

3M (Minnesota Mining & Manufacturing Company), 192

Thurber, Donald, 217, 232, 234, 250

Time, 160

Times Literary Supplement, 231, 274

Times (London) 127-28, 273

Tisserant, Father, 150

Todd, Congressman Paul H., 288, 295

Tokyo, Japan, 267, 301

Torch Lake, 51, 58

Touring Boys Camp, 75-76

Traverse City, Michigan, 1, 40, 42, 43, 64, 67, 204, 208, 253-54, 258, 345, 347

Traverse City Chamber of Commerce, 256, 259

Trevelyan, Sir Humphrey, 298

Trinity College, Cambridge, 280

Turner Construction Company, 68-69

UAW, 207, 213

Uganda, Africa, 313

U.S. Customs, 175

U.S. Embassy, London, 134, 149

U.S. Office of War Information, 134-35

unions, 206-8, 213; attitude towards, 257

University College, Oxford, 224

University Microfilms, Inc., 2-3, 4, 87, 95, 147, 158, 164-69

Air Force work, 142

American Culture Series, The, 118, 119

American Periodical Series, The, 118, 119

Biblioteca Nazionale (Florence, Italy) newspaper filming, 304-5

building expansion, 193, 195, 196, 204-5

cafeteria, 169, 233-34, 263

conflict of interest, 214, 215, 263-67, 268-69

dissertation business, 89-93; American Research Libraries (ARL) endorsement, 165-68. *See also* Ellsworth, Ralph

Dolph's Funeral Parlor, 31

Editions of One, 228-33

First Street building, 35, 319, 329

founding of, 2-3, 34-35

Golden Anniversary, 369-72

holding company formation (E &S Realty), 228

Justice Department contract, 140-42

merger and acquisition offers (pre-Xerox), 234-37

non-union, 213

Office of Strategic Services (OSS) work, 128, 134, 136, 138, 148

O-P (out of print) book service, 230-32

periodicals business, 154-62, 164

personnel policies, 242

post-war slump, 152

preservation of British manuscripts during war, 134, 142

pricing, 242

436

INDEX

V-Mail. *See* Microfilm developments during WW II
Von Hatingberg, Dr. Hans, 107-8

Wageman, Connie, 35, 119
Wagman, Frederick, 264, 265
Wainger, Jim, 242, 243, 244
Wall Street Journal, The, 267
Walton, Ivan, 124
Washington, D. C., 28, 128, 136, 190, 288
Wayfarer, 245
Wayne State University, 206
Weaks, Don, 56
Webster papers, 288
We-Que-Tong Club, 49, 51, 55
West Baffin Eskimo Cooperative, 182
West, Oscar, 68
Western Foundation Company, 68
Westernland, S. S., 83
Wheeler, Ben, 97
Whitaker, G. C. "Gee," 236, 237
White, Lee, 111-12
Williams, G. Mennen (Michigan governor), 188, 209, 288
Williams, Nancy (Mrs. G. Mennen), 288
Wilson, David, 139, 150
Wilson, Joe, 239-40, 241-42, 244, 245, 247, 250, 261, 276, 304, 313
Windsor Tractor Equipment, 6, 78
Windt, Valentine, 197, 198
Wing, Donald, 231
Wolbach, Fritz, 138
Wolff, Fred, 69-70

Wolff, Vera (Mrs. Fred), 69-70
Wolverine Broadcasting Company, 251-52, 260, 315
World War II, 117-42, D-Day, 143, 148; declaration of war by England and France, 117; Hitler and the rise of Nazism, 105-11; Invasion of Poland, 107, 117; Pearl Harbor, 128; Schweinfurt, daylight bombing raid, 135
Wright, Hart, 199
Wright, Louis, 356
Wright, Phyllis (Mrs. Hart), 199
Wunche, Alex, 208

Xerox Corporation, 4, 241, 247, 261-63, 304, 313; Century 21 exhibit, 239; mandatory retirement policy, 317-18; and the profit motive, 249, 315; UMI merger offer and agreement, 239, 242-45, 247-48; and UMI reprint business, 316-17, 331. *See also* Haloid Company; Haloid Xerox; Rank-Xerox
Xerox 914 copier, 240
Xerox stock, 254, 256, 343

Yale University Library, 18, 94n, 100
Yocum, Clarence (Dean, U of M Rackham Graduate School), 91
Yost, Joyce, 75

Zurich, Switzerland, 103, 280

438